GENEALOGIES OF THE WEST

Civilization, Religion, Consciousness

JAUME AURELL

ANTHEM PRESS

Anthem Press
An imprint of Wimbledon Publishing Company
www.anthempress.com

This edition first published in UK and USA 2023
by ANTHEM PRESS
75–76 Blackfriars Road, London SE1 8HA, UK
or PO Box 9779, London SW19 7ZG, UK
and
244 Madison Ave #116, New York, NY 10016, USA

British Library Cataloguing-in-Publication Data
A catalogue record for this book is available from the British Library.

Library of Congress Cataloging-in-Publication Data
A catalog record for this book has been requested.
2022919277

ISBN-13: 978-1-83998-757-1 (Pbk)
ISBN-10: 1-83998-757-X (Pbk)

This title is also available as an e-book.

CONTENTS

List of Figures   v

Acknowledgments   vii

Introduction   1

PART I   **FOUNDATIONS**   23

CHAPTER 1   **Jerusalem**   25
CHAPTER 2   **Athens**   35
CHAPTER 3   **Rome**   45
CHAPTER 4   **Christianity**   57

PART II   **MATURATIONS**   69

CHAPTER 5   **Clash**   71
CHAPTER 6   **Expansion**   83
CHAPTER 7   **Shift**   93
CHAPTER 8   **Exuberance**   111

PART III   **DEVELOPMENTS**   121

CHAPTER 9   **Modernity**   123
CHAPTER 10   **State**   131
CHAPTER 11   **Capitalism**   143
CHAPTER 12   **Science**   155
CHAPTER 13   **Reforms**   167
CHAPTER 14   **Enlightenments**   177

PART IV	**REVISIONS**	**189**
CHAPTER 15	**Ideologies**	**191**
CHAPTER 16	**Crisis**	**203**
CHAPTER 17	**Liberations**	**217**
CHAPTER 18	**Challenges**	**235**
Epilogue		**247**
Suggested Bibliography		259
Detailed Table of Contents		275
Index		283

LIST OF FIGURES

1.1   The Dome of the Rock on the Temple Mount in Jerusalem.   26
2.1   Details of the Caryatid Porch on the Acropolis in Athens, Greece.
      Ancient Erechtheion or Erechtheum temple.   39
3.1   Caesar Augustus, the first emperor of Ancient Rome.
      Monumental bronze statue in Rome.   48
4.1   Thirteenth-century mosaic of Jesus Christ in the temple of
      Hagia Sophia in Istanbul, Turkey.   59
5.1   The Hagia Sophia (The Church of the Holy Wisdom or Ayasofya),
      Istanbul, Turkey.   74
6.1   Medieval knight's sword, of uncertain date.   89
7.1   Sculptures on the western facade of the Cathedral of Chartres:
      Matthew, Charlemagne, or Constantine I, and Hildegard
      of Anglachgau or a queen, ca. twelfth century.   96
8.1   Basilica of St. Francis of Assisi (Italy).   114
9.1   Drawings by Leonardo da Vinci for the anatomical study
      of the hand.   126
10.1 Illustration of the cover of Hobbes' Leviathan.   132
11.1 A young merchant working on his beads, with coins and an
      open book in his hands. Pieter Gerritsz van Heemskerck, 1529,
      Dutch painting, oil on panel.   146
12.1 The cartographer Gerardus Mercator, on a commemorative
      gold coin.   157
13.1 Statue of King Henry VIII, King's College, Cambridge (England).   169
14.1 Fragment of a monument to Immanuel Kant against
      the background of the sky. Kaliningrad (Russia).   181

15.1 Portrait of Karl Marx, around 1875.   199
16.1 Effects of a bombing in the city of Guernica (Spain).   204
17.1 View of the aisle of a restored 1959 city bus. Just like the
      bus Rosa Parks made it stop with her dignified and courageous
      gesture.   222
18.1 Berlín Wall.   237

ACKNOWLEDGMENTS

These pages reflect ideas that emerged from long conversations with colleagues who share with me a passion for history, as well as a conviction that historians are responsible for contributing to society's improvement by relating past experience. Among these colleagues, whose echo is undoubtedly found in these pages and whose friendship I have treasured for many years, I owe a special acknowledgment to those who have reviewed the manuscript: Robert A. Rosenstone, Montserrat Herrero, Peter Burke, Rocio G. Davis, and Peter Fritzsche. They have agreed or disagreed with me on the points I make in the book, but their suggestions have been invaluable to me. José Enrique Ruiz-Domènec and Henry Odell decisively encouraged this project from the beginning. Gabrielle M. Spiegel, Anthony Adamthwaite, Marisa Galvez, Carlos Eire, and Julie Fairman contributed to my determination to finish the book. Christa Byker's and David Ronder's suggestions helped to improve the manuscript.

Another important source of inspiration and gratitude for the ideas contained in this book corresponds to the *Religion and Civil Society*, Institute for Culture and Society at the University of Navarra. This project is an example of truly interdisciplinary dialogue, without which it is simply impossible to interpret the great questions of the past or present. During the process of writing the book, I have been especially grateful for the valuable suggestions made by the director of this project, the political philosopher Montserrat Herrero.

I am especially grateful to Yury Contreras-Vejar for encouraging me to go ahead with this project from the beginning and for the countless hours spent revising my manuscripts that were never quite final. In the end, we both agree that our succulent conversations, many of them sustained during the painful period of the pandemic, have been the best reward of this stimulating and fruitful intellectual venture.

My father, Toni Aurell, also reviewed the manuscript of this book in detail—shortly before his death. He has been a constant source of inspiration for me as an example of how to combine a passionate professional life with extraordinary sensitivity for the cultivation and promotion of culture, a passion that he constantly transmits to his children. My mother Victoria Cardona, to whom this book is dedicated, has now finished her eighth book. I also owe to her many of the ideas contained in this book, fruit of our long conversations, and I hope I inherited something of her passion for writing and her *joie de vivre*. I have seen reflected in my parents and grandparents the richness of the Western tradition that I have tried to describe in this book. If what I have written here holds some weight and inspires conviction, it is not just because I have long studied Western values in books and archives, but because of the example of various people with whom my path has crossed, relatives, friends, and colleagues.

INTRODUCTION

This book presents a new look at the West by tracing the still-recognizable footprints of the past and reflecting on what the present challenges are facing. It attempts to decipher traces of the places, characters, events, and intellectual trends that the West recognizes as its own. It tries to shape something like a genealogy(es) of the West, starting from the conviction that the knowledge of the past is essential to our enrichment as citizens and, ultimately, for improving our society.

I wrote this book for readers who seek a synthesis of Western legacy to rethink it, and who, like me, remain unsatisfied with either of the two opposed directions that threaten the continuity of this secular culture: self-flagellation and exclusivism. On the one hand, the West experiences an artificial, and politically correct *meaculpism* that besieges it and leads to pessimism and inaction. On the other, it suffers from the radical positions of politicians who advocate for a 'pure' Western civilization that is exclusive and exclusionary. This attitude has proven sterile, and is, in the end, in direct contradiction of the West's ability to welcome and integrate other cultures, assimilating the best of them and expunging the worst.

To achieve this purpose, I propose to embark on a journey that reaches back to the foundations of the Western civilization such as Jerusalem, Athens, Rome, the early Christianity, the fusion between Latin and German societies, and the painful split among Rome, Constantinople, and Mecca. It connects the great values of the Middle Ages—from the chivalrous spirit to the scholastic rationality—to the present. It shows the faces of the modernity and its most relevant achievements—the state in politics, the capitalism in economics, and the science in knowledge—and how they are being revised nowadays by postmodernity. It finally examines the twentieth- and twenty-first century self-questioning of the West, which has revised its previous tradition and heritage, and threatens the entire civilization to disappear.

I have written this book driven by the persuasion that it is not possible to preserve one's own tradition and culture when knowledge of it widely disappears and people fail to appreciate or develop it. The image chosen as the cover of this book—an aquarelle by Salvador Dalí of one of the most sublime scenes from the Dante's *Divine Comedy*—reflects this attitude. Dante's marvelous journey through purgatory is coming to an end. The poet's conversation with Virgil takes on an increasingly intimate and nostalgic tone. One senses the pain of separation. Only a baptized person can cross the threshold of paradise. Dante will have thus to abandon his guide and master, whose role will be taken over by Beatrice in Paradise. Finally, a farewell is called for. Virgil does not consider it necessary to say a word. Instead, Virgil just crowns Dante "with crown and mitre" ("per ch'io te sovra te corono e mitrio").

This scene contains many lessons. The gesture that Dante attributes to Virgil belies the supposed suspicion of the medieval world toward the classical tradition. We already had plenty of evidence: the continuity of Romanization in Byzantium, the Roman restoration of Charlemagne, the recovery of Roman law, the rationalization of philosophy, and the classical substratum of scholastic philosophy. This sublime poem confirms this continuity, as Virgil, the most classic among classic poets, hands over to Dante, the most sublime medieval poet, the crown of his mysterious literary reign. The scene stages the natural connection between the classical, medieval, and modern worlds of the West, connected by their sublime artists (the crowner Virgil, the crowned Dante, the witness Dalí), which seems to me an accurate icon of the spirit in which this book is written: an appreciation for tradition and a pragmatic vision of the present to gain a better future.

Hence the importance of recovering the West's confidence as a civilization, which necessarily requires knowledge, appreciation, affection, and cultivation of its own history and tradition. When examining wars and humanity's other misfortunes, historians are like doctors—they outwardly seem remote and detached from the terrible diseases that they must investigate and cure. Indeed, as historians, it is our duty to analyze, interpret, and relay the past formally and honestly (and as beautifully as possible), precisely so that its lessons reach society. But the historian's job is also painful in that we continually attest to humanity's seemingly unending ability to fall into repetitive patterns of conflict and violence, as well as its inability to learn from these mistakes. Blinded by flippancy, superficiality, laziness, or simply deliberate manipulation, society often does not even bother to analyze its mistakes—and greatness—in depth.

The history of the West is marked by the contrast between success and failure, idealism and realism, compassion and cruelty, peace and violence, reform and revolution, unity and diversity, creation and destruction, innovation and tradition, and defiance and submission. This book tries to identify and interpret these two sides of the coin. This *civilization of extremes*—to paraphrase the great British historian Eric Hobsbawm—has led to make compatible objective achievements such as the welfare state with the most atrocious events such as the unspeakable horror of the Holocaust.

History is never an absolute good and evil, like people is never definitively good and bad. If the shadows of the Western tradition are evident, the positive aspects and good contributions to the humanity are not fewer: the creation of effective public institutions, the cooperation between private initiative and public planning, the legal security, the preservation of civil rights, the establishment of a universal educational and social assistance network, the dignified pension system, the promotion of free speech, the increasing respect for ethnic and religious diversity, the acknowledging for minorities, the separation between church and state, the appreciation for art and culture, the compatibility between the particular and the global, the division between the public and the private, the separation of powers, and a civic sense of coexistence and solidarity.

History helps us examine our collective past, just as our memory helps us examine our personal experiences. As the famous saying goes, "Those who do not learn history are doomed to repeat it." Personally, I prefer a more positive spin on this sentiment, namely that examining and caring about the own collective past enriches people because we get to know one another better, confirm our identity, learn from the mistakes, buttress the self-esteem from the greatness, and seek to improve upon the past. Historians deal with what actually *happened*. This realist stance—based on a weighted analysis of the past—safeguards them from both the extremes of the utopian escapism of populists' demagogy and the paralysis of fear of the traditionalists. Historians are intimately aware of what has worked (or not) in the past and are pained when society foolishly returns to disastrous ideas and ideologies that creep back in due to forgetfulness, cunning, deception, or simply to the imposition of higher interests.

However, on the other hand, historians' amassed experience should not turn us into skeptics (there is nothing to be done) who see all battles as lost, or into rigid traditionalists (there is nothing new under the sun) ready to fight and armed against the windmill of novelty as the new *Quixotes*. Our experience studying the past indicates that humanity's most formidable advances in the most diverse fields (political theories, social reforms, economic progress, scientific discoveries, and technological improvements) have arisen from illustrious minds capable of honoring the best of their tradition and applying it to something in need of innovation. As the medieval scholar Bernard of Chartres put it,

> We are like dwarfs on the shoulders of giants, so that we can see more than they, and things at a greater distance, not by virtue of any sharpness of sight on our part, or any physical distinction, but because we are carried high and raised up by their giant size.

In politics, reforms have had more long-lasting effects than revolutions—democracy was solidified more through English reforms than through French revolution. In economics, reformed theories such as Keynesianism—from its founder, John M. Keynes, who first challenged the radical ideas of the neoclassical liberalism—and social democracy have shown themselves in practice to be much more effective and viable than those related to unrestrained capitalism, radical communism, or revolutionary populism. In science, researchers who keenly understand and recognize the advances of their predecessors lead great revolutions (Newton, Einstein, Bohr), building their own theories on those that came before—as the historian of science Thomas Kuhn has persuasively shown.

Historians are of course aware that certain political ideas, social theories, and economic practices that failed in the past perhaps may work in the present when applied to different circumstances and contexts. Or, conversely, something that worked in the past will not necessarily work in the present. Authoritarian monarchism might have been the lesser evil of political systems when most of the population was illiterate, and might have been efficient to control unjust local mafias, but it is unjustifiable in contemporary societies. Slavery and feudalism might have found legitimation at some point in their ability to protect a security that no one else, apart from masters and feudal lords, could guarantee, but there is no way to defend them now. In the US-Great Depression and European postwar periods, the Great Deal and the Keynesianism, which advocated for a highly regulated capitalist system, were useful instruments for reconstruction, but its modeling needs constant reform and era-specific reformulation to be truly effective.

The moral of these historical lessons is that a balance between thoroughgoing knowledge of the past and interest for the present experience prevents society from interpretations that are paralyzed by nostalgia or utopianism. The complexity of the problems facing the world requires decisive responses, based on an adequate diagnosis, but also on a determined attitude. Neither *meaculpism*, so typical of the contemporary West, nor resignation is the right way to go. The former is impractical since it employs wrongheaded strategies that divert attention from the real problems. The latter engenders passivity. As I will argue in this book, the West needs to recover a weighted self-esteem based on their own history and tradition. In my view, this attitude does not necessarily lead to hegemonism or supremacism. But at the same time it is urgent that the West recovers its central role in respect for human dignity; fight against any discrimination of race, nation, or genre; defense of human rights, and protection of freedom of speech, thought, and religion.

In the remainder of this introduction, I intend (i) to justify the choice of the subject of the book (the West); (ii) to review the main challenges facing the West, and how they might be overcome; (iii) to develop the way I have approached them (genealogically), and (iv) to define and justify the relevance of the three concepts included in the subtitle (civilization, religion, and consciousness). Therefore, some readers might prefer to skip this more theoretical part and go directly to the actual narration of the genealogies of the West, starting with Chapter 1.

I

I am aware that choosing the idea of *The West* as a central point of the book can be problematic nowadays. In a certain sense, this concept is an amalgam of intellectual constructs created by the scholars' imagination and people's abstract ideas. Since it is not properly a geographical space, it owes its existence to the *difference* from the opposite concept of the *Orient*, as Edward Said explained in his *Orientalism* in 1978. Two decades earlier, Carl Schmitt had pointed out in his text on *The Planetary Tension between Orient and Occident* (1955) that the differences between orient and occident were not due to a 'polar tension' like that of the north and south pole. Earth does not have an absolute East or West. Rather, "the West" is a space of experience that endures over time, in the sense that some of the past events of that particular cultural delimitation remain active in our present experience. The West exists because there are individuals who *continue* to consider themselves Western. Western are those who find themselves under the weight of a specific history when it comes to understanding themselves: that "effective consciousness" that Hans-Georg Gadamer spoke of, the sense of a history pressing down. Thus, the West has to do with a historical consciousness (something that is always perceived in the present), and not with the construction of a *canon* of historical events in an *a posteriori* reading.

For a long time, the inhabitants of Western Europe have strengthened their identity as a civilization in contrast to other Eastern civilizations such as the Persians, the Byzantines, the Islamic, the Russians, and the Chinese. At the same time, the category of the West has been recognized from the outside, even if—as I will try to show in this book—it is not fruit of a single tradition, a unique genealogy, or a simple shared space, but of a complex amalgam of traces. It is therefore the result of a fusion of some ancient peoples of the eastern Mediterranean, the Greco-Roman legacy, Judeo-Christian heritage, the long maturation of the values generated by medieval and Early Modern European society, the material and technological development of the industrialization, the secular legacy of the Enlightenment, the late-modern tendencies and ideologies of liberalism, and the postmodern radical challenging of the Western tradition stimulated by postcolonialism, poststructuralism, transculturation, deconstructionism, and gender theories.

Even acknowledging the West's achievements, an account of its legacy may be read as a supremacist transgression in our global, transcultural, transcultural, postcolonial, and transnational world. Assuming and synthesizing this general trend of thinking, Yuval Noah Harari explains in his *Homo Sapiens* (2011) that "the place of racism in imperial ideology has now been replaced by *culturism*. Among today's elites, assertions about the contrasting merits of diverse human groups are almost always couched in terms of historical differences between cultures rather than biological differences between races." Harari is arguing that to highlight Western cultural values and achievements could degenerate into a hegemonic position towards other civilizations parallel to that what racists used in the past. Yet Harari and others who follow this approach are paradoxically imbued of what they want to denounce, since they implicitly assume that there is a kind of *ranking* among all past and present societies. However, through my rereading and reevaluation of Western history and genealogy, I would like to claim that visiting the past is not about who is better or worse, superior and inferior, civilized or uncivilized, hegemonic or subaltern, or developed or underdeveloped. It is not a question of judging or ranking, not least because all these categories are relative depending on who is designing them. It is rather about contextualizing the past, trying to explore roots, thinking about collective heritages, considering shared traditions, and recovering history—even if one shares this tradition with other cultures or ethnicities, and whether or not one identifies with these values. The reexamination of this collective experience leads to what classic historians called the function of history as *Magistra Vitae*, history as learning, the position I take in this book, rather than history as judgment.

In my exploration of the West, I do not see the book's chapters as interlocking parts of a rigid chain whose authority must be upheld. Neither do I think that the outline of traditions and values of Western civilization that I propose is an authoritative interpretation. Rather, I present these reflections as an apprenticeship for myself, and a way to dialogue with my interlocutors, my readers, who will certainly not agree with me on all the ideas argued in this book. My point is that our tradition should be critically revised once again, questioning these Western values and wondering which of them should remain and which of them should be expelled. To me, this is precisely one of the main qualities of Western spirit: its ability to constantly question its own principles, as we have experienced in the last hundred years, with the crisis of modernity of the interwar period (Chapter 16), the cultural revolution of the 1960s (Chapter 17), and the current postmodern critique with its manifestations such as gender and postcolonial theories (Chapter 18).

This Western strategy of critique/counter-critique, of love/hate of its own tradition, is replicated in its two-stroke strategy of inclusion/exclusion. This comes from very far. Herodotus, who has been known as "the father of [Western view of] history," begins by reminding the Greeks of what they owe to Egypt while at the same time establishing the borders between Greece and Persia. This all-inclusive/all-exclusive approach is reflected in my own decision to include *Jerusalem* as the first link of my genealogy. Some of my fellow historians would probably better opt for a 'Christian West' rather than 'Judeo-Christian West'—and others would argue that Islam should be included in this equation. For that reason, I try to justify the conceptual connections among the different chapters of this book, which I consider the steps of a chain rather than disconnected and arbitrary links.

We can discuss up to what extent the Western values remain authoritative, if this authority has led it to a supremacist attitude, and whether this authority must be questioned as a whole. But it seems to me obvious that, whether or not we accept the category of the West and its values, the *West* is a category that was recognized by people in the past so that it possesses, at the very least, *historical* existence. In fact, the topic of *The History of Western Civilization*, which was included in many programs in American Universities in the twentieth century, has certainly been disappearing during the last thirty years, having gradually been replaced by more global or transnational approach. Yet it is very symptomatic that its interest is still intact because some universities have kept it, and that two respected historians like Anthony Grafton and David A. Bell have recently published a well-conceived handbook titled *The West: A New History* (2018), in order to replace William H. McNeil's classic *History of Western Civilization: A Handbook*, published originally in 1949 and having been reissued numerous times.

Courses on Western civilization have been abandoned specially for their alleged Eurocentrism and Occidentalism. This disinterest for the history of Europe might be explained by the Old Continent's decreasing power in international politics. But I do not think the emergence of the new cultural and demographic tendencies are enough to justify eliding the value of the Western tradition and legacy. By arguing that it is worth reflecting again on the past and the present of the West, this book operates with the conviction that no era is better than another: they are simply different. Manichean judgments are usually capricious generalizations motivated by the need to legitimize some contemporary practice driven by personal interests, usually of a political or ideological nature, when in fact every era contains both good and bad elements. And on this point, we cannot just look the other way since our era has arguably been not better than others. The last century has witnessed some of the most horrifying events imaginable, including the Armenian genocide, the Nazi Holocaust, atomic bombs, Stalinist famines, Mao's purges, the Khmer Rouge's atrocities in Cambodia, and genocides in Rwanda and the Congo. But it has experienced great achievements too: many battles for racial liberation, gender claims, and social equality, which until recently seemed unthinkable, have been won. In addition, unprecedent levels of material comfort, health care, education, and retirement security have been attained.

Recounting each historical epoch inevitably leads to uncovering both positive and negative elements. The Middle Ages, for example, do not have a great reputation today mostly because the Enlightenment portrayal of it has endured, defining it by its most perverse elements, such as the limitation of religious freedom, feudal networks that were often inhumane, and impoverished material conditions. Yet, at other times, such as at the beginning of the nineteenth century, the Middle Ages was idealized because other more positive aspects were valued, such as authenticity, empathy with nature, loyalty, commitment, chivalric code, solidarity, the value of one's word, and other high ideals.

Together with each era's ups and downs, it is also evident that humanity (and more specifically the West) has experienced moments of cultural splendor in which history seems to intensify and human progress to expand, for example, Pericles's Athens, Augustus's Rome, Justinian's Constantinople, Leonardo's Florence, Michelangelo's Rome, Velázquez's Spain, Rembrandt's Amsterdam, Victorian London, Vienna *fin-de-siècle*, Paris *belle-époque*, or Berlin between wars. In short, history is not an Olympic competition where only rankings and medals matter. Rather, it invites us to correct the mistakes and learn from the successes that each era offers. But this requires a respectful and empathetic approach to the own past, rather than a blind, decontextualizing, and vindictive revisionism of it.

II

This is the spirit that enlivens this book, even if it is no secret that Western civilization is currently undergoing severe reappraisal, if not under open attack. This aggressive maneuver has gone so far as to deny its own existence. When that has proved impossible to deny, its sense of mission has been condemned and its very right to survive as a specific civilization questioned.

This is by no means a new phenomenon. As far back as a century ago, there was already talk of the 'crisis' or 'decline' of the West—which was, in reality, a crisis of Western modernity rather than of the West itself as a whole. In the interwar period, relevant thinkers, artists, and writers expressed their unease with the more inhuman implications of rationalization, urbanization, industrialization, and massification, all processes associated with modernity. Oswald Spengler let out a howl of despair in his *The Decline of the West* (1918), analogous to that other scream made famous not long before by the Norwegian painter Edvard Munch (1893). The multiple literary and artistic currents associated with *modernism* or the *avant-garde* declared themselves openly critical of modernity, despite their potentially misleading *ultramodern* label. Thinkers, artists, and writers such as Friedrich Nietzsche, Marcel Proust, Virginia Woolf, Pablo Picasso, and Frank Kafka stressed the ill ease, suffering, or tedium of the West. I can find no other icon that better expresses this anxiety than Picasso's *Guernica* (1937), in which the horror of war is represented by the disfigurement of the image. Others such as Stefan Zweig, who had given his memoirs the nostalgic title *The World of Yesterday* (1934), chose suicide as the only way out of their inner tragedy—in his case out of fear that even in Brazil, where he was exiled, he was not safe from the Nazis.

This tendency toward self-flagellation and radical self-questioning increased after World War II. From the 1960s onward, emerging from the increasing realization of the horrors of the Holocaust, the global tensions of the Cold War, the tyrannies established in so many countries, and the cultural revolution, the expression *postmodernity* came into general circulation to define a supposed superseding of the main values associated with modernity: religious subjectivism, philosophical rationalism, economic capitalism, and the political state. This time it was a French intellectual, Jean-François Lyotard, who nailed the diagnosis with his *The Postmodern Condition*, originally published in French in 1979, which is a sound diagnosis that we can still read with great interest today.

In those years, the processes of decolonization encouraged the cultural indigenization of many Asian and African peoples. They investigated their own roots in a natural reaction against the colonizing West. These processes of self-recognition and self-awareness, perfectly justifiable and understandable, were radical to varying degrees, but all shared a certain anti-Western sentiment, usually manifested as anti-American rather than anti-European. The transcultural and postcolonial movements of the new millennium are undermining not only the modern values inherent in colonization but also the very foundations of the West. Their strategy is to emphasize the most perverse effects of the West's global expansion, such as its ethnic hegemonism, colonial supremacism, savage capitalism, and predatory exploitation. Two pioneering authors for the intellectual legitimization of postcolonialism and transculturation were the American-Palestinian Edward Said (*Orientalism*, 1978) and the Indian Gayatri Spivak (*A Critique of Postcolonial Reason*, 1999), to whom we owe the development of the concept of 'subaltern.'

These intellectual movements and their activist offshoots argue that today we are no longer living through either the crisis of modernity of the first half of the twentieth century or the critical postmodern era of its second half, but a post-Western, postcolonial, and post-Christian period unique to the twenty-first century. The new trends have ended up promoting an openly anti-Western movement, dedicated to demolishing its historical foundations, its secular tradition, its specific religiosity, and its civilizational values. Without perhaps reflecting too deeply on the fact that they themselves owe their existence to the West's permanent predisposition toward self-awareness and self-criticism, they have challenged the very existence, identity, and values of what has traditionally been regarded as *The West*, of which they are certainly victims but also, paradoxically, both heirs and debtors. One of the main demonstrations of this fact is the paradox that many of these anti-Western intellectuals owe their academic and intellectual training to the best American and European universities: The Ayatollah Khomeini, with his studies in Paris, is the first exponent of a long list.

Prompted by the analytical and historical observation of these upheavals and paradoxes, informed by an openly revisionist attitude, and trying to understand the noble motivations of these anti-Western movements, this book is devoted to a reexamination of the historical existence of the West, the meaning of its mission in the world, its potential validity today and, of course, to contribute to raising their self-esteem in these difficult times. My approach is based on the four concepts that appear in the title and subtitle: genealogy, civilization, religion, and consciousness. The following pages of this introduction are devoted to defining what I mean by each of these four concepts.

III

The title of the book refers to the concept of *genealogy-(es)*. Differently from history, the genealogy proceeds retrospectively. It typically starts in the present and from there backtracks through each family branch, reaching as far as memory or documentation goes. In terms of the objectives of this book, it relates to the Western traditions and legacies, their presence in the present, and their integrity of the past. This is why I choose the label 'genealogy,' rather than 'history' to entitle this book. Legacy and tradition are not dead realities frozen in the past but live memories adapted to new contexts in the present. They are that part of the past living in our present. This book also aims to reexamine, explore, and reevaluate our own heritage so that we may eventually identify some implicit cultural patterns that help shape individual and collective identity. Socrates's dictum that "un examined life is not worth living," reminds us how important it is to examine one's own heritage—or at least one's *shared* heritage. The Western tradition has conditioned our past, and whether or not we are aware, it conditions our present and future.

By choosing the genealogical method, I have aimed to approach the past through the filter of the present. I am thus interested in the political, social, economic, cultural, intellectual, artistic, and religious aspects of past civilizations, focusing especially on those that have in some way shaped the values of the present. However, I try not to approach the past to justify or legitimize the present, which would potentially lead to manipulate or distort my evaluation. Rather, I do so to better understand who we are, where we come from, how we are wired, and what we owe each period of the past. My presentism, in as far as it exists, manifests itself in the criteria with which I select historical events, rather than in their manipulation to legitimize the present. Thus, this book is not a systematic history of the past or a universal history but rather an account of the processes, ideas, and events that the West has experienced and that have become part of its identity today— and for this reason, we consider them relevant and worthy of consideration today.

Genealogy is something more (or less) than a purely historical analysis. At the end of the twentieth century, Michel Foucault reacted against the traditional progressive vision of history, re-signifying the concept of *genealogy* as expounded by Nietzsche a century before. These two intellectuals—recognized as heroes of postmodernity—created a new mode of tracking philosophical concepts in their development over time, demythologizing their origins and tracing a crooked rather than a continuous line. This enables the detection of the various points of emergence, the multiple influences and sources, the continuities and discontinuities, and creating new interpretations and meanings for our present.

Genealogy invites the author and the reader to revise their point of view and destabilizes rather than harmonizes. It never hides behind its supposedly objective and scientific character, an impossibility in history as it is written not by an object but by a subject—its method being narrative rather than scientific. Genealogy is a concept derived etymologically from *genesis* and *logos*. Genesis refers to the birth of an event and logos to the primordial co-implication of all the partial meanings that produce or give rise to that birth through their historical experience.

I have not wanted to enter into contrasts, antitheses, or oppositions to the other great civilizations such as the Slavic-Orthodox, Chinese, Hindu, or Islamic. Not wanting to make this dialectic a central theme, it seeks rather to inquire how the West has gone about responding to the challenges posed by its lasting historical existence, not necessarily in conflict with other parts of the world. This is compatible with the fact that the identity of the West has been historically forged by contrast with other, neighboring civilizations, following the dialectic of the friend–enemy and civilized–barbarian: Israel versus Egypt, Greece versus Persia, Roma versus Germania, Early Christians versus pagans, medieval Western Christianity versus Islam, and early modern Western monarchies versus the Turks. But the West generally followed its own path—with the sole exception of the failed experiment of the twelfth-century Crusades—until the global expansion of its sixteenth- and nineteenth-century colonizations.

The specific responses to those great challenges were made manifest in some foundational events that have been fixed in the *historical* canon, such as the flight of the Jews from Egypt, the battle of Thermopylae, the birth of Jesus, the coronation of Charlemagne, the founding of the medieval nations, the conquest of America, the battle of Lepanto, the founding of the United States, the railroad, and the 1968 revolution. But they have also been embodied in the life of some memorable Western individuals, idealized and mythologized to a greater or lesser degree: David, Pericles, Socrates, Augustus, Jesus, Justinian, Agustine, Charlemagne, Abelard, Dante, Giotto, Columbus, Leonardo, Shakespeare, Luther, Copernicus, Newton, Locke, Smith, Marx, Washington, Robespierre, Tocqueville, Picasso, Einstein, and Churchill. Events, figures, ideas, and works were bringing to fruition what we commonly known as the West. The West itself has reflected systematically on the historical development and the nature of those specific responses through the question–answer logic discussed by Robin G. Collingwood, or the challenge–response of Arnold Toynbee, among many other methods.

In pursuing the genealogical approach, the weight of history cannot be evaded. My own experience as a medievalist has convinced me of the extraordinary capacity of origins to generate a specific civilizing condition in a given community.

Certainly, those origins need to be confirmed by the unfolding of a consciousness that can be rendered more or less explicitly in its narration, in the form of myths, legends, or histories. It is no coincidence that the Book of *Genesis* is the first one in the Bible or that every nation in the West has its founding heroes—explicitly recognized as the founding fathers in the United States, and likewise the Norman William the Conqueror in England, the Germanic Clovis in France, the Asturian-Leonese Don Pelayo in Spain, King Boleslaw in Poland, and, more recently, the founding fathers of the European Union such as Konrad Adenauer, Alcide De Gasperi, and Robert Schuman. In the end, civilizations are consolidated through sharing certain histories and a discourse community. The historian Robert A. Rosenstone has expressed this reality in his family autobiography *The Man Who Swam into History* (2005): "Ultimately it is not the facts that make us what we are, but the stories we have been told and the stories we believe."

The assumption of a discourse community refers to the natural tendency of civilizations to universalize their values, in a bid to expand and legitimize the boundaries of their discourse. The criticism of the West as expansionist is somewhat paradoxical, since no relevant civilization has been able to exempt itself from this natural tendency to expand. So, the historian of civilizations must trace the cultural emanations and the spiritual motivations that begin to spread beyond a local tribe, a family lineage, an ethnic group, a socio-professional group, a socioeconomic class, a complex community, or a complete society. Historians should therefore not confine themselves solely to the study of a civilization's origins—essential though those are—but also analyze its modes of expansion, the strength of its cohesion, the permanence of its existence, its modes of transformation, and its ability to survive in the face of the changes that affect it, external attacks, and its own internal contradictions.

IV

Based on the adoption of genealogy as the book's central axis, the subtitle introduces its three other key notions: civilization, religion, and consciousness. The first of them, civilization, has long been a basic conceptual tool in the methodology for analyzing the identities of societies. The concept is gaining even more popularity today, with BBC programs such as those of Mary Beard's and Simon Schama's *Civilisations* (2018), which is reminiscent of Kenneth Clark' *Civilisations* (1969). Certainly, regardless of the extent to which one identifies with its values, the historical existence of Western civilization is hard to deny. But how far does civilization continue to be a valid concept and method for defining what we know as the West?

Civilization (in the singular) was a term ignominiously popularized in the eighteenth century by French thinkers of the Enlightenment, as an alternative form of life to primitivism or barbarism, offering literacy, urbanization, modernization, and consensus among its component values. This concept emphasized the superiority of Western civilization, then at the zenith of its self-esteem and self-satisfaction, and was reduced to a hegemonistic meaning: the West possessed *the* civilization, a more advanced and *civilized* culture, in contrast to other supposedly more primitive ones. The celebrated film *My Fair Lady* (1964) in its apparently naïve production—emphasized by Audrey Hepburn's memorable performance as a *primitive* who is civilized thanks to a sophisticated educational process—shows how deeply this vision permeated the West until the 1970s.

This sense of civilization had a strong racial, moral, and Manichean component, as Western predominance was a direct consequence of the hegemony of the *white man* over other races. The first major reaction to this Enlightenment's reductionism approach to the concept of civilization came from the classical sociologists such as Max Weber and Émile Durkheim at the beginning of the twentieth century. They began to emphasize the plural 's' in 'civilizations'—as used today in the aforementioned BBC documentaries—and re-signified the concept to define and distinguish the six or seven great cultures that structured the world they knew. They built a theoretical framework that was put into practice by various intellectuals who, over the course of the twentieth century, have reflected on this concept and its practical consequences, such as Arnold Toynbee, Christopher Dawson, Benjamin Nelson, Fernand Braudel, William McNeill, Immanuel Wallerstein, and Felipe Fernández Armesto.

These authors emphasize that there is not *one* ideal civilization surpassing all others, but diverse civilizations, each with its own culture, religion, worldview, customs, institutions, tradition, and, crucially, its own self-identification (*consciousness*). The unfolding over time of these shared values forms a kind of historical whole, which ultimately generates a more far-reaching sense of belonging than that of nations and states. Civilizational identity is also formed and shaped by exclusion and differentiation from other civilizations, in a typical dialectical relationship of friend–enemy, as happened between the Jews and pagan Babylon, the Greek cities confronting the common Persian enemy, or the Romans the Germanic barbarians.

This new and more comprehensive concept of civilization was also more all-encompassing than those of race or nation, transcending its reductionism and privileging the religious and cultural spheres. It involves a broader cultural grouping and also one of longer duration (*longue durée*), becoming a privileged supra-state and supra-racial tool of analysis. It allows societies to be combined into identity groups that reflect major symbolic systems and go beyond more traditional nation-state groupings. It offers a viable alternative to the more apparently realistic and operative one of states, since it provides an easily intelligible conceptual structure for understanding the world in its entirety. It distinguishes the major from the more local conflicts, outlining the future, and directing rulers in more positive and constructive action. One fact that attests to the enduring relevance of civilization is that, just as wars were between dynasties from 1350 to 1500, religions from 1500 to 1650, princes from 1650 to 1800, peoples from 1800 to 1918, and ideologies from 1918 to 1989, in today's post-1989 world, they are between civilizations. This meaning of civilization also prevails over that of ideologies in terms of magnitude and duration, as ideologies—even if they have global aspirations—are much more determined by their conjunctural and contextual conditions, and the passage of time erodes them much more easily, as has been shown in the recent case of Fascism and Marxism.

In this broad concept of civilization—the 'civilizational complex'—the analysis is not reduced to the sociocultural processes of great nations but rather concerns dense structural systems that can contain within them diverse countries, nations, classes, institutions, and even a wide variety of cultural expression. Within their huge diversity, the multiple countries that form part of a civilization usually share origin and end time myths, a symbolic universe, a common tradition, religious beliefs, logical procedures, and, last but not least, structures of consciousness. It all coalesces in some systems of social and cultural action, which in the West are as follows: the assumption of rationality as logic of analysis, action, and operation, giving rise to the state, capitalism, and scientific exploration as its main achievements; the belief in Christianity, in its various confessions, as religion; the obsession with technical application as guarantor of comfort and happiness; the commitment to representation as political tool; the preference for institutionalization, with a tendency toward bureaucracy; the conviction of the necessity of a legal system to preserve society from chaos; and individual consciousness and freedom as hegemonic moral criterion.

This new notion of civilization(s) established by the modern Western sociologists, and recently recuperated by historians such as Niall Ferguson in his *Civilization: The West and the Rest* (2012), had the additional virtue that it could be used as a tool for comparing the West with other civilizations (especially the Chinese, Hindu, Islamic, and Slavic), seen for the first time as *equals*, though with a different history and values. The comparative perspective expanded as the sense of unease and crisis in the West grew in the interwar period, leading to research into other civilizations informed by both creative curiosity (wonder) and a genuine desire to learn some lessons. These approaches did not always emerge in the academic sphere, but also at the popular level: the fascination of the Beatles for Hindu culture, during their phase of musical maturation around the year 1967, stands as an iconic manifestation of this reality.

The fall of the Berlin Wall in 1989 represented a turning point, ushering in a period of apparent Western hegemony, however ephemeral it would subsequently prove to be. This sort of *pax romana* stimulated new reflections from the civilizing perspective. The interpretations of Francis Fukuyama in *The End of History and the Last Man* (1992), and Samuel P. Huntington in *The Clash of Civilizations* (1996), gained especially wide currency. Both reflected a striking state of euphoria—something like a swan song—prior to a period of deep depression. The former constituted something like a birth certificate—at once naïve, certain, and doomed to expire—of the definitive hegemony of Western civilization. The latter appeared to offer a more somber, realistic outlook in the face of pressure from other civilizations such as the Islamic and Chinese, but ended up arguing for the advisability of boosting Western influence to the maximum.

The ethnic-nationalistic-religious wars of Yugoslavia in the 1990s, the attack on the Twin Towers in 2001, and the Russian invasion of Ukraine in 2022, as well as many other dramatic events related to political tyrannies and religious terrorism issued the death certificate of the Fukuyama construct and confirmed that Huntington was closer to reality in his gloomy diagnosis. What has followed is now no longer history, but current affairs: the desperate, and rather despairing, defense of the West against the challenges of Islamic, Slavic, and Chinese civilizations seeking to break its hegemony.

What all these twentieth-century diagnoses make clear—comparative in the case of sociology and hegemonistic in that of political science— is that the concept of *civilization* can still be salvaged today as a tool not only for a better understanding of the world, but also as a means of improving it. Toby E. Huff has argued that civilizational identities are based on historical experiences of centuries mediated through language, custom, law, and religion that transcend village and state and that have powerful galvanizing effects that continue to shape international cooperation and conflict. Benjamin Nelson adds that civilizations are configurated of identities of language, the central patterns of reciprocities including juridical rules, the fundamental canons governing the decision-matrices in the spheres of opinion and act, the common structures of consciousness, the comprising cultural worldviews and images of experience, and shared logics, of the self and time.

Civilization still matters. Some civilizations are still operative today, sustained by the common experience of certain symbolic systems of a religious, legal, and philosophical nature, as indeed the Western, Slavic-Orthodox, Chinese-Confucian, Islamic, Hindu, and African-Sub-Saharan civilizations are. As a critical framework, civilizational analysis is more useful than the more traditional nation-state, and more reliable than the global, since its inherent decontextualization makes it less viable for highlighting specific differences and the frequency of discontinuities. The civilizational approach, heir to the French historical school headed by Fernand Braudel in the mid-twentieth century, is also more aligned with the working hypotheses postulated more recently in the influential Cambridge *History Manifesto* (2014) by Jo Guldi and David Armitage, who clearly advocate long-term over short- and medium-term history.

The great paradox, and an even clearer demonstration of the timeliness of continuing to maintain this conceptual category, is that the great civilizations have proved extraordinarily resistant to the galloping globalization we have experienced this past century. Non-Western have perhaps proved vulnerable in their adoption of some global principles originating from the West, above all capitalism as an economic system, liberalism as a way of life, and Marxism as an ideology. But their values—religious, cultural, and idiosyncratic—have shown a striking impermeability and resistance, especially those of the Chinese, Hindu and Islamic civilizations. As a consequence, beyond some superficial assimilations arising more from the historical experience of Western colonization processes than from globalization, Islamic civilization has continued to be essentially Islamic, Chinese civilization essentially Chinese, and Hindu civilization essentially Hindu. I will try to analyze the extent to which Western civilization continues to be essentially Western, though of course its own revisionist and self-critical bent has enabled its adaptation to the new global conditions without losing—as I will argue in the following pages—anything essential.

The second concept that appears in the subtitle is that of religion, which has traditionally functioned—and continues to function—as an essential value in civilizations. The apparent processes of secularization are more simply skin-deep transformations, which, paradoxically, maintain historical and systematic analogies with the religious processes that founded their specificity. Religion constitutes the most essential part of the values that make civilizations specific, and therefore distinguishable from others: Judeo-Christian in the West, Orthodox in the East, Muslim in Islam, Confucian in China, Hindu in India, and animist in sub-Saharan Africa. To varying degrees, these civilizations have undergone secularizing processes that have sought to demolish the integrity of their own religion, or have at least revised their fundamentals through reform—as was the case with the emergence of Protestantism in the West or the division between Shiites and Sunnis in Islam. But the most visible historical experience confirms that these *processes* of secularization have not been either progressive—given that they have had many ups and downs, advances, setbacks, and recoveries over time—or all-encompassing, since those religions continue to mark the life of those civilizations to a significant extent. The concept of secularization itself should recognize continuities underlying changes.

The continued relevance and eternal return of religions in those civilizations is compatible with the greater or lesser adhesion of individuals to their more explicit moral rules, as Émile Durkheim set out in his *Elementary Forms of Religious Life* (1912), or with varying levels of participation in sacred rites, as the symbolic anthropologists have confirmed more recently, especially Cliffort Geertz, Victor Turner, and Mary Douglas. The British historian Christopher Dawson stated that the great religions constitute the foundations on which the four great civilizations rest: Christianity, Islam, Hinduism, and Confucianism. In the ancient axial age, as originally conceived by Karl Jaspers (*The Origin and Goal of History*, 1949), the transcendental myths were shared by the Jewish prophets, the Greek philosophers, the Chinese scholars, the Hindu Brahmins, the Buddhist *sangha*, and the Islamic *ulema*. With the passage of time, they became more and more differentiated, until their evident diversification today, but their foundational myths are still alive in the imagination of the people.

In Western civilization itself, there has been a notable diversity in the essence of Christianity, depending on historical period, as some scholars have conveyed, that is, Ludwig Feuerbach's *The Essence of Christianity* (1841), Adolf von Harnack's *What is Christianity* (1901), Romano Guardini's *The Essence of Christianity* (1929), and Joseph Ratzinger's *Introduction to Christianity* (1968). But the Christian values of charity, fraternity, solidarity, justice, freedom, universality of rights, and tolerance of beliefs have remained standing over the centuries in the West. Succeeding generations of Western have inquired into the nature and essence of Christianity. This is a very Western move: to inquire into the rational roots and spiritual mysteries of their own religion.

The third concept that appears in the subtitle is that of *consciousness*. English in its richness distinguishes between *conscience* and *consciousness*, which other languages—including the Latin ones—do not. Beyond its application to the reflective capacity of individuals, consciousness is a term that refers to the capacity of certain collectives—whether an ethnic, class, national, state, religious, linguistic, or civilizational community—to recognize themselves as a unit through a self-perception that is deliberately constructed rather than passively encountered. A classic study of the formation of such a consciousness, in this case of a social class, is Edward Thompson's *The Making of Working Class* (1963).

Civilizations are, in this context, structures of consciousness, to borrow Benjamin Nelson's expression. The use and application of this concept in the analysis of Western civilization is essential not only for thinking critically about its existence but also for recognizing the diverse cultural manifestations that these self-knowledge and self-perception have generated. Throughout the book, I will argue that a passion for rational knowledge, a profound self-critical tendency, and consequent scientific development are some of the clearest expressions of this Western consciousness. For that reason, the periods which saw revolutions in knowledge—the Athenian rationality of the fifth century BC, the legal reforms of the classic Rome from the first century, the logical thought of the twelfth century, and the Scientific Revolution of the seventeenth century—will merit detailed commentary.

A society is never truly known and recognized in its singularity until the contours of its own self-knowledge can be traced. From the *Confessions* of Augustine and Jean-Jacques Rousseau, through Abelard's *Historia Calamitatum*, Teresa of Ávila's *Book of Her Life*, and François-René de Chateaubriand' *Mémoires d'Outre-Tombe*—all of them true masterpieces that every Western student should be familiar with from secondary school onward—the West has developed a striking propensity for autobiography, fruit of its passion for self-knowledge and self-recognition. These works are recognized for their sublime literary value, yet they also say much about the Western character. This passion for self-perception also manifests in the pronounced Western tendency to theorize about—and constantly question—the very foundations of its own philosophy (through metaphysics and the theory of knowledge), its religion (theory and history of religions), and even its scientific disciplines (theory and history of the sciences, scientific epistemologies). This has a certain over-sophistication effect and can generate a sterile tendency toward narcissism and formalism, but it has of course immunized the West against stagnation. To survive, any civilization needs to maintain a judicious equilibrium between tradition and innovation, between respect for the most salient values of its identity and the need to adapt to new times, fostering healthy self-criticism through free intellectual debate. In the end, this self-reflective tendency—or should I perhaps say obsession?—was exalted at the zenith of modernity in the theories associated with Freudian and Lacanian psychoanalysis and its later echoes, which continue until today.

V

The central point of my argument, and what justify this book, is that it would be anachronistic to deny the historical reality and current existence of the West, both as an event and a meaningful entity. Put in graphic medical terms, a poor diagnosis fatally leads to the wrong therapy. The current situation is too severe for a diagnostic error to occur. I therefore argue that it is possible—is even, perhaps, the only method available—to write a specific history of the West without reducing it into elitist exclusivism or flagrant supremacism, or into sterile archaeologism or ideological presentism.

Declaring the reality of the West does not necessarily imply being anti-anything, extra-anything, or post-anything. Moreover, my approach is compatible with the historical reality of an 'axial age'—an idea originally developed by Karl Jaspers with regard to Antiquity—in which there co-habited in Eurasia a plurality of civilizations with similar degrees of cultural and scientific development. However, it is a verifiable historical fact that not all civilizations are equal. For instance, the artistic and cultural achievements have differed greatly. Why Florence, Venice, and Barcelona continue to attract so many millions of tourists a year, without being major state or financial capitals themselves, is something that should lead one to reflect on the sublimity of their artistic, cultural, and historical heritage. As Benjamin Nelson has argued, all great peoples, such as China, India, Greece, and Israel, may be said to be possessed of a potential to engender universal structures, but few have gone so far in articulating effective institutions in the spheres of social relations and cultural designs.

The diversity of civilizations does not legitimize the compiling of a *ranking* or a *canon* of civilizations, as some pro- and anti-Western intellectuals seek to do. It is simply a matter of going deeply into the existence of the West by means of a genealogical rather than a properly historical method in order to extract certain notions of identity. My intention is to create a narrative for all those who, in one way or another, identify with the values of the West that will enable them to critically approach, examine, explore, question, revise, maintain, and update their own civilization.

Excessive detachment, frivolous disregard, or superficial disinterest in one's own tradition can degenerate into irreparable losses of values that have taken centuries to consolidate, from liberalism to democracy. The question is not so much whether our civilization is the ideal one, but to what extent it wins the comparison with other civilizations, whether its ways of life generate more adherence than others. From the inductive data we have on migration processes today—most of the migrators pointing to North America and Europe as true paradises for those who aspire to them, even worth risking one's life for—we should not doubt too much the effectiveness of the West. In this book, I would like to share these thoughts with readers who identify with Gustav Mahler's paraphrase of Thomas More: "Tradition is not the worship of ashes, but the preservation of fire." Every tradition requires updating, assuming the risks that entail, if it does not want to die of starvation. But updating is not synonym of self-demolition.

In the end, this book does not seek to *construct* or *de-construct* an identity, and far less to defend an identity that might be assumed to be natural, essential, exclusivist, supremacist, or hegemonic. On the contrary, these *genealogies* simply try to show the complex reality of the West to reassess what type of tradition is weighing on the present of those of us who consider ourselves Western, what possibilities of continuity that tradition offers, what alternatives and improvements might materialize, what challenges are facing, and, finally, what the price of rupture would be.

PART I

FOUNDATIONS

CHAPTER 1

JERUSALEM

These *genealogies* begin with King David's conquest of Jerusalem around 1000 BC, a fundamental milestone in the history of Israel and the West. David decided to make Jerusalem the capital of the Jewish people because of its strategic location, as well as its neutrality and ability to bring together the scattered tribes of Israel. He also started plans to build a great temple in Jerusalem, the new holy city of the Israelites, to preserve the Ark of the Covenant in a dignified place, to centralize the worship of Israel's God, and to establish a center of spirituality and pilgrimage for all of his people. Ultimately, built by David's son Solomon, the Temple reflected Jerusalem's majesty and beauty (Figure 1.1). It gave testimony of the history of Jerusalem and Israel for 1,000 years until it was demolished in AD 70 by troops of the general and future Emperor Titus, at the time of Emperor Vespasian. Jerusalem was devastated and the Jewish people dispersed throughout the Mediterranean. These 1,000 years of history—and its projection on the spirit of the Jewish people throughout history—are one of the pillars of Western civilization and require special attention.

Relatively small in number, the Jewish people were of Semitic origin and suffered under the yoke of Egyptian slavery until about 1300 BC. They freed themselves under the leadership of their patriarch Moses, who spoke with the God of Israel 'face to face.' From Egypt, they traveled eastward and, over the next two centuries, colonized an area between the Mediterranean Sea and the Jordan River with the conviction that it was the Promised Land that God provided in fulfillment of His promise to their ancestor, the patriarch Abraham. Yet, occupying that land was by no means easy, not only because the small towns that had previously colonized it resisted (the Gibeonites, Amorites, Hittites, Canaanites, and Jebusites), but also because the surrounding powers (the Egyptians, Assyrians, Babylonians, Persians, Greeks, and Romans) pressured and harassed them for the next ten centuries, starting from the conquest of Jerusalem until the destruction of their temple in AD 70.

FIGURE 1.1 The Dome of the Rock on the Temple Mount in Jerusalem.
© Shutterstock.

Who were these neighboring powers? To the west, on the banks of the Nile, the Egyptian pharaohs—essentially deified leaders—had built a great empire with admirable agricultural activity and commercial vitality. To the east, on the banks of the Tigris and Euphrates rivers in modern Iraq, the Mesopotamian, Sumerian, Akkadian, and Babylonian civilizations were creating prosperous urban communities with a sophisticated political organization. To the north, on the Mediterranean shore, the Phoenicians in Tyre and Sidon, present-day Lebanon, were building a commercial center and are credited with creating the basic structure of the alphabet that we use today. Their alphabetic script surpassed other forms of writing in Antiquity like Babylonian cuneiform, Egyptian hieroglyphs, and Chinese logosyllabic. Israel was also located next to several Southern nomadic Arab tribes which, while unable to organize politically, had valiant warriors. Farther east, in present-day Iran, the formidable Persian Empire was growing and would eventually expand beyond proportions ever imagined, from Egypt to present-day India.

Despite its small size compared to these great powers, Israel soon distinguished itself based on a religion with a completely different foundation, namely a belief in one God who created all things and kept them alive through His providence and love. All the surrounding civilizations believed in higher beings, commonly called 'gods,' but thought of their existence as removed from men, who only knew of these gods through stories told from generation to generation presented in the form of myth or legend. Poets retold these stories, which priests and chiefs often represented during complex, participatory rituals. These civilizations never formulated the idea of just one God or of a god who could be close to the humans. Moreover, the Israelites claimed to have an especially intimate relationship with their God, who spoke to their prophets and priests, a claim that garnered hostilities and misunderstandings from the beginning. Unfortunately, anti-Semitism is, after all, an ancient matter.

In addition, the Jewish people believed their God to be separate from the world, transcendent, and to have an existence of His own apart from His creation. His people owed Him a singular form of adoration, distinguished from myths and legends and beyond human understanding. Thus, they opposed reducing their God to a certain image, and rather preferred to describe and narrate Him with words, which also clearly differed from their neighbors' practices. Egyptians, Sumerians, and Babylonians represented their gods in anthropomorphic or animal images, such as Anubis who was portrayed with the head of a jackal. For their part, the Israelites' most important temple, in the city of Jerusalem, lacked any image whatsoever and instead housed the Ark of the Covenant, which contained tablets engraved in stone listing the Ten Commandments that their own God, whom they respectfully pronounce the name ('Yahweh'), delivered to their first prophet, Moses.

Most importantly, for posterity, the Jewish people handed down the Bible, a combination of books woven together by the narration of God's revelation to his chosen people. It is the most-read book in human history and its stories, using symbolic, conceptual, poetic, and narrative language, reveal deep truths about human nature and its historical experience. From the point of view of Jewish tradition, there is only *Tanakh*, an acronym that indicates the composition of the Hebrew Bible of three types of texts: *Torah* ('teaching,' also known as the Five Books of Moses), *Nevi'im* (Prophets), and *Ketuvim* (Writings). Tanakh, moreover, is not the Old Testament as known by the Christians. The confusion and selection of texts and notably different, for example, in the Hebrew Bible, the book of Daniel is in Ketuvim and not in Nevi'im.

Yet, from the point of view of the Christianity, the Bible is divided into two books: the first, the Old Testament, recounts the events from the creation of the world up to 135 BC, when the Jewish warriors, the Maccabees, rebelled against the Hellenistic Seleucids. It contains 46 books with diverse themes that can be divided into four major groups: Pentateuch (from Genesis to Deuteronomy), historical books (from Joshua to the Maccabees), prophetic books (from Isaiah to Malachi), and sapiential books (from Job to Sirach). The latter, unlike Genesis and other historical books, contain a Hellenistic and Greek, rather than Mesopotamian and Persian, influence and depict sublime realities such as the meaning of wealth and success, the experience of suffering, the struggle between good and evil, what virtuous men and women are like, and achieving inner peace, with beautifully poetic and highly suggestive language. It is striking that, after so much time, these books still inspire reflection; indeed, their advice goes far beyond the concrete historical circumstances in which they were written.

The Bible is not an insular account from obscure sages of Israel, but rather a deep reflection on the exchange of ideas that took place between Israel and its neighboring peoples. The books of the Bible appear to be an intentional compilation rather than a random assortment of texts from individual authors. The narration of humanity's origins in the first book of the Bible—Genesis— is based on a careful selection of literary elements that explain the original message that God wanted to transmit to the people of Israel and, through their experience, to all of humanity. Thus, the models, themes, and symbols it employs reflect the contact that Israel had with neighboring peoples. The Babylonian poem *Enuma Elis*, composed many centuries before Genesis, contains a beautiful account of creation and begins thus:

> When on high the heaven had not been named,
> Firm ground below had not been called by name,
> Naught but primordial Apsu, their begetter,
> (And) Mummu-Tiamat, she who bore them all,
> Their waters commingling as a single body;
> No reed hut had been matted, no marsh land had appeared,
> When no gods whatever had been brought into being,
> Uncalled by name, their destinies undetermined—
> Then it was that the gods were formed within them.

(Beginning of the *Enuma Elis*, quoted in James B. Pritchard, ed., *Ancient Near Eastern Texts Relating to the Old Testament* (Princeton, Princeton University Press, 1969), pp. 60, 61)

Unlike Jewish monotheism, the poem expresses clear polytheistic content, but its parallelism with Genesis' creation narrative is evident. Genesis also conveys that God "formed a man from the dust of the ground and breathed into his nostrils the breath of life, and the man became a living being" (*Genesis*, 2: 7). The serpent, which appears in Genesis as the personification of the devil, is a symbolic element from the ancient East's mythical accounts too, for example, in the *Epic of Gilgamesh*.

The oral transmission of stories is an essential act for all peoples, and ancient Israel was no exception. However, Israel's desire to determine a tradition for subsequent generations is quite specific and original to it, and could not have been accomplished without writing. Oral transmission has tremendous expressive force, but the content it contains changes almost every time it is recited in the form of poem, song, or story, at a family or community gathering. The written word, however, has enormous potential for more effectively establishing an enduring norm, law, or way of acting. The English anthropologist Jack Goody used the concept of 'structural amnesia' to distinguish oral fluidity from written fixity.

In establishing this written tradition, the Israelites were inspired by the wisdom of one of their neighbors, the Phoenicians, who first used writing as it has been used in the West from then. They were merchants and well connected with the Persian, Babylonian, Egyptian, and Greek civilizations because of their frequent commercial relations on the coasts of the Italian and Iberian peninsulas. They differentiated themselves with dedication to trade over military campaigns and pillage. This commercial ambition motivated their development of a form of expression to record transactions more reliably than with the spoken word, which is easily manipulated and hard to remember. Thus, they created the basic form of the alphabet as we know it today in Western civilization, that is, by separating speech into letters and attributing a written symbol to each phonetic sound. This was a revolution and a radical alternative to text based on the most accurate representation of an idea, a concept or an object through drawing (Chinese characters), of puzzle-like riddles (Egyptian hieroglyphics), or schematic symbols (Babylonian cuneiform script). The Phoenicians created these new symbols, which we now recognize as *letters*, some 3,000 years ago. As we will also see, commercial activity has always been an essential element of not only economic development but also cultural enrichment, assimilation of other civilizations' values and respect for other traditions, as the Greeks and Romans experienced in Antiquity.

The Israelites were especially fond of understanding their origins, which clearly signals their profound sense of identity. In addition, they had the audacity to connect their particular history to the very creation of nature and humans. Their neighbors had the same fixation, and all of them have left us beautiful stories about the creation of the world and of the first human beings, but none were able to generate a story as full of meaning and symbolism as the one found in the first three chapters of Genesis. This book relates, in luminous language and with a singular mixture of simplicity and depth, the story of the creation of the universe in its different stages: "In the beginning, God created the heaven and the earth" (*Genesis* 1: 1). God first created light, a recurrent theme in the West's spirituality and philosophy, to dissipate the darkness that covered the earth, thus distinguishing day from night. Then God formed the heavens, separating the sky from the earth. He then gathered all the water that covered the earth into one place, distinguishing it from the earth. God then created vegetation and animals. Finally, Genesis narrates the creation of man and woman, who were assigned the task of dominating and subduing the rest of creation. But men abused God's trust and their nature was damaged by 'original sin,' inclining them toward evil, pain, and shame based on the experience of weakness and death. From there, the Old Testament narrates a long history of Israel's dialogues, alliances, allegiances, betrayals, encounters, and disagreements with their God during one millennium.

Origin stories are enormously relevant for all peoples because they directly connect with the question of identity. Suffice it to recall the cultural appreciation that historical figures and national heroes found in origin stories enjoy, for example, Romulus and Remus in Rome, Charlemagne in Europe, William the Conqueror in England, Hugh Capet in France, or Pelayo in Spain. However, these origin stories often refer to a very distant past and we usually know very little about these people and their era. Thus, instead of employing a strictly historical narrative, a kind of mythological, symbolic language marks these stories. Biblical stories about the origin of the world and humans use a language common to myths—a symbolic expression of realities that cannot be expressed in rational and scientific language and that do not fit into the categories of ordinary history. This does not necessarily negate truth; rather, in the absence of reliable testimony and written documentation, language that is schematic, simplified, and based on simple binary categories—God and man, male and female, angel and devil, good and evil—helps trace the truth. To understand this language, we must break away from a rational and scientific mentality, and open ourselves up to other languages that better reflect spiritual realities.

This symbolic language also has the advantage of being easily recognizable by all. By expressing meaning through symbols, it appeals to the deepest values and beliefs intimately connected to our identity. If we think of the country to which we belong, the institution for which we work, or the family in which we grew up, we can distinguish, on the one hand, their origin stories (which usually refer to the founding heroes or first conquerors of a nation, the creators of a company or institution, or original family ancestors) and, on the other, related 'historical' stories that refer to verifiable realities.

Along with all these experiences, over the centuries, the Israelites developed an unusual awareness of being specially chosen by God, a favored people. Neighboring civilizations did not acknowledge this sense of privilege from a people whom they (rightly) considered the least powerful among them and reacted with varying degrees of envy, sarcasm, and contempt. This attitude generated distaste toward this small population, whose demographic reach, political relevance, commercial volume, and military might contrast sharply with its self-proclaimed status as a chosen people. We will never know exactly when anti-Semitism commenced, but it clearly did not take that long. From the first centuries of its existence, neighboring powers showed little mercy toward the Jewish people in a way that seemed to go beyond mere military competition. In addition, the brutality of Egyptian, Babylonian, and Roman domination was compatible with their curiosity before such a clever people. Perhaps for this reason, Persia (Iran today) was the only empire against which Israel did not clash head on; the Persians tolerated Israel's customs and traditional worship, allowing them to rebuild the Temple in Jerusalem around 536 BC. In this regard, Israel likely benefited from the Persian tendency to constitute 'federations' of subjugated states rather than to centralize power, as well as from the fact that Israel was geographically located halfway between Persia and Greece—the true enemy of the Persians.

The Jewish people endured domination with mixed feelings, ranging from providentialism to fatalism. These two extremes gradually led to paralysis, either based on the belief that God would finally redeem them from brutal domination (providentialism) or on the conviction that their status as a chosen people made it impossible to change course (fatalism). But, around 1000 BC, the Israelites decided to change the course of their history in a quest for greater autonomy in political decision-making. For temporal issues, they decided to appoint an intermediary between God and the people, a king. Seen in perspective, establishing a monarchy in Israel was not terribly original since neighboring civilizations had already instituted it in one way or another. In addition, it reflected well on Israel's progress after its liberation from Egyptian domination since a tribal confederation (governed by 'judges') already proved itself insufficient in the face increasingly complex societal structures.

The Israelites asked their God to adopt the political systems their neighbors were effectively practicing. This part of the history of the Jews is graphically narrated in the First Book of Samuel. God warns them, through the priest Samuel, that if a monarchy is established, kings will select their best sons for the military and bring their most beloved daughters to court. However, the Israelites, who portray themselves in the Bible as an stubborn people, reiterated their request. God then instructed Samuel to choose a courageous soldier, Saul, to be the first king of Israel. Saul was succeeded by King David, whose reign was of great significance since he conquered Jerusalem, established it as the capital of the new kingdom, converted it into a holy city, unified the twelve tribes of Israel, and territorially expanded the kingdom, building long-lasting institutions. His memory is exalted as a model of a wise and holy ruler. In addition, he took the crucial step of transforming the monarchy from elective to hereditary, a change that all sovereigns seek, in one way or another, when they appropriate the title of monarch by choice, marriage, or usurpation. David's son and successor, King Solomon, was also wise and courageous at first, but eventually degenerated into hedonism and distanced Israel from God's favor. After his death, the Kingdom of Israel collapsed and never regained its previous splendor. The stories of these kings are recounted with extraordinary realism and energy in the books of Samuel, Kings, and Chronicles, in narrations that many medieval and modern Christian kings, as well as their chroniclers, considered models for learning and practice.

Israel did not establish a hereditary monarchy as an original contribution to posterity (its most powerful neighbors had already practiced it for many centuries), but Israel's kings used it to legitimize their sovereignty. The Israelite monarch was not seen an ordinary citizen. From the moment that the priest Samuel anointed Saul with sacred oil, choosing him from among his brothers, even though he seemed the least gifted of them, he corroborated a divine election and consecrated him. The custom of anointing kings held enormous symbolic relevance among medieval and early modern European monarchies and became an essential rite in their accession to power. Many centuries after King David, the Visigoths of Spain resumed the practice of royal anointing. In AD 672, the Bishop of Toledo anointed King Wamba in a solemn enthronement ceremony explicitly modeled after David's anointment narrated in Samuel. The Carolingian dynasty consolidated this custom, which then spread throughout medieval Europe. These rites are characterized not only to reinforce the citizenry's solidarity but also to produce a *transformation*—a change of era, the recovery of health, or crop improvement. The king's anointment was also seen as bringing about a transformation in that he became a sacred person with the qualities needed to exercise divine authority. The rite of royal anointing also had obvious parallels with the anointing of priests, although it was clear that consecration enabled two different powers, temporal (whose proper ceremony is the coronation) and spiritual (whose proper ritual is the anointment), respectively.

While the kings of Israel needed the help of priests to legitimize their authority, they also sought counsel from prophets to correctly establish their government. In reality, prophets advised kings, but also rebuked them when they performed poorly. Nathan seriously admonished King David after he plotted Uriah's death in order to marry his beautiful wife, Bathsheba. Ahijah predicted Israel's decline after King Solomon's death because the latter fell into idolatry and temptation. Some, like King David, were repentant and corrected themselves, becoming models for their entire people in spite of their weaknesses. Others, like Solomon, did not make amends and received divine punishment, which the prophets foretold. Over time, in the West, specialized personnel supplemented prophets' function as advisers, but kings still desired to act with prudence and justice, and medieval kings even aspired to wear the crown of holiness. Thus, the model of ancient and modern kings oscillated between wisdom (an ideal associated with prophets) and holiness (an ideal associated with priests).

Israel's second monarch, King David, is widely considered a prefiguration of the Messiah, a mysterious character who the prophets progressively proclaimed and hoped to come in the future. Many of Jesus' contemporaries believed in him not only because of the authority with which he preached and performed miracles, but also because they were astonished that many of the things they had read and heard about the Messiah for so long, and written many centuries before in the Bible, were fulfilled with Jesus, including minor and symbolic details. Others converted to Christianity later by carefully comparing the Old and New Testaments with the conviction that the coincidences found there could not be the result of mere chance. Even King Herod, a bloodthirsty, cruel, and antireligious ruler, displayed respect for the Scriptures by bringing together "the chief priests and the teachers of the Law" to clarify where the Messiah was to be born because he was afraid that the Messiah would compete with his power (Matthew, 2:4). This gesture clearly shows the then-widespread belief that the Bible was a reliable prophetic source with real stories told through poetic and symbolic language. After Herod listened attentively from his advisers, he learned that—according to the prophet Micah—the Messiah was to be born in Bethlehem. Trusting this indication, he acted accordingly, calling for the slaughter of all male children under two years of age residing in Bethlehem and surrounding areas. Jesus, who was born in Bethlehem, was spared due to the fact that his parents escaped to Egypt before Herod's order was fulfilled.

Although the prophets often spoke of a 'redeemer' in the strictly spiritual sense, the Jewish people never quite agreed on whether the redeemer's scope of action extended to the political sphere. At the time, many Jews recognized Jesus as the true Messiah based on his miracles and the consistency of his actions and words with Elijah and Isaiah's prophecies. Many, however, were disappointed because they expected a political and military messiah to free them from Roman imperialism. Jesus was eventually condemned to the humiliating and cruel death of torture on the cross, a punishment normally reserved for the most dangerous of criminals. Jesus did not resist with force, and at a crucial moment in his trial, he summarily declared before Pontius Pilate that he was indeed king, but that his kingdom was not of this world.

After Jesus' death and the spread of the news of his resurrection, around AD 30, the Jewish people were painfully divided, concluding this first chapter on the history of the West. Those who recognized Jesus as the messiah, savior, and redeemer of the world soon received the name 'Christians' in Antioch of Syria and spread a religion with universal reach that is unrestricted by race or nation. Those who did not recognize Jesus continued practicing Judaism as a religion circumscribed to the people of the Hebrew race. Yet, if Judaism was circumscribed to the Jewish people, it was from the beginning intended as a call to salvation to anyone who decided to follow the way of Abraham and Moses: the tension between universalism and particularism was present from the origin of Judaism, and transferred to Christianity from its beginnings. They suffered General Tito's brutal destruction of the Temple in Jerusalem in AD 70, and their subsequent diaspora throughout the Roman world.

Since then, although Jews and Christians certainly share many basic values vis-à-vis civilization, they walk diverse religious paths. Christianity took several centuries to consolidate and never ceased to be plagued by divisions and conflicts. The same happened with Judaism. For a couple of centuries, the distinction between Judaism and Christianity was hard to delimitate. When this divergence became effective, Jews and Christians followed divergent paths to this day, although they have certainly shared many basic values that are at the foundation of Western civilization.

CHAPTER 2

ATHENS

By the year 500 BC, the Persians, the only empire that respected Jewish practice, dominated the entire known world—from Afghanistan to the territories that we currently known as Iran, Iraq, Arabia, Turkey, the Balkans, Egypt, and Libya. A glance at a map suffices to grasp the enormous extent of this empire. How had such an expansion occurred? For a long time, the Persians waited in the background, checked by Assyrian and Babylonian hegemony, until a courageous sovereign, Cyrus the Great, launched westward on an unstoppable conquest during the sixth century BC. First, he took the city of Babylon and its kingdom. He freed the Jews and allowed them to return to Jerusalem, as well as to reestablish their religious practice. After his death, his son, Cambyses II, conquered Egypt and dethroned the Pharaoh, bringing a 3,000-year-old empire to its end.

One of Cambyses II's successors, King Darius, known as 'the king of kings,' further expanded the empire, conquering Asia Minor to the north and reaching the borders of India to the east. At the same time, he accomplished extraordinary administrative feats, promoting the construction of roads that facilitated the execution of his orders around the extents of his vast empire. Eventually, Darius also wanted to conquer the cities settled in present-day Greece, but the inhabitants of the Greek colonies were accustomed to governing their businesses independently and were proud of their autonomously functioning independent states. These tenacious merchants refused domination from a sovereign who dictated laws at will, spoke a different language, and directed affairs from afar.

The confrontation between the Persians and Greeks, known as the Persian Wars, inspired some of the most beautiful historical and epic stories, and remains collective memory as the prototypical confrontation between barbarism and civilization. Darius equipped a massive fleet with the intention of eliminating Athens and conquering all of Greece. After a failed first attempt, a renewed Persian fleet landed next to the city of Marathon, located just over forty-two kilometers from Athens. Miltiades, a brave and intelligent general who headed the Athenian troops, caught the Persians by surprise and defeated them. Realizing that the Persians had not fled, but actually set out for Athens, he sent a messenger to run as fast as possible and alert the Athenians of the imminent arrival of the Persian fleet. The messenger arrived faster by land than the Persian ships could by sea, so he fulfilled his mission, but his heart did not withstand the grueling trip and he died as soon as he communicated the news. The marathoner's herald, together with the arrival of Miltiades's troops, gave the Persians reason to back down from their attempts to conquer Athens. The victory of the Athenians was absolute, and in 490 BC the Persians had to return to their lands accepting their defeat.

Darius's successor, Xerxes, however, was too ambitious to forget about the Greeks. He organized a massive army that set out by land and sea for Greece. In the north of Greece, they met unexpected opposition—a group of brave Spartan soldiers who tried to stop them at the Thermopylae Pass. The Persians threatened to launch so many arrows that they would darken the sky, but the Spartans replied that they preferred to fight in the shade. The Persians ultimately won because a traitor showed them a path through the mountains that allowed them to surround the Spartans. But the Battle of Thermopylae delayed Xerxes's army, which contributed to the preparation of a better Athenian defense, led by General Themistocles. After Marathon, Athens had built a new fleet. Before receiving news of the Persian army's advance, Themistocles evacuated the entire population of Athens and took refuge in the neighboring island of Salamis. When the Persian army arrived to Athens, it was empty and undefended. Meanwhile, Athens' allies began to fear an impending Persian attack by land and sea, but Themistocles maneuvered astutely so that they did not have time to jump ship. He sent an emissary to Xerxes, whose army was already encamped near Salamis, to announce that the Greeks were going to escape once more and were set to flee the next morning. Xerxes fell into this trap and prepared to act as soon as possible. When the Persian fleet arrived at Salamis, it confronted the Greek one. The Greeks had already prepared boats with better mobility than the enormous Persian ships with four rows of oarsmen and they defeated the Persians. The Greeks also defeated the Persian land army shortly after at Plataea.

In 480 BC the Greeks had won against the Persians for a second and definitive time, opening up a glorious period for Athens, which lasted approximately a century and is considered one of the most extraordinary moments in human history because the things that were thought, written, depicted, and experienced have proved to be perennially relevant and sublime. The words Marathon, Thermopylae, and Salamis are a part of Western collective memory. These battles have remained a symbol of resistance to death in hopes of saving people from foreign domination and despotic rule. The question of what would have happened to the world if the Persians had defeated the Athenians has always weighed in the back of Western minds. According to popular accounts spread by the winners, a handful of Greek soldiers' valiant performance saved Greek civilization from annihilation and submission to the (alleged) chaos of Persian brutality.

Beyond their evident historical interest, the popular interpretation of the Persian Wars as a confrontation between civilization and barbarism, between good and evil, incites reconsideration of the creation and transmission of historical accounts. Throughout history, manipulation of narratives related to barbarism vs. civilization or good vs. evil has often shamefully legitimated stronger powers' abusive conquests of weaker territories. In the case of the Persian Wars, this narrative is justified by the fact that one of the peaks of civilization would not have existed without Salamis and Marathon. But this already implies a first assumption based on a 'what if...' which is not an appropriate starting point. In addition, these narratives are often exaggerated, and it is impossible to verify if Greek forces were really ten times smaller than the Persians, as the Greek chronicles relate, or if the account aimed to further exalt the heroic nature of the Greek victory over the Persians.

However, even with their tendency toward simplification, no one can deny the Greeks' extraordinary ability to generate stories that have been transmitted from generation to generation. These legendary narrations begin with an event that took place in the past and endow it with legend based on a remarkable symbolic meaning and importance for identity. Even today, large audiences continue to enjoy the stories created in Antiquity. Hollywood has deftly updated the battles of Troy, Salamis, Marathon, and Thermopylae, thus immortalizing them even more. The effectiveness of these stories, like the medieval accounts of King Arthur, Robin Hood, Roldan, or El Cid Campeador, is based on the inclusion of heroes that capitalize on the action and connect with listeners or readers. In classical Greece, Homer's Trojan heroes Hector, Ajax, and Achilles have nurtured the imagination of millions of readers (and film audiences nowadays) over the ages. The epic of Ulysses, meanwhile, inspired many literary varieties on the question of the travel and odyssey that, in one way or another, each individual undertakes to reconnect with his or her origins and identity.

As we saw in the chapter on Jewish history, the creation and operation of these timeless literary models is common to many cultures. Thus, it is worth examining in more detail the main contributions of what is considered Athens's classical period, also known as the Pericles era. Pericles's expertise in public affairs earned him great respect from his citizens. Beginning in 444 BC, he ruled Athens, ensuring that the city remained a maritime power, defending it from external attacks and effectively promoting the intellectual, artistic, and cultural initiatives outlined below. As happened in other places with cultural golden ages—such as the Rome of Augustus, Renaissance Florence, early modern Flanders, seventeenth-century Spain, and Vienna's fin-de-siècle—Athens' extraordinary cultural expansion was made possible by the profits it earned from taxes imposed on other Ionian populations in exchange for military protection. In any case, the height of Athenian civilization did not last long—most estimates give it some forty years—but this time was enough for its permanent inscription in the book of world history.

The Greeks created sublime art and inspiring literature that deserve the adjective of 'classic,' that is, it produced canons of beauty and models that have never gone out of style and that have served as a model for all subsequent eras. The beauty of Greek art perplexes historians, obsessed with an Enlightenment-inspired idea of progress, who seek to identify antecedents and consequences. But things do not usually work that way, nor are they so simple. Good artists are too original to be predictable or to be boxed in by preestablished categories. The models on which Phidias relied to produce beautiful sculptures for the Parthenon friezes—preserved in the British Museum and thus divorced from their original context—remain a mystery, and will likely remain so. The sculptors of classical Greece managed to reproduce the human body with a naturalness and beauty hardly otherwise expressible. Sculptures like Myron's *Discobolus*, which conveys a movement that its contemporary spectators would have identified with the excitement of Olympic competition, managed to enhance and idealize beauty, in comparison with everyday and natural forms. Historians are left with a (somewhat painful) curiosity surrounding Greek painting, which, although we can roughly decipher it in beautiful figures on ceramics, vases, and urns, did not survive the passage of time, like, unfortunately, so many other cultural, intellectual, and artistic products.

The same can be said of Greek temples' perfect proportions, which have inspired architects throughout time. In his *A Little History of the World*, Ernst Gombrich gives an explanation as to why the temples are still standing and admired after so many centuries:

> However, the temples are still standing. Even in Athens. And best of all, the citadel of Athens is still there—the Acropolis—where new sanctuaries made of marble were erected in the time of Pericles, because the old ones

had been burnt and destroyed by the Persians while the Athenians watched from the island of Salamis. The Acropolis still contains the most beautiful buildings we know. Not the grandest, or the most splendid. Simply the most beautiful. Every detail is so clear and so simple that one cannot imagine it otherwise. All the forms which the Greeks employed in these buildings were to be used again and again in architecture. You will find Greek columns – of which there are several kinds – in almost every city of the world, once you have learnt to recognise them. But none of them is as beautiful as those on the Acropolis where they are used not for show and decoration but for the purpose for which they were invented: as elegant supports for the roof.

The Acropolis is imposing from a distance, but beautiful and proportional at close range. Anyone who has approached it with even a minimal sense of the sacred can attest to Gombrich's words, and to how deeply stirring those stones built about 2,500 years remain (Figure 2.1). It invites the observer to discard once and for all the unpleasant tendency that our contemporaries have of confusing the new with the good or the best.

In addition to a talent for storytelling and the sublimity of their art, the Greeks were also well known for their philosophical speculation. Socrates is usually presented as a model of the good citizen and teacher of coherent thinkers.

FIGURE 2.1 Details of the Caryatid Porch on the Acropolis in Athens, Greece. Ancient Erechtheion or Erechtheum temple. © Shutterstock.

Plato and Aristotle are among the first names that appear in almost every history of philosophy. These two thinkers' influence is so manifest that some have tried to simplify the whole history of thought by separating it into two camps along Platonic-idealist and Aristotelian-realist lines. Like all generalizations, this is a simplification and there are realities that do not completely fit into such an overarching dual framework, but, in any case, the ability of the classical Greek world to build models for posterity is worthy of admiration in this area as well. Greek philosophical speculation should be considered the first Enlightenment, experienced twenty-three centuries before Voltaire's birth.

The Greeks also succeeded in distinguishing between mythical thought, typical of neighboring nations like the Jewish one, and strictly rational reflection. This did not involve substituting one for the other, as many assume with the expression "from myth to logos," because the Greeks also managed to echo mythical thought in literature and theater. It is rather an acknowledgment of the peculiarity of "myth *and* logos," and, therefore, of the appropriate distinction between them. Based on this distinction, the Greeks developed a kind of rational thought that the West widely developed from scholastic and Cartesian thought, all the way up through the Enlightenment and the slightly more-tormented forms of existentialism and postmodernism in force today. But they also created literary genres—for example, the epics of Homer and the tragedies of Sophocles—that responded to society's need for legendary and mythological narratives.

Mythological stories respond to people's deep need for ideal models of behavior. When these models are plausible and have a moral basis, they allow people to understand the world and, simultaneously, look to sublime models that they aspire to imitate, for example, medieval epic poems, such as *The Song of Roland* or *The Poem of the Cid*, the legend of King Arthur's Round Table, the modern novel in its multiple manifestations (from *Don Quixote* to *Lord of the Rings*), and contemporary films, from *Star Wars* to *Batman*. All of these examples reveal values such as chivalry, heroism, tenacity, commitment, loyalty, and courage. These messages are difficult to communicate otherwise since only the language of fiction can transmit these values simply enough to be understood widely.

Georges Lucas acknowledged that *Star Wars*' story is shaped by *The Hero with a Thousand Voices* (1949) by Joseph Campbell, in which he discussed on theories of the archetypal hero shared by world mythologies:

> I came to the conclusion after *American Graffiti* that what's valuable for me is to set standards, not to show people the world the way it is. Around the period of [*Star Wars'*] realization, it came to me that there really was no modern use of

mythology. The [film genre of] Western was possibly the last generically American fairy tale, telling us about our values. And once the Western disappeared, nothing has ever taken its place. In literature we were going off into science fiction, so that's when I started doing more strenuous research on fairy tales, folklore, and mythology, and I started reading Joe [Champbell]'s books. It was very eerie because in reading *The Hero with a Thousand Faces* I began to realize that my first draft of *Star Wars* was following classic motifs. So I modified my next draft according to what I'd been learning about classical motifs and made it a little bit more consistent. I went on to read *The Masks of God* and many other books. (Quoted in Stephen Larsen and Robin Larsen, *Joseph Campbell: A Fire in the Mind*, Inner, 2002, p. 541)

In fact, two manifestations in classical Greece perfectly express the complementarity between myth and logos, between mythological language and rational language, namely history and theater. One Greek sage, Herodotus, is considered the founding father of history. He chronicled the Persian Wars, referred to above in connection with historical narration as one of the spoils of the victors. In his *History* (a word whose etymology in Greek corresponds to the contemporary concept of 'inquiry'), Herodotus intended to recount those battles as objectively as possible. For this, he systematically interviewed the protagonists involved or, at least, those who heard first-hand stories, engaging of course mostly with Greeks.

Even with all the limitations of his rudimentary methodology, contemporaries were able to distinguish Herodotus's real descriptions from other narratives, such as Homeric legends or poems, which did not have the same need to accurately reflect events exactly as they happened. Herodotus, along with other famous Greek historians such as Thucydides and Polybius, broke with another convention by avoiding poetic verses and instead employing a succession of sentences that we now call 'prose,' which served as an external sign to distinguish his historical narratives from the poetic form of legendary and mythological narratives. The Greeks were fond of fabled narrations of extraordinary events with gods and heroes in the form of verse and which were often set to music in order to better retain them and thus be able to transmit them across the generations. A similar phenomenon exists today with music—although our memories are relatively poor, we manage to remember the lyrics to songs from our favorite bands because they are presented in short verses and are set to musical rhythm. But Herodotus dealt in real events with flesh-and-blood people, not in the supernatural feats of heroes and gods, which is why he chose the form of prose. Additionally, with this tool, he was able to extend his moral reflections. He saw his historical prose as facilitating reflection on the ideas and moral consequences associated with events, rather than word-for-word retention, which he saw as secondary.

Historians generally agree that nineteenth-century Germanic historicism, particularly the work of Leopold von Ranke, led history's true revolution and ushered it into the pantheon of scientific disciplines. They also, however, firmly attribute to Herodotus the first separation between history and literature, honoring him with the title of "the father of history." After him, history and literature were separated in theory, but since both are presented as a narrative, it is not always easy to distinguish between them. Historians' most important task comes in the form of committing themselves to an honest search for historical reality. Concern for narrative beauty, even in the case of a history book, has existed since ancient times. For example, the last historical book of the Bible, II Maccabees, composed around 100 BC in an unmistakably Hellenic environment, ends with an exhortation to historians to present their stories not only truthfully but also beautifully:

> This, then, is how matters turned out with Nicanor, and from that time the city has been in the possession of the Hebrews. So I will here end my story. If it is well told and to the point, that is what I myself desired; if it is poorly done and mediocre, that was the best I could do. For just as it is harmful to drink wine alone, or, again, to drink water alone, while wine mixed with water is sweet and delicious and enhances one's enjoyment, so also the style of the story delights the ears of those who read the work. And here will be the end. (2 Maccabees, 15: 37–39)

Today, historians would only disagree with the above quote concerning the harmfulness of drinking wine alone. These words are a model to follow for those dedicated to historical writing, although of course it is another matter to be able to emulate the beauty with which this idea is expressed.

Along with written history, the Greeks made another important contribution, namely the use of stage interpretation, which they called theater, to transmit the deepest truths embedded in human condition. The Greeks realized that they needed a system capable of sharing the content of their most important myths, that is, those that referenced their society's values. Some anthropologists have defined Greek theater as a "rationalization of ritual" since all its external forms (communication between actors and spectators, transmission of profound realities through a fictional plot, and the drama of representation) resemble the forms found in rituals, but are detached from any mystical connotation. These plays were originally rather brief, but soon extended to the whole day, usually on holidays. Performances transpired in places with good acoustics and that facilitated a view of the stage from a variety of angles. For this, spaces already in the form of a half circle were used, as still visible today in the ruins of many ancient Greek and Roman cities. Actors wore large masks that covered their faces because, among other reasons, they prevented the audience from identifying actors with the characters and, importantly, allowed their voices to reach everyone in attendance.

Slowly, genres within the theater began to emerge, which, in turn, responded to different audience demands. The most popular genre was tragedy since it employed a solemn and majestic tone, but was graphic and understandable at the same time, to explore some of the great human dilemmas, such as fate, good and evil, and death. Even today, classic tragedies, such as Sophocles' *Antigone* and *Oedipus Rex* or Euripides' *Orestes* and *Medea*, remain relevant. The ancient Greeks also very much appreciated comedy since the irony it employs allows the audience to face serious issues and profound political and moral content with a bit more levity than tragedy allows for. Aristophanes was the most representative comic playwright with plays like *The Knights*, a satirical work that, using a fictional mask, is a brutal satire against Cleon, one of the most influential politicians in the period immediately after Pericles. Comedies allowed the Greeks, who presented themselves as very serious people, to relinquish their calculated severity for a while, giving them a chance to laugh at themselves—a strategy we can continue to learn from.

Finally, the Greeks also possessed an acute practical sense of existence. Confronting the Persians protected them from anything approaching tyranny because they became very protective of their freedom and autonomy. The organization of completely autonomous *poleis* (cities), rather than large and extensive empires, made a more rational organization of government possible when compared to their contemporaries. The first Constitution of Athens dates from 594 BC, a century before the battles of Marathon and Salamis. A nobleman named Solon proposed a formation that became known as the 'Solonian Constitution,' which established that citizens must decide for themselves how to organize their city. As a result, this political system earned the name democracy, literally, 'government of the people.' Distinguished Athenians met periodically in the market square to make decisions and then chose qualified men to put them into practice. It was certainly not a 'democracy' as we understand the concept today because only an elite group of so-called citizens made decisions, while most other residents (notably slaves and women) were left out. This nascent system sufficed nonetheless to function as a model in the fierce struggle against tyranny and despotism that all societies wage in one way or another.

Classical Greek civilization had, like all cultures, its bright spots and its shadows. Slavery was deeply rooted there, tyranny largely won out over good governance, and its golden age was truly ephemeral, broken up prematurely by internal struggles among perpetually dissatisfied elites and by the irreconcilable breakdown between the Athenian and the Spartan models. But, in the balance of what it bequeathed to posterity, successes outweigh Athens's failures, and this is so not just because it left us the Olympics, which we continue to celebrate every four years, but also because we continue to collectively applauding its many examples of excellence and nobility. At the end of the day, the Greeks were the first to offer a classic model of action in public life, art, and thought worthy of inspiration for generations to come.

CHAPTER 3

ROME

Legend has it that Rome was founded in 753 BC. In popular wisdom, Rome embodies the practical aspects of existence, just as Jerusalem embodies religiosity and Athens embodies wisdom. The figure of the Roman jurist is seen as one of the paradigms of this new civilization, as had been the case of the Jewish prophet and the Greek philosopher. Like all generalizations, nuance is required, but this one works to start off a chapter dedicated to Roman civilization, which continues to serve as an inspiration and model for some of the West's most ingrained values, including rational planning of the means for certain ends, the practical and legal sense of existence, and the unrelenting search to apply theoretical and technical advances.

The term that best expresses the Roman contribution to posterity might well be *civilization*. This concept reminds us of values, such as respect for previously agreed-upon rules, administrative planning, the protection of basic rights, skilled road construction, political representation, social stability, economic development, hygiene, clothing styles, basic educational norms, and the promotion of culture and education. Obviously, the Romans did not necessarily achieve excellence in all these areas, but they did try to promote them not only in their capital, Rome, but also in all the territories they conquered. For this reason, the concepts of Romanization, civilization, acculturation, progress, and development are today nearly synonymous.

Like Israel, Rome cared about its origin story and transmitted it in mythological and symbolic language. But, while the Jews referred to the origins of humanity, the Romans were satisfied with going back to origin of the Trojans. As the legend goes, a Trojan, Aeneas, fled and took refuge in Italy. His two most notable descendants, Romulus and Remus, were fathered by Mars, the god of war, and were nursed in the forest by a wild wolf. One of the brothers, Romulus, founded Rome in 753 BC. The Romans structured their calendar starting from that date (*Ab urbe condita*, "from the foundation of the city"), in the same way that the Greeks did so starting from the first Olympics and later the West would do so beginning with the birth of Christ or the Muslims from Muhammad's Hegira.

For some centuries, the Etruscans dominated the Italian peninsula, and therefore the Romans were their subjects. But the city was soon organized around a monarchy, the system that predominated in the great civilizations of the time. This structure ended up being ineffective, however, for a city that, starting from its foundation, was extremely dynamic. The last king of Rome, Tarquin the Proud, died at the hands of a nobleman named Brutus. Next came the establishment of a government of 'patricians,' who were usually large landowners and effectively dominated the poor, called plebeians. The patricians elected the main city officials, called consuls. At first, the plebeians had no rights and, of course, were excluded from the city's government, but later, after a struggle that lasted for centuries, they managed to have their rights recognized as equal to those of patricians and to share in city governance. From then on, each year, two consuls were elected—one patrician and one plebeian.

This happened in the fourth century BC, between the Gauls' humiliating sack of Rome in 390 and the beginning of Alexander the Great's conquests in 336. At the end of the century, the Romans began to aggressively expand along the Italian peninsula, an effort that lasted until approximately the year 250. During that period, the Romans consolidated their conquest model, which unfolded during the following seven centuries. Unlike Greek, Persian, and Hellenistic strategies, Roman expansion aimed at sustaining stable colonization rather than merely military presence. Territorial annexation happened often through alliance, coalition with a city that requested military protection, or by Roman legion conquest.

After conquering the Italian peninsula, the Romans fixed their eyes on the rich island of Sicily. When Roman generals set their eyes on any land, they had a good chance of victory. This new land was famous for its grain production and for having been one of the most renowned Greek colonies. But the island, which since Antiquity was accustomed to continuously changing rule, had passed into the hands of the Phoenicians, who dominated it from the great North African capital of Carthage. Thus, it ensued a fierce struggle between the Romans and Carthaginians for the control of Sicily, known as the Punic Wars because the Romans used the adjective 'Punic' for the Phoenician inhabitants of Ancient Carthage, modern Tunis. The battles were fought between 241 and 202. The Carthaginians had a courageous, audacious, and intuitive leader, Hannibal, who nearly destroyed Rome, but the Romans ultimately prevailed and Hannibal committed suicide rather than submit to their power. The Punic Wars became a reference in the Romans' collective imagination, similar to what the Persian Wars represented for the Greeks.

Starting with that decisive victory, territories along the Mediterranean continued to fall like dominoes into the hands of Rome. Greece was next, having been subdued by the Macedonians and greatly weakened by internal division. This conquest had significant cultural consequences because, although Athens' political power was weakened, incorporating it into the Roman Empire resulted in the Hellenization of Roman territory. Greek spread throughout the Mediterranean as a sophisticated language, its most renowned literature was translated into Latin, and its art was taken as a model, when not simply imitated. Without the mediation of the Romans, it is possible that very little of classical Greek civilization would have been transmitted to later generations. In fact, many Greek sculptures that we admire today in museums around the world are not original in the strict sense, but rather faithful copies made centuries later by the Romans.

The Romans devastated Carthage in 146 so that they could occupy the North of Africa and conquer Hispania, after challenging its Celtic and Iberian inhabitants. After a long period of progressive expansion, Rome became the most powerful city in the known world. The formidable general Gaius Julius Caesar initiated the next great expansion. Between 58 and 51, he captured Gaul and part of Germania. Shortly afterward, he conquered Egypt by maneuvering skillfully with Queen Cleopatra. Julius Cesar not only proved to be a wise and courageous warrior, reflected in the powerful war memoir he left for future generations, but also a good administrator. He reorganized the calendar, establishing a division by months and years, still in use today. Although the official political system in place corresponded to Consuls, and the Senate had a monopoly on power, Julius Cesar earned authority and respect from his people. Many senators became suspicious of him and, in the year 44, they assassinated him—his own friends brutally stabbing him on the Senate floor. This assassination has been preserved in the popular imagination of the West with the phrase that Caesar supposedly uttered to one of the conspirators, at the moment of his death: "And you too, Brutus?" (*Et tu, Brute, fili mi?*). The inclusion of this story in William Shakespeare's *Julius Caesar* is a good illustration of the typical process of invention and transmission of stories that are told over and over again as guarantors of Western tradition, without being quite sure of their historical veracity. This shows that tradition is composed, at the same time, of verified historical realities and unverified legends. But, regardless of their veracity or not, they all tend to have a notable exemplary capacity. This story, for example, has given rise to countless theories about the morality of assassination, when the ruler becomes a despot who harms the lives of his subjects.

FIGURE 3.1 Caesar Augustus, the first emperor of Ancient Rome. Monumental bronze statue in Rome. © Shutterstock.

Julius Cesar's adopted son, Cesar Augustus, took control of Roman territory and was declared its first emperor after nearly unceasing struggles against other generals (Figure 3.1); he ruled from the year 31 BC until AD 14. Although the empire continued to expand during the next two centuries, Augustus' reign is considered the peak of Roman civilization, with extraordinary cultural flourishing and achievements, in addition to expansive territorial dominance that became known to posterity as the era of *pax romana*. The Latin adage *si vis pacem, para bellum* (if you want peace, prepare for war) was more relevant than ever. The Romans had fought for centuries to achieve the peace they then enjoyed, which was the result of military domination and effective colonization rather than of universal harmony.

We tend to associate the idea of empire, together with that of civilization, with Rome. The centralization of sovereignty, authority, and government in a single person may seem intolerable today, since we identify such a system with dictatorship and tyranny. The West has advanced in terms of mechanisms that check rulers, due to centuries of political experience. But, at that time, a centralized domination that worked well, that brought many peoples together, and that was based on a solid legal system like that of the Romans was usually more just than a decentralized government in small sovereign units. These decentralized systems often degenerated into very despotic, mafia-like governments whose power was backed by the ability to generate more violence than their opponents. The real social problem in Rome was its inability to overcome the slave system, which was only abolished much later with the mass assimilation of Christian ideals.

Notwithstanding, the Roman Empire's prestige was so great that, once it disappeared, all subsequent sovereigns tried to imitate it in one way or another. Charlemagne designed the idea of *transferring the Empire* and organized a solemn coronation in Aachen at Christmas of AD 800. He tried to promote a continental rather than a maritime empire. Sovereigns assumed that being in possession of this imperial crown entitled and legitimized them to limitless territorial expansion since their model, the Roman emperor, possessed universal jurisdiction. As could not be otherwise, this led to tension between the emperor of the Holy Roman Empire (Charlemagne's successors who inherited the imperial crown during much of the Middle Ages) and the papacy, the other institution with universal jurisdiction, although the spiritual and religious realm, rather than the temporal or political one. The tension between the papacy and empire, which had been building since Constantine's conversion in the fourth century, was constant in the medieval era and culminated in political-religious strife during the early modernity—the Thirty Years' War. Because of some dynastic problems, court upheavals, and military victories, the imperial crown moved from Germany to Spain in the sixteenth century, finding in Charles V and Philip II worthy heirs. The legitimating idea of the imperial crown was again echoed in Napoleon's 1804 coronation as emperor in Paris. Hitler then latched onto it, establishing the Third Reich, a supposed restoration of the medieval Holy Roman Empire. As history reveals to us, legitimizing universal territorial expansion has terrible consequences for humanity, and we must firmly relegate any aspiration that resembles it to the past.

Returning to Roman politics, how did Rome effectively manage such an enormous amount of territory? They only had one precedent to look to, namely Darius' Persian Empire, mentioned in the context of the Persian Wars, which stretched from Egypt to the borders of India, a nearly unbelievable expanse. Darius based this control on two pillars, namely the construction of roads to facilitate interaction and the establishment of a network of officials (known as satraps) to ensure political cohesion and administrative efficiency. Following in part this model, assimilated especially through the Alexandrian system found in Hellenistic territories, the Romans established, first of all, an extraordinary network of roads, whose outline is visible today in physical remains and urban networks, and from which modern roads have benefited in terms of impeccable design (many modern roads were built on ancient Roman routes, such as the Via Apia in Rome, the Watling Street in England, and the Via Augusta in Barcelona). The construction of these roads required Roman ingenuity to overcome formidable physical obstacles. When the Romans set a goal, it seemed that nothing and no one could get in the way of their tenacity and ambition, which resulted in the accumulation of immense technical and applied skill. Roman engineering was so extraordinary that it built various public works of such size and quality—bridges, roads, and aqueducts—that they are still usable today.

In addition to their roads, the Romans also exemplified meticulous and effective administrative organization based mostly on territorial structure and decentralization. The empire was organized into provinces, based on conglomerations of cities, which, with their peculiar urban fabric and demographic concentration, were key to Roman administrative rationalization. This process involved the appointment of political, military, and legal representatives, who ruled through imperial delegation at the provincial and local levels. Securing the roads and rationalizing the administrative framework ensured the emperor and his closest collaborators' centuries-long control of the empire. Written orders reached even the farthest provinces in a short period of time with the help of fast and efficient messengers.

The power and duration of the empire was also based on the establishment of a well-organized fiscal regime, which guaranteed reasonable and lasting economic sustainability. Rome was a pioneer in this field, as the first major political entity to implement a rational, proportionate, and systematic tax collection, which charged not only individual persons but also commercial transactions. We too often forget that the walls surrounding old cities, both in Antiquity and in the Middle Ages, served not only a defensive but also a fiscal function. The intense monetization that the empire underwent also decisively contributed to its commercial flexibility and effective fiscal system, but it had its negative side in the form of continuous inflation that the emperors sanctioned to counteract cyclical financial crises. Rulers were able to continuously play with the Roman coin's two sides (gold and silver) and assign each a value according to the needs at the time. The Romans thus became the first people in history to systematically understand the harmful effects of a deregulated economy that lacks control and efficient regulation.

Finally, the establishment of a legal order, whose solidity and brilliance is still admired, supported this massive framework. Roman law was based on the premise of citizens' equal condition before the law. This equality before the law was certainly restricted to a minority, namely Roman citizens (*cives*), thus excluding a large swath of the population, namely slaves and a sizeable part of the provinces. Still, the determination with which the Romans preserved the rights of their citizens, even those who were far from the capital, is praiseworthy. After two thousand years, the *Acts of the Apostles* detailed account of Saint Paul's appeal to his Roman citizenship in order to be treated according to the provisions of the law continues to amaze.

After a violent altercation with the Jews at the Temple of Jerusalem, soldiers chained Paul "with two chains" and took him to prison, but the tribune allowed him to say a few words in his defense from the stairs leading up to the prison. After carefully listening to his defense, his fellow Jews became even more enraged and wanted to beat him again. The tribune, somewhat bewildered, decided then to lead Paul inside the jail to obtain more information through torture, which, as narrated in the *Acts of the Apostles*, was likely habitually practiced among the Roman soldiers, namely they were to stretch him with straps and whip him. The tribune directed the centurion to carry out this torture, but Paul quipped at the centurion, "Is it legal for you to whip a Roman citizen who hasn't even been tried?" These words were like a magic spell. The centurion hurriedly went to the tribune, who was waiting outside to avoid directly viewing the torture, and asked, "What are you going to do? This man is a Roman citizen." The tribune entered the torture chamber and asked Paul if he was really a Roman citizen since he himself had obtained citizenship with a large sum of money. Paul replied that he had obtained his citizenship at birth. The tribune, "frightened to learn that he was a Roman citizen," warned of a Jewish conspiracy to assassinate Paul and carefully organized his transfer from Jerusalem to Caesarea. He then prepared an escort of 200 soldiers, 70 horsemen, and 200 spearmen, commanded by two centurions. A long legal process then ensued, culminating in Paul's appeal to Caesar, a right reserved exclusively to Roman citizens. After being interrogated once again by the new governor of Judea, Festus, and King Agrippa, great-grandson of Herod the Great, Paul was transferred to Rome. He remained there for two years under house arrest until he was ultimately released. This story, and the reverberation of the Roman civilization's prestige, lasted centuries. In 1850, when both classical and biblical references were better known than today, Lord Palmerston quoted St. Paul—and Cicero's *civis romanus sum*—in Parliament, comparing British citizenship to Roman.

Roman legislation was comprehensive and applied to the most varied spheres of life, from family to trade. It ensured public order and guaranteed the rights of its citizens although, as seen in St. Paul's case, such protection required activating extraordinary means and mobilizing hundreds of soldiers. Of course, the Romans did not practice separation of powers, a principle that is the legacy of contemporary societies, due to the pioneering work of the American founding fathers and French thinkers like Montesquieu and Tocqueville. Nor did the Romans seek to overcome the obvious discrimination that the exclusion from their legal system meant for those who did not benefit from the status of citizen. But they managed to make effective legislation of universal value guaranteed by objective legal practices. Roman law is still studied at the most prestigious universities because its wisdom and practicality have not waned over the centuries. Most of the Mediterranean European countries based their legal system on Roman law, while other such as Britain and the United States follow a "common law" tradition, originally developed in medieval England.

Notably as well, the Roman Empire also left us the dream of a united Mediterranean Sea. Today such a dream seems out of reach because of the two consecutive schisms that happened in the Mediterranean (the division between a Christian north and an Islamic south in the seventh century and the division between an Orthodox East and a Catholic West in the eleventh century), which have marked its history in recent centuries. In addition, today, the Mediterranean is typically seen as poorer than the most culturally and economically advanced Atlantic and Central European countries, but this was not always so. Rome's territorial and military expansion also manifested itself in cultural, linguistic, and commercial unity of the Mediterranean (sea between lands), a space for union and exchange. Thus, the Mediterranean was referred to as *Mare Nostrum*. The most prestigious historians of the twentieth century, especially Fernand Braudel and Georges Duby, narrated the effectiveness of thinking of the Mediterranean as a space of unity rather than of fragmentation.

The cultural unification of the territories around the Mediterranean leads us to the concept of Romanization. Today, this concept is associated with that of civilization since military conquest and Roman acculturation were two sides of the same coin under Roman expansion. Unlike their Egyptian, Babylonian, Persian, and Macedonian counterparts, the Romans did not plan to build a single empire where all people enjoyed the same rights. They preferred to convert conquered territories into provinces that could maintain their customs, religions, traditions, cultures, and languages. But these provinces were required to respect Roman authorities, submit to their troops, pay taxes, and organize according to the urban model. At first, inhabitants of the occupied territories detested their conquerors' impositions, but were eventually seduced by the new urbanized and civilized ways of life—including customs, language, and law system—that were incorporated into their daily existence. Thus, along with military conquest and political subjugation, an imperceptible, yet deeply assimilated, civilizing process went on. Rome's practical genius was thus naturally incorporated when locals began to enjoy comfortable routes, public entertainment buildings, sporting events, running water, thermal baths, and even pagan temples toward which to direct their religiosity. In this way, even if only for practical reasons, Latin became a *lingua franca*, like English today.

The longevity of Roman domination was based on a sequential strategy that was repeated unfailingly in each expansive process, as follows: First, military conquest, then institutional and administrative settlement which guaranteed political stability, and, finally, a civilizing process that we know as *Romanization*. When Romanization became effective in a province, the maintenance of an exceptional order ceased to be the only pillar holding things together. Thus, resources were liberated to lead military forces toward other expansion fronts and centers of tension, which were increasingly located in the eastern frontier with the threat that the vigor of the emerging Germanic peoples posed. This strategy made the Romans stand out since most empires that have emerged throughout history have had to content themselves with a military presence and a police order of control. When it faded or was weakened, it provoked insurrection and the empire's quick and subsequent collapse. Certainly, modern empires have sought alternatives, or tried to apply their own brand of Romanization, for example, evangelization in the Spanish Empire, commercial activity in the British Empire, revolutionary fervor in the French Empire, and communist sentiment in the Soviet Union. All empires have needed their own form of Romanization to legitimize, justify, and consolidate their territorial expansion and political control. But, to date, it is difficult to identify an empire whose cultural implantation has been as effective and as long running as the Roman one. For this reason, Rome continues to captivate intellectuals and scholars alike.

With all these values examined, we can define Rome's legacy. Politically, Rome implemented the three forms of government (monarchy, republic, and empire) that have been a source of continuous inspiration for subsequent civilizations. Intellectually, it provided an amazing payroll of inspiring intellectuals and poets, from Seneca and Cicero to Tacitus and Virgil. Administratively, it achieved extraordinary rationalization, which allowed it to consolidate its conquests and immediately implement an effective system of government therein. Economically, it built the first global economic space, the Mediterranean, in which an ostensibly natural border became a space ripe for exchange not only of material products but also of ideas. It designed legislation and an enduring penal system so effective and precise that contemporary jurists continue to study and admire it. Further, it based its territorial expansion not only on military supremacy but also on values of civilization inherent in the imposition of a language (Latin) and religion (paganism and later Christianity), making its longevity possible. Artistically, it emulated Greek aesthetics as no one did in the future until Renaissance Florence and Rome. Finally, it developed the first technological society, characterized by a rationalized public works plan and the construction of roadways that ensured speedy messaging, travelers' safety, the promotion of trade, and the exchange of ideas.

Roman-occupied territories welcomed these values more or less enthusiastically, but eventually assimilated the language, legal system urban development, and, toward the end of the empire, the official religion. Later, when Germanic kingdoms settled in the former territories of the Roman Empire, they generally maintained basic Roman values. Henri Pirenne showed, in his remarkable but controversial book *Mohammad and Charlemagne* (1937), that Roman values did not actually break down under Germanic invasions, but rather under Islamic expansion. This has led to intense debate over whether the West is the heir of Roman or Germanic legacy. Where did feudalism come from in the West? What was the West's legal foundation? Were not European monarchies more resonating of Germanic monarchies than of Roman governance models? These discussions were initially limited to academics, but soon entered the public sphere because the answers to these questions are more than a purely scholarly issue. German historical accounts, which were extraordinarily powerful in the nineteenth century, logically opted for Germania, trying at the same time to discredit the Roman tradition, which it identified with the Roman pontificate. Time put things in their place, and specialists generally agree that Rome prevails over Germania. But this debate among cultural German or Roman hegemonism remains a model of how the attempt to legitimize a present reality (political, cultural, or religious) can completely distort an objective view of the past.

Beyond the debate between the legacy of Rome and Germania, a question of much greater importance emerged during the long centuries of Roman decadence, namely the dilemma between paganism and Christianity. Constantine was the key figure in this process. His conversion at the beginning of the fourth century meant the Roman Empire's *de facto* assumption of Christianity—although its official recognition would arrive with Theodosius a century later—and the abandonment of paganism. But, as often is the case, things were not quite that simple. Constantine himself, convinced of the need to adapt to the times, and perhaps also stirred by a genuine spiritual conversion, decided to end persecutions and take on Christianity as the empire's official religion.

Yet, he also tried to harmonize this new religion with ancient pagan forms of worship. His collaborators built a conversion story that vividly reflects his intention to reconcile these two religions: the old pagan with the new Christian. In that story, Constantine saw a cross inscribed on the sun right before defeating his opponent Maxentius in the Battle of the Milvian Bridge, an event that led to his own conversion. The overlap of two symbols that were essential to each of these religions (the sun for pagans, the cross for Christians) is a graphic and effective embodiment of the desire to bring them together and satisfy both peoples. In any case, Constantine's bold decision to legalize Christianity brought Christians out of hiding and allowed them to assemble in the capital of world power, further consolidating a religion that was founded by a Jewish carpenter four centuries before. The glaring question remains: How did such a prodigious expansion happen?

CHAPTER 4

CHRISTIANITY

The first three chapters of this book initiated with the conquest of Jerusalem around the year 1000, the clash between Persia and Greece around the year 500, and the legendary foundation of Rome in 753, all of which occurred before the Christian era. Starting with these dates was a more or less arbitrary decision. By contrast, there is no doubt that the birth of Jesus, which opened the first year of the Christian era, marks a before and after no only in the history of the West but for the humanity, establishing the chronology we still use today. Given Christianity's enormous influence, this chapter is devoted to analyzing its first centuries and the keys to its global expansion.

The birth of Jesus marks the transition between the Old and the New Testaments, the distinction between Jewish and Christian religions. Our main sources for Jesus' life and teachings—and the first books of the New Testament— are the four Gospels. Matthew writes a testimony as a Jesus' disciple, and he is therefore a direct witness of the events he is narrating. Mark leaves a succinct account of the events and teachings he heard from his master Peter, the first of the Apostles. Luke tells also his story based on his master Paul's teachings. These three are known 'the Synoptic Gospels,' since they have lots of similarities and parallelism, both in the stories they tell and in the doctrine they state. John left the fourth of the Gospels, written some decades after the other three, around the end of the first century. He was the youngest of the Jesus' disciples, influenced by the Hellenistic thought when he designed his Gospel. In contrast to the Synoptics, he tends to be more discursive, doctrinal, and theological than soberly narrative. Thus, he introduced some key concepts—such as the identification of Jesus with the *Verb* (the word) as Son of God and as the *Logos*—which were intensively debated by the early theologians of the Church from the second to fourth centuries.

The founders of the great world religions were usually people of notable origin. Before the penitent phase during which he devised his doctrine, Buddha grew up in the midst of luxury and wealth; it is said that he had three palaces where the most delightful music continuously played. Confucius was the son of a rich official. Muhammad was the son of Abd Allah, a distinguished man who was nonetheless not very wealthy. Jesus, by contrast, was not a rich or notable person, and was described by his peers as "the carpenter's son" (Matthew 13: 54–58). He was born in a small village, Bethlehem, whose only claim to fame was that it was King David's city. During his childhood, his parents had to flee to Egypt and experienced the hardships common to all immigrants. In his adolescence and youth, he worked at his father's small business in the humble village of Nazareth. During the period of his life dedicated to manual labor, he observed Jewish practices and customs, and went completely unnoticed to the point that when he started preaching and working miracles, his own relatives doubted him (Mark, 3: 21).

When he was about thirty years old, he began publicly preaching the message he had received from his Father God, from that God who the Jews knew well and of whom they were protective. Jesus proclaimed himself the Son of God, and therefore the Messiah for whom the Jewish people had waited so many centuries. Some of his contemporaries began to call him 'the Anointed One' (Christ), referring to one of the best-known Messianic biblical images. Thus, the name Jesus, which he had received from his parents, Mary and Joseph, was joined to that of 'the Anointed One,' giving rise to the name Jesus Christ (Figure 4.1). Jesus lamented Jewish religious authorities' rejection of his status as Messiah despite demonstrating it with authoritative preaching and miracles.

Some Jewish sects, such as the Pharisees or Sadducees, and the priests' princes, not only did not believe in his divinity but also plotted to execute him for heresy. These groups were unable to agree on doctrinal questions, but joined forces to capture Jesus because they saw in him a spiritual leader with real authority, which endangered their political-religious monopoly. They captured him, using the betrayal of one of his closest disciples, Judas, in Jerusalem. Since the Jews were completely subject to the Rome at that time, they could not condemn him, so they went to the Roman governor in Judea, Pontius Pilate. But since they could not argue before the secular power on strictly religious grounds, they argued that Jesus had crowned himself king, and therefore might try to compete with the emperor. They thought, rightly, that this argument would impress the governor, an ambitious man eager to maintain public order

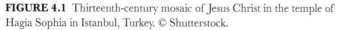

FIGURE 4.1 Thirteenth-century mosaic of Jesus Christ in the temple of Hagia Sophia in Istanbul, Turkey. © Shutterstock.

in a region in which so many other governors had failed. Christ certainly saw himself as royalty, but, when questioned by Pontius Pilate, he replied:

> My kingdom is not of this world. If it were, my servants would fight to prevent my arrest by the Jewish leaders. But now my kingdom is from another place […] I am a king […] For this reason I was born and have come into the world, to testify to the truth. (John 18: 36–37)

These words are essential for understanding the subsequent rise of Christianity since its doctrine is theoretically situated in the realm of truth, goodness, faith, and morality, and not in any political faction. In fact, a few years prior to that, those who falsely accused Jesus of failing to pay taxes had argued with one of his wise paradoxes: "Give to Caesar what belongs to Caesar and to God what is God's," ratifying the autonomy of the spiritual and temporal realms. Some of the Jews that were contemporaries of Jesus, specially the religious authorities, did not understand his spiritual message because they expected a Messiah in the form of a political liberator rather than a spiritual redeemer. After many centuries of hostile foreign domination, perhaps they had their reasons to expect a political leader, but Jesus was far above political partisanship or national exclusivism. The Gospels never refer to his opinion on the delimitation of national borders, the type of taxation that citizens should pay, or his political opinion regarding a certain ruler.

Notably, he did not even venture to denounce the dominant social system, slavery, or at least there is not a single mention of the issue in the Gospels, except when he stated: "Whoever wants to become great among you must be your servant, and whoever wants to be first must be your slave" (Mt, 20: 26–27). His contemporaries, thus, did not recognize him as a revolutionary or counterrevolutionary, nor as someone seeking to subvert the established order, although in reality he heralded the most profound revolution in history. Slavery, like so many other reprehensible customs in Antiquity, collapsed precisely when the spirit of Jesus's preaching on Christian fraternity and love took such deep hold in European society that it could no longer be tolerated, and alternatives to this unjust system were sought.

Nor did Jesus particularly attack the Romans for having occupied the Promised Land. One of his first miracles was actually the cure of a Centurion's son in Capernaum, as told in Luke 7: 1–10. Rather, he asked rulers to be righteous, subjects to be loyal to them, and soldiers to avoid brutality and corruption. He forcefully denounced moral degradation, as when he called the bloodthirsty Herod "that fox." His doctrine aspired to universality, and taking sides with a political faction or temporary solution would have effectively cut him off from one group or another. His preaching was exclusively spiritual—those who accept his teachings were meant to try to improve society from their respective social situations and professional positions. However, they did not receive any specific indication regarding the strategies they should follow in its pursuit.

He had a clear affinity for children, the poor and marginalized, and interacted with the downtrodden, blind, handicapped, lepers, and prostitutes. He reproached a lack of generosity on the part of those who, blinded by wealth, were insensitive to the material and spiritual needs of others. He explicitly stated that "it is easier for a camel to go through the eye of a needle than for a rich man to enter the Kingdom of God" (Matthew 19: 24). But he never presented rhetoric that pits the rich and poor against one another or irremediably condemns the rich. He did not turn his back on the rich who showed genuine interest in his preaching, trying to convert them as well. He accepted invitations to the homes of the rich, such as Zacchaeus, Matthew, and Lazarus, knowing that Jewish religious authorities would not approve some of these relationships. He has friends among the most notable Jews, Joseph of Arimathea, an illustrious member of the Sanhedrin, and Nicodemus, a wealthy man.

During the long judicial process that would lead to his death, Pontius Pilate did not exactly believe Jewish leaders' version, but he feared that disorder would break out again, since the accusers were a restless people and given the nature of their religion that was so unlike the eclecticism of Roman paganism. Pilate literally "washed his hands" off the matter in everyone's presence and ordered Jesus to be executed by crucifixion. This death, which involves slowly suffocating after long hours of physical torment, was reserved for non-citizens, especially murderers and criminals, and was mostly practiced in the provinces to make an example of the sentenced. The torment took place on a hill near Jerusalem called Golgotha (place of the skull). Only his mother, Mary, a small group of brave women, and his disciple John remained by his side. They were overcome with grief, but attended the execution and later gave an account of what they had seen and heard. Most of his disciples, themselves humble fishermen, fled in fear of reprisal from the Jews or Romans. Only his Jewish friends, Joseph of Arimathea and Nicodemus, were courageous enough to present themselves to Pontius Pilate after the crucifixion and ask permission to bury Jesus. This was not given in the case of a man condemned to the most ignominious of deaths. Pilate acceded to their request.

At the request of the Jewish leaders, Pilate sent soldiers to guard Jesus' tomb. But the body of Jesus mysteriously disappeared, despite these security measures. Two explanations were given: that the disciples stole his remains or that Jesus rose from the dead, a resurrection that many claimed to have witnessed. The first version was soon discarded since it was hard to believe that poor fishermen could win a group of professional and experienced Roman soldiers who risked their lives if they were judged to have abandoned their duties. After forty days, these same disciples, who had fled in terror days before, were found preaching the doctrine of Jesus with enormous energy near the temple in Jerusalem. Having mysteriously overcome their fear of the Jewish and Roman authorities who had prompted their flight from Golgotha weeks before, they began to base their preaching on the historical fact of the resurrection of Jesus, whom they recognized as God and therefore referred to Him as Jesus Christ. Paul, who was not among those first witnesses, but to whom Christ appeared some eight years later, accurately expressed this conviction in a letter to a group of Christian faithful: "If Jesus Christ has not risen, our faith is in vain" (1 Corinthians, 15: 17).

With a firm belief in the resurrection and in the truths they had directly received from Jesus, and willing to give their lives for the faith they preached, Christ's followers started expanding. As their numbers rose, they began to be called 'Christians' in Antioch of Syria. Their preaching began in Jerusalem and spread throughout the Palestine region. Toward the year 61, the same year as Paul's first trial in Rome, Christians were already in the most prosperous cities of Syria, Asia Minor, Greece, Macedonia, and Italy. Christianization first took place in cities rather than in rural areas, which is likely why inhabitants of the countryside (*pagus*) began to be called 'pagans' based on their later Christianization. It is an irony of history that, in Antiquity, Christianization began in cities and that modernity's de-Christianization and secularization also began in cities. Rural areas have always sought to preserve their values and traditions, whatever their stripe. Early Christians, most of them Roman citizens, also clearly knew how to take advantage of the Roman framework of maritime and terrestrial communication routes.

As the Gospels tell the story and teachings of Jesus, the book of *Acts of the Apostles* succinctly narrates the first Christian expansion between the years 30 and AD 60. Its author, Luke, a physician who also wrote one of the four Gospels that narrates the life of Jesus, employs a style that all historians could learn from, namely one that is objective, concise, and expressive. His historical prose is extraordinarily precise when necessary (his long description of one of St. Paul's shipwrecks is a unique source of knowledge related to navigation in Antiquity), and always takes great care to project chronological accuracy. It introduces dialogues and brief contextual explanations when appropriate and is remarkably sober in the narration of events.

Paul of Tarsus is a key figure in this expansion. Jewish by religion, a Roman citizen by birth, and Hellenistic by culture, his own background accurately reflects the early evolution of Christianity. He inherited some of the values corresponding to the process of Hellenization of some Jewish currents, which had begun several centuries before Christ. Discussions about the nature of the covenant between God and the Jewish people never actually ceased to be at the center of intellectual discussions in the history of Judaism. This discussion intensified with the destruction of the second Temple in the year 70, but it was already established in the communities of the Diaspora. An outstanding example of these cultural interactions between Hellenism and Judaism is Philo of Alexandria, whose work is key to understanding Paul of Tarsus.

Paul was first educated by observant Jews (Gamaliel, a famous Pharisee, doctor of the law and member of the Sanhedrin in Jerusalem), but gradually began to mainly interact with the 'gentiles,' that is, those outside of the chosen people of Israel. Some early Christians, among them some of the twelve Apostles, believed that Jesus Christ's message should be restricted to this chosen people, and therefore could not conceive of interacting with the gentiles. This amounted to a very serious debate about the direction of the church and, of course, resulted in a transcendental resolution. It was the cause of the first great disagreement between the early founders of the Church (Peter, James, John, and Paul), but all finally agreed in what has been called the first council of the Church, which took place around the year 50 in Jerusalem. They decided that Christianity should surpass the narrow boundaries that confined it to Judaism, making it thus a universal religion. The Old Testament began to be read with this new perspective, and many of its prophecies were reinterpreted in light of a new meaning. Christianity began to spread beyond a single people (Hebrew) and became a multiethnic religion, which opened the door to the educated Hellenistic elite that populated Asia Minor, Greece, and Macedonia. Paul knew Greek, which, together with the careful selection of Hellenized representatives like Timothy, contributed to the Christian's expansion beyond a specific cultural sphere (from educated to ignorant, from literate to illiterate), ethnic condition (from Jewish to Roman and Germanic people), political boundaries (from Lisbon to Jerusalem), or social class (from rich to poor, from landlords to peasants, from lords to slaves).

Together with this evangelization process, materialized in universal Christian baptism rather than in the purity of a certain race, and with the institutional consolidation of the Church, Christianity began laying down the foundations of *Tradition*, just as Judaism had previously done. This first occurred with a written narration of the most important Christian events (the four Gospels and the *Acts of the Apostles*), with systematic explanation of the truths required of believers and practitioners (the epistles of St. Paul and of other apostles) in order to receive Christian baptism. All these books were grouped in later centuries in a canon known as the New Testament, which aimed to clarify the Old Testament in light of God's revelation through His son Jesus Christ. Divine revelation and Apostolic Tradition are two key Christian concepts that interact continuously with each other.

Christianity preached the power of love over hatred, as well as the recognition of human dignity beyond any political, social, or economic category. Undoubtedly, these represent two substantial developments in terms of humanity's beliefs and practices. In addition, the Jewish people's God-Justifier (YHWH, Yahweh) and the pagans' distant gods became for Christians God the Father, an ever-present being, and God the Son, who was a man himself. This approach signified a real revolution since every ancient civilization, from Egypt to Persia to Mesopotamia, founded their respective religions on the belief in a god or gods who did not interact with human beings. The only exception to this rule was Greek polytheism (their gods were so passionate that they were in fact akin to men) and Hebrew monotheism whose God, unlike neighboring civilizations, identified with their people alone, but He could be frightening and terrifying. The audacity of the Christian faith was based on the conviction that God had come to dwell among men, infinitely lowering himself to take on the human condition and thus experience its limitations and suffering. Jesus Christ, God and man, not only testified to the truth, but was also a model for correct action. This contrasted radically with all the religions of the past, as well as with those that came after it.

To be sure, the doctrine of Christian Trinity has been a point of friction and debate within Christianity from its beginnings, and a permanent stumbling block. The Gospel of John seems to indicate that the logos, Jesus, is God, but the very nature of Jesus is and has been a matter of doctrinal disagreement, especially in Antiquity. It was not by chance that almost the most part of the immense work of Origen (around 184–253) was destroyed and yet Arianism appeared supporting ideals against the trinity and the divine nature of Jesus. These heresies will periodically appear during the Middle Ages so that the hierarchy had to fight against them.

Around the year 60, Christians suffered the first of the brutal persecutions that took place in the first three centuries of their existence. The Emperor Nero was set off by a false accusation that Christians had started a devastating fire in Rome. Other emperor-backed persecutions followed with varying duration and brutality, whether religiously motivated because Christians refused to worship the Roman emperor's image, or politically motivated since Christians were seen as trying to compete for the Roman sovereign's power. In both cases, they endured these persecutions with renewed strength and were proud witnesses of their faith. The word 'martyr' etymologically means 'witness.' These witnesses, who gave their lives for the Church, were immediately viewed as the saints of this new religion, worthy of both imitation and praise.

Persecutions of Christians lasted until the beginning of the fourth century. Even though they were extraordinarily cruel and radically unjust, the Church was not in a permanent state of hiding or imminent danger during the first three centuries of its existence. Instances of violent persecution were intermingled with ordinary life. Certain belligerent emperors, like Nero and Diocletian, persecuted them, but others were gentler or simply tolerant of Christians. Ultimately, Constantine granted Christians the freedom to worship with the Edict of Milan in the year 313. He himself was baptized at the end of his life. This freedom was a mixed blessing because it also ushered in the instrumentalization of Christianity for political ends. This trend, initiated by Constantine, worsened in 381 when Theodosius recognized Christianity as the official religion of the empire. This ushered in a problem that has, since then, been constant throughout Western history, namely the relationship between the temporal (represented by the sovereign) and the spiritual (embodied in the papacy).

Although Christ's doctrine is quite clear (give to Caesar what is Caesar's and to God what is God's), sophistry abounded and it was not always easy to act rightly and prudently in this complex space. The fourth century was witness to both Cesar-papism, with Constantine presiding before the bishops gathered at the Council of Nicaea (325) and clericalism that led Ambrose, bishop of Milan, to publicly humiliate Emperor Theodosius, forcing him to kneel in his presence to publicly acknowledge his repentance after violently suppressing sedition in Thessalonica (390). From one extreme to the other, the Church and State searched for middle ground until resolving, many centuries later, the Investiture Contest thanks to the Concordat of Worms (1122)—and the issue extended until the seventeenth-century European Wars of Religion.

In late Antiquity, approximately between the third and fifth centuries, a powerful intellectual phenomenon emerged, which has been called 'the second Enlightenment,' the Classical Greece one being the first. During its first centuries of existence, Christianity fought to steer clear of two extremes. On the one hand, Christian thinkers had to overcome excessive Gnostic spiritualism (a kind of acute Hellenization of Christianity) that would have led Christianity to a radical departure from the world and left its doctrine with little rational basis. On the other hand, they had to avoid excessively imitating the world, which would have bunched Christianity with other pagan religions that had developed in ancient civilizations. Both forms of Hellenization would have led Christianity to the same impasse, namely secularization. Although early Christian thinkers, known in the broadest sense as the Fathers of the Church, did not seek familiarity in Jewish synagogues or pagan temples—aligning them with Christianity would have undermined the specificity of this new religion— they certainly tried to assume and integrate their best cultural achievements. The way early Christians chose to construct their houses of worship confirmed this choice—as an exact transposition of the Roman basilica's architectural structure, one of the most recognizable civil buildings at the time that differed significantly from synagogues and temples. This adoption was both formal and functional because it signified the transposition of a commercial and legal edifice to a sacred structure.

This architectural move embodies what the Fathers of the Church did with their theological writings, namely to combine the best of what they had received from Greek philosophy with the truths revealed in the Scriptures. A combination of Greek thought and Biblical faith was already present in the Old Testament, whose Wisdom books have a strong Hellenistic imprint. The church of late Antiquity developed an intercultural meeting point anchored in biblical faith. The first four Ecumenical Councils of the Antiquity (Nicaea in 325,

Constantinople in 381, Ephesus in 431, Chalcedon in 451) fixed the most crucial theological dogma of the Church based on rational criterial. To do this, they did not reduce the faith to philosophical theory, nor did it distort philosophical theory to adapt it to the faith, nor did they limit it to purely symbolic and mythological interpretation, as was often the case among the religions of the time. Rather, they endowed it with as much realism as possible by attempting a first synthesis between supernatural revelation of Biblical tradition and Christ's preaching, on the one hand, and rational, Hellenistic thought, on the other. This combination is clearly based on the Christian borrow, use, and adaptation of philosophical concepts from Greek philosophy that are explicitly found in its original dogmatic formulation, for example, 'nature,' 'person,' 'essence,' and 'substance.' Yet, influential early fathers such as St. Augustine had no knowledge of Greek and their philosophical formation was fundamentally Latin. Concepts such as *ousia* and *hypostasis* presented a series of problems once they had to be translated into Latin. *Substantia* is a good translation of the Greek *ousia*, but other concepts had to be adopted to the new Christian realities—*sacramentum*, for instance, was taken from a secular-political context by Jerome, since it was originally related to the oath of the emperors when they enter the office. Translations created and still create innumerable theological controversies, and it is an interesting field of *political theology* understood in the scholarship as a way of analyzing the transferences between the temporal and the spiritual spheres.

Without this initial fusion between Hellenistic tradition and revealed truth neither thirteenth-century medieval scholasticism nor eighteenth-century Enlightenment thought would have emerged, and Western thought most likely would have drifted toward radical rationalism (a dream-like rationalism that inspired Nazism or Stalinism) or toward abstract mysticism of an Oriental stripe, sometimes deriving in tyranny. Were Christianity incapable of verbalizing truths with dogmatic content or institutionally organizing itself to preserve that tradition, it would have ultimately merged with the mystical religions of Asia such as Hinduism, Confucianism, and Buddhism, with their renunciation of dogma and limited institutionalization, or with the West's secularized enlightened humanism. The corollary is that Christianism, and Western civilization, owes much of its specificity to the thinkers and scholars of the Late Antiquity such as Tertullian, Ambrose of Milan, Jerome of Stridonium, Augustine of Hippo, and Gregory the Great in the Western tradition, and Basil of Caesarea, Athanasius of Alexandria, Gregory of Nazianzus, and John Chrysostom in the Eastern tradition.

In addition to influencing the course of Western thought, Christianity also shaped social life. Slavery was contrary to Christian beliefs. Although Jesus's preaching in texts from the first disciples do not contain explicit condemnation of slavery, his doctrine of love quite obviously laid a theoretical and practical foundation for its abolition. Around the year 60, Paul wrote to one of his disciples, Philemon, about his slave fugitive named Onesimus. In that letter, Paul prefers pastoral advice to authoritarian imposition and does so "in the name of charity," that is, on the basis of charity instead of justice. Paul could have retained or freed Onesimus, but he did not want to do anything "without your consent so that your good deed is not forced, but voluntary." That is, the exercise of freedom is combined with the practice of charity when deciding Onesimus's fate. Finally, Paul exhorts Philemon to receive Onesimus "forever, not as a slave, but as more than a slave—as a dear brother." We do not know the effect of Paul's letter on Philemon, but it certainly expresses Christians' attitude regarding the problematic subject of slavery. Furthermore, many slaves, as this Pauline letter attests, were baptized into Christianity with the same rights and duties as the rest of the faithful.

Christianity's influence was so wide-reaching that slavery ceased to be an extensively recognized reality starting in the fifth century. Some other factors contributed to its effective disappearance, such as the Germanic peoples' tendency toward family and tribal organization, as well as the progressive introduction of a different social and economic structure, but Christianity's conviction of love and equality before God was much more effective in the long term than any other factor. Slavery as a system was replaced in the medieval centuries by feudal-vassal ties and in the modernity by labor contracts. But the struggle for its psychological and legal abolition was not simple. Sixteenth-century Spanish theologians of the School of Salamanca, led by Francisco de Vitoria, argued for the first time for an international law and challenged the idea of slavery. They did not achieve their objectives, but their theoretical reflections set the grounds for future claims. In early modern Europe, supposedly Christian political systems began to promote slavery again, such as in the modern Spanish, Portuguese, and British empires. Slavery was not formally abolished in Britain until the mid-nineteenth century, due to the courageous effort of a few English parliamentarians, popularly reflected in the movie *Amazing Grace* (2006), and in Brazil in 1889. Serfdom was abolished in Denmark as well as Russia as late as the mid-nineteenth century. The struggle against racial discrimination was hard in the United States, as we recount in Chapter 17, and is still a lot to do. Doubts remain about the current practice of slavery in Brazil and Cuba. Unfortunately, the history of unofficial slavery continues to the present in many parts of the world.

Any social system can degenerate into radically unjust practices, and the imprints of slavery are easily recognizable in certain contemporary contractual practices—for example, trafficking in children, child labor, or abusive labor contracts in certain countries that lack a legal framework to protect workers. To promote social justice, it is not enough the implantation of a particular type of system or a prevailing social, economic, and legal structure, which should adapt as well as possible to the times and, therefore, change. Rather, it rests in the conviction that people should be treated with the dignity they deserve, and laws and practices should increasingly adapt to this reality—no matter what their ethnic reality, political tendency, religious belief, or social condition is.

After St. Peter's martyrdom in Rome, his successors at the See of Rome began to inherit the title of Supreme Pontiff, nomenclature that was imported and transferred, once more, from the Roman civil world. Other great cities of Antiquity, such as Constantinople, Jerusalem, Alexandria, and Antioch of Syria, received, together with Rome, the title of Archbishop, and their bishops received the title of Patriarchs. But Rome preserved its primacy over the others, and its bishop, also known as the Pope, was endowed with universal jurisdiction. This did not generate much controversy until the fourth century, since the supremacy of the See of Rome was proportional to its status as the greatest political, military, economic, and cultural capital in the known world. But as the Western empire declined and finally disappeared, Rome became a second- and third-order power. Other cities, first in order Constantinople, then achieved political supremacy and began to fight for ecclesiastical supremacy.

The roads to Rome and Constantinople became politically, culturally, and religiously diverse, constituting themselves as two divergent legacies (the Latin in the West and the Greek in the East) of the Roman tradition. Soon after, toward the beginning of the seventh century, a third great front unexpectedly arose in Arabia, namely Islam. Charlemagne, Justinian, and Muhammad represent these three divergent traditions and civilizations, whose division we can still perfectly delineate—perfectly visible even today—as the Catholic-Protestant West, the Orthodox East, and Islam. They governed the history of the West from the fourth to the eighth centuries, in a period known as Late Antiquity. This rupture opened a whole new chapter for the West and posed a challenge that almost wiped it out as a specific civilization as we know it today.

PART II

MATURATIONS

CHAPTER 5

CLASH

This chapter focuses on late Antiquity, a crucial period in world history since it cradled the formation of three great civilizations—Latin-Western, Greek-Orthodox, and Islamic—that have spread throughout the world to this day. It began with the fall of the Roman Empire in the middle of the fifth century and lasted through the consolidation of the Carolingian Empire at the end of the eighth century. Key dates include Justinian's reign (527–565), which recovered much of the empire's greatness and Byzantine culture reached the height of its splendor; Muhammad's Hegira (622), which is considered the starting point of the expansion of Islamic civilization; and the coronation of Charlemagne as emperor (800), evidence of the influence of values associated with the Western Roman Empire. With Justinian, Muhammad, and Charlemagne as main historical characters, the leading ethnicities were the Slavic, Arab, and Latin, while the respective languages and cultures were Greek, Arabic, and Latin.

How did this radical diversification occur? How did the empire lose its unity so rapidly? Although people then were not entirely aware of it, a triple fracture began to permeate the empire, developing three areas that are still enormously influential today. The first front was heir to the western part of the empire, culturally and linguistically Latin, ethnically Latin-Germanic, and Roman Catholic in religion. Its symbolic capital was Rome. Its influence is still perceptible today in Western Europe and America, reaching global dimensions from the nineteenth-century with the European colonization of Asia and Africa. It corresponds to what we know today as Western civilization and is unique among the three regions formed in late Antiquity in that, after intense struggle, it managed to preserve the autonomy of the political and religious, the temporal and the spiritual. It is thus defined with a geographical concept, 'The West,' and not a religious one, as is the case of the Orthodox and Islamic worlds.

The second region, heir to the eastern part of the empire, is culturally and linguistically Greek, ethnically Slavic, and confessionally Christian-Orthodox. Its symbolic capital was Constantinople, which during the Middle Ages was known as Byzantium and, after the Turkish invasion, as Istanbul. The Islamization of Byzantium brought its symbolic capital to Moscow, considered by many to be 'the third Rome.' Its influence remains in Eastern Europe, from Greece to Russia, and most widely expanded during the second half of the twentieth century with the rise of communism.

The third great front of late Antiquity's diversification was located at the southeast corner of the empire, although it corresponded to much more heterogeneous ethnic and cultural heritages going back to Arab nomadic tribes and with imprints from the ancient Egyptian, Mesopotamian, and Persian empires. Its unification was originally religious with the expansion of Islam, a religion that managed to strengthen ties between an amalgam of very diverse ethnic groups, such as the Arabic, Persian, Berber, Hindu, and sub-Saharan tribes.

The deep cultural differences between these three areas make it impossible to unify them, at least in the medium or long term. Significantly, the great confrontations of the twentieth and twenty-first centuries are defined by clashes between these three civilizations: the confrontation between Slavic-Orthodox East and the Western European countries during the Cold War (1945–1989) and the confrontation between Islam and the West at present, especially since September 11, 2001. The entire globe, except for China and India, could be included in one of these three categories.

When did these three areas begin to diversify given that they were all at one point part of and unified by the Roman Empire? Henri-Irénée Marrou and Peter Brown have explained the history of divergence in late Antiquity, and its specificity as a historical period. They argue that the history of the world after the year 400 basically implies understanding how Eastern and Western societies adjusted to the Germanic population's growth and expansion ('barbarians,' as they called them), which arrived in waves from the northern and northeastern parts of the empire. At first, it only involved more or less transient violent raids of a military nature. But, over time, Germanic peoples began to establish themselves, adjusting to and settling in lands that a central authority (Rome) had controlled but which had ceased to exist. Different reactions (adaptive in the West, traditionalist in the East, and disruptive in Islam) in the face of these huge migratory waves sharpened the differences between these three areas. The West demonstrated its proverbial capacity for acceptance and integration, and the Germanic peoples eventually fully assimilated Roman culture, contributing their own traditions, values, and style, such as the consolidation of the monarchy, the assimilation of Christianity and Roman civilization, and a strong sense of solidarity. The lands that had belonged to the East part of the Empire, politically consolidated around Byzantium, reacted with a radical return to Roman origins, forcefully opposing any type of ethnic, religious, or cultural fusion with other groups. The peoples of the south and east of the former Roman empire embraced Islam, a new religion that was incompatible with any remnant of Roman or Christian tradition.

The Byzantine civilization was the first to emerge. It did so around the undisputed authority of Constantinople, a city founded in 330 by the Emperor Constantine. Once designated the imperial seat, Constantinople permanently brought together the full weight of the empire's tradition. Its civilization did not present any special novelty because it explicitly intended to eternalize Rome's legacy. Yet, the originality and beauty of some of its cultural and artistic manifestations are undoubtedly extraordinary, characterized by variety and a baroque style. Even today we recognize this tendency in Orthodox liturgy's pageantry, with all its accouterments, splendor, sumptuousness, attire, and incense. The Basilica of San Vitale's magnificent mosaics in Ravenna, Italy, in which the Emperor Justinian appears with Empress Theodora and her courtiers, illustrate the courtly majesty of Byzantium. This tendency toward ceremonial sumptuousness, full of a symbolism that its members fully appreciate, contrasts with the Western liturgy, both Catholic and Protestant, which is much more sober and conceptual. The famous Byzantine icons, on the other hand, represent one of the best examples of art's ability to unite the natural with the supernatural, the temporal with the spiritual, and the prosaic with the sublime.

Constantine chose a strategic location in the Bosporus Strait that connects Asia Minor with Europe, which ancient Byzantium once occupied. Thus, the different names of this capital city perfectly identify the three great traditions that have occupied it, namely Byzantium (Greek-pagan), Constantinople (Roman-Christian Orthodox), and Istanbul (Turkish-Islamic). Constantine chose well because the city he had founded soon became a true capital of the eastern part of the Roman Empire. A distinction between east and west did not just respond to the need to divide the empire to achieve greater governmental, strategic, and administrative efficiency. Rather, it reflected the progressive divergence between the Greek-and Latin-speaking worlds, which pertained to two very different cultural traditions.

Constantinople's center corresponded to the *polis* founded by the Greeks, but was enriched with the construction of new neighborhoods, palaces, and churches, and with consequent demographic expansion. It became known

FIGURE 5.1 The Hagia Sophia (The Church of the Holy Wisdom or Ayasofya), Istanbul, Turkey. © Shutterstock.

as "the second Rome" and, starting in 476 with the fall of Romulus Augustulus, the last Western emperor, it became the visible head of the Roman Empire during one millennium, and it was the seat of the emperor until its fall to Turkish powers in 1453. In the sixth century, Justinian was a key emperor in the consolidation of Constantinople as guarantor and heir to the Roman Empire and its civilization. Along with his military (he led successful campaigns in Italy, North Africa, and Hispania), and construction work (he promoted the construction of the Saint Sophia Church with its immense dome), he aimed to revive the faded magnificence of ancient Rome (Figure 5.1). He ordered ancient Roman law to be recompiled, including observations, comments, and annotations from relevant scholars and jurists. This resulted in the volume universally known as the *Corpus iuris civilis Justiniani*, a source of inspiration for jurists that law students continue to study even today, because it remains the foundation of many laws and, above all, the philosophy that underpins them.

This effort toward legal universalization was beneficial for the entire Byzantine Empire. Thanks to this work, Justinian also succeeded in establishing a more rational and centralized administration, controlled by officials with specific education for performing these functions. When a sovereign strives to establish legal principles, he does so with the intention of guaranteeing universal rights for all citizens, circumventing despotic and tyrannical tendencies at all levels.

His colossal work of legislative compilation, based on the study of more than 2,000 texts, was carried out in his first years as emperor. The main parts of the *Corpus Justiniani* include the Code of Justinian (a compilation of imperial constitutions from the time of Adrian), the Digest (a compilation of all legislation that came before the empire), and Justinian's Novels (a compilation in Greek of the decrees Justinian himself set forth). This project's importance to Eastern and Western civilizations cannot be overestimated.

Along with all these contributions, Byzantine civilization nevertheless had some derivations that negatively affected the peoples that originally formed it. One of them is the slippage of the figure of the emperor, supposedly the heir of the Roman emperor, to a *basileus* figure, the title with which one of Justinian's successors, Heraclius, wanted to be recognized at the beginning of the seventh century. Carrying a clear Hellenistic foundation and Eastern tone, this title had political-religious connotations that promoted the increasing sacralization of the Byzantine emperor, well illustrated in his portraits, especially those in which he appears to be directly crowned by Jesus Christ. This sacralization led to a tendency toward autocracy and tyranny on the part of the emperor, whose actions could be easily legitimized, even religiously, despite being unjust or despotic. The assumption of the title of *basileus*, with all its semantic and symbolic weight, implied the progressive submission of the ecclesiastical hierarchy to the emperor. This, in turn, generated notable anomalies regarding the natural autonomy between the temporal and the spiritual realms, imbalances that are still very visible today in countries that are heirs to the Slavic-Orthodox tradition.

However, although progressively circumscribed to quite limited borders, the influence of the medieval Byzantine Empire, both in the East and in the West, is immense. Legitimated by its scrupulous preservation of Roman tradition, its influence is seen above all in realities of a symbolic nature. Since we are now more accustomed to everything being explicit, we fail to totally understand the scope of these realities, but in a largely illiterate world, symbols, schematic images, iconographies, simple words, and legends about the past were enormously powerful. European kings modeled their coronations and other rites to the throne after Byzantine ceremonies, as well as imperial vestments, basic iconographic themes, liturgical development, and diplomatic practices, among many other manifestations.

Over the centuries, Byzantium circled in on itself, viscerally (and increasingly anachronistically) comfortable in a tradition that Latin and Islamic fronts continually threatened. On the first of these fronts, the religious division between East and West deprived Byzantium of indispensable allies when confronting surrounding Islamic powers. This separation fully emerged in the Catholic-Orthodox schism of 1054, which Ecumenical Patriarch Michael Cerularius encouraged and whose effects are still felt in today. The Crusaders' conquest of Constantinople in 1204 was a calamitous event for all of Christendom since these deviated from their true goal, the sacred city of Jerusalem, out of greed and ambition. It confirmed, however, that the schism between East and West was rooted in the development of diverse cultural traditions. On the latter front, Byzantium was increasingly unable to stop the momentum of new Islamic powers (from the hegemonic Caliphate of the Abbasids in the eight century to the Turks in the fifteenth century), which eventually led to its demise and conquest in 1453.

This leads us to inquire into the circumstances of the birth of Islamic civilization. Where did unstoppable force that successfully engulfed the Byzantine Empire come from? It emerged somewhat mysteriously from Arabia. Throughout Antiquity, civilizations expanded across Persia, Mesopotamia, Syria, and Egypt. The Arabian Peninsula did not play a leading role, most likely because of its challenging environmental conditions, including arid deserts, high temperatures, a lack of water, and the inability of its tribes to get behind a common objective. It is no doubt surprising then that, in the midst of these conditions, the seventh century saw the emergence of a religion that expanded into more than half of the known world in the West.

Where did the Arab world stand before Islamic expansion? Beyond belonging to a common ethnic group and the relative similarity of Arab dialects, unity was elusive due to tribal structures—whose ties were based on consanguinity—that shaped social and political life. Each tribe was subject to a main family and its sheikh. In contrast to almost all its neighbors, these tribes were eminently nomadic, although that account is somewhat nuanced. Southern tribes were more fixed since their main economic activity was agriculture, tending to well-irrigated oases with palm and other aromatic trees. In the west, with more traffic and better roads, merchants, moneychangers, and loan sharks flourished, as commerce proliferated. People in the areas next to the Persian Gulf were mainly seafarers. Nomads in the middle of the Arabian Peninsula bred camels and practiced a subsistence economy. Finally, Bedouins in the desert left a mark on Arabic culture, a facet of this culture that soon became widely known. They were fearsome warriors that either protected or plundered caravans, revenge was one of their most deeply rooted values, leaders gained authority based on prestige in battle rather than on consanguinity, they had a deeply rooted sense of honor and respect, a great appreciation for hospitality, and, lastly, disdained organized, rigid, civilized, or controlled ways of life.

Muhammad's preaching provided these scattered tribes, who previously had no shared belief system, a unique opportunity to unify and strive toward a common goal. The simplicity and cohesion of the Muslim religion was instrumental in helping the Arabs overcome their chronic inability to organise themselves politically, to form a hierarchical body or to plan rationally for long-term action. Islam's ability to organize social life explains its tendency toward being a political-religion because its original followers were unable to separate these two fields. The religion that Muhammad revealed, his example, and his governance style in Medina bestowed upon the Arabs a common ideology, a shared goal to fight for—the expansion of their religion—and a strict regulation of spiritual, political, and social life, which, in turn, guaranteed its preservation.

Who was Muhammad? Born around 570, he was orphaned at a very young age and was then educated by an uncle with whom he traveled throughout Syria on commercial business. Years later, he began to work for a rich businesswoman, named Jadicha, a widow who was much older than him and whom he eventually married. When he was about forty, around 610, the archangel Gabriel appeared to him in a vision and he decided to retire from business to reflect on his life and the world around him. During long nocturnal meditation sessions in a cave, he again heard the word of God, through Gabriel, who spurred him to fight the pagans who no longer feared God. From that moment on, Muhammad declared himself a prophet, a spokesman through whom God announces his will to men. A little later, he began to preach a belief in one God, the resurrection of the dead, God's fearful judgment, and, finally, eternal peace for the inhabitants and pilgrims of Mecca. He was at first met with violent opposition from rich merchants because his passionate and aggressive preaching threatened the great pagan pilgrimages of the time and all their commercial potential. He was thus forced to desist. Only his wife and some relatives, including his cousin Ali, believed him.

His enemies eventually wanted to assassinate him, and he quickly fled Mecca on July 16, 622, which marks the *Hegira* (the exodus) and the beginning of the Muslim calendar. The new city in which Muhammad settled received the name Medina, that is, the city of the prophet. There, he consolidated his preaching, especially in terms of the existence of a single God (Allah in Arabic) without Christian Trinitarian theology. Muhammad also preached that God determines our destiny in advance and that our death is fixed from the beginning, making it foolish to worry much about it. He exhorted his followers to fight for this doctrine, if necessary to the death. He did not consider it a sin to kill a pagan who refuses to recognize Allah as God and Muhammad as his prophet.

Any courageous warrior who died fighting for those ideals would go directly to paradise, while the pagan would descend to the underworld.

His first major invasion was precisely an attack on Mecca. Although he failed in his first attempt, he eventually took over the city, became a powerful man, and shortly before his death in 632, preached to some 40,000 pilgrims gathered there. The core of his preaching is very simple, which may in part explain its enormous effectiveness. Islam is the submission or surrender (which is what the word Islam means in Arabic) to a single God whose will and instructions only the Prophet knows and interpret. All those who refuse to submit to Islam deserve death. The submission of women to men practiced therein was not an essential doctrinal matter, but the experience shows that much of how religion in a certain place is lived is based on how the culture of that place is. The interaction between culture, tradition, and religion (particularly intense in Islam) is one of the more complex problems in history and deserves special attention, examination, and revision.

Because Islam lacks a mechanism for setting tradition (as Judaism did with the Scriptures or Christianity with the magisterium of popes and bishops, its authorized interpreters) and since the Koran is more an exposition of general principles than the enumeration of specific mandates, the force of practice has been enormous in Islam. Logically, then, many doctrinal divisions sprung up in Islam from very early on, leading to a loss of political unity given the difficulty of specifying praxis or morality. And this continues today, with the added difficulty of the pronounced division between Shiites and Sunnis, and the diversity among countries as different as Sudan, India, Morocco, Indonesia, Nigeria and Chechnya in spite of a common religion.

Spurred by a religion that legitimized them militarily and inspired them psychologically, Arab peoples took vast territories from Byzantium, invaded the Persian kingdom, and founded an immense empire in only two decades, between 636 and 655. In the next century, conversions to Islam increased considerably and conquest moved farther, to ancient Romanized Africa, the Iberian Peninsula, and Sicily. Around the year 800, just a little more than 150 years after its foundation, the Muslim regimes were nearly unstoppable, occupying present Portugal to India and then began to expand through Africa. While this enormous expansion occurred, the original empire began breaking up based on the ethnic particularism of the provinces, the most prominent lineages' internal quarrels for power, and the emergence of political divisions and heresy. Overall, however, the Muslim religion's consolidation was so robust that it was destined to play a defining role in world history for ages to come.

But Islam cannot be boiled down to doctrinal explanation and military expansion. It also had its cultural Golden Age. Classical Islam—constituted during the first centuries of its existence—left us, for example, the decimal number system (Arabic numerals), which was an essential discovery for scientific and technical development in the West from the sixteenth century onward. From an artistic point of view, Islam did not produce images because of its radical iconoclasm (prohibition of any image of a spiritual nature), but this accentuated its imaginative and varied plaster work, as we can still admire in some of its architectural gems, such as at the Alhambra in Granada. The West later learned from Islam's structural and aesthetic solutions in architecture, such as geminated columns and multiple domes. From a philosophical perspective, the classical Arab tradition turned its gaze toward Greek culture through luminaries such as Avicenna and Averroes. Although this classical tradition disappeared shortly thereafter due to Islam's progressive abandonment of rational speculation, its sophisticated schools of translation contributed decisively to the later recovery of classical thought in the West from the twelfth century onward. The Western imaginary understands the medieval Muslim Empire as quintessentially *oriental*, as Edward Said explained in his book *Orientalism*. However, Islam's power to fascinate the West was due not so much to its warriors' adaptability in the seventh century, but rather due to the resurgence of Persian traditions between the eighth and ninth centuries and the Golden Age of Arab culture in the ninth to twelfth centuries.

Around year 800, while the Byzantine Empire hid within its borders to preserve millenarian Roman tradition and Arabic Islam expanded around the world, the West seemed mired in a process of political division and economic decline. A ruler then emerged who many considered 'providential,' a worthy protector of Christendom and regenerator of the Roman imperial crown: Charles the Great or Charlemagne. The imperial crown had dispersed until Charlemagne undertook the task of rehabilitating the empire. What had happened, in the meanwhile, in the lands that had inherited the Western Roman Empire?

From the fifth to the eighth centuries, the native population of the western part of the empire assimilated the Germanic peoples, with whom they eventually merged ethnically. Peoples capable of psychologically assimilating immigration waves and generating multiethnic societies tend to experience tension early on, but soon thereafter generate an appreciation for diversity, internal dynamism, social mobility, and adaptation. This endowed them with enormous creative and expansive energy in the medium and long term, as experienced, for example, in the United States in the twentieth century. As a result of this convergence of civilizations, new political entities emerged, such as the Visigoth kingdom in ancient Hispania, the Frankish kingdom in ancient Gaul, the Ostrogoth kingdom in ancient Italy, and the Saxon kingdom in old Britannia. Faced with this political dispersion, the Latin language was the only cultural element that remained in educated spheres like courts and monasteries. The different Germanic languages waned or, at least, were only used colloquially rather than in writing or in official and literary documents. Latin thus continued to preserve cultural hegemony.

This was the situation when Charlemagne began to reign in 768. He was the grandson of Charles Martel—whose prestige was heightened by being the first Christian sovereign to halt Islamic advances in the Battle of Poitiers in 732—and son of Pepin, the first Frankish king anointed by the bishop in the year 751. This practice originated with the kings of Israel, and the Visigoth kings had briefly reappropriated it a century before. Charlemagne relied on three pillars—dynasty legitimation, military prestige, and religious justification—to establish the basis for his sovereignty. He inherited a kingdom made up of much of current France and Germany, and managed to consolidate and expand it, giving it a political, cultural, and religious identity that the West had lacked since the Roman Empire, although it had become a continental empire more than a maritime one. It is not surprising, then, that many consider him 'the father of Europe' in political and cultural terms (the typical 'founder-hero'), and that a global publication like *The Economist* would publish a weekly section, entitled *Charlemagne*, devoted to discussing important European matters.

During the course of his reign, Charlemagne expanded his empire to the area that currently covers France, Belgium, Germany, Italy, Austria, and northern Spain. This unification was based on military drive, administrative efficiency, and the ability to unify Christians, who considered Charlemagne a protector of their religion. His coronation as emperor of the Romans, held at Christmas in 800, was enormously symbolic and legitimating, authorizing him in fact as heir to the emperors of the ancient Roman Empire. He was thus considered the first emperor of the Holy Roman Empire, made in the image and likeness of his ancient predecessors, but distinguished by the fact of his sacredness as ruler of a fully Christianized world.

The pope hadanointed Charlemagne's father, Pepin, and many later monarchs of the various European kingdoms were anointed. The sacredness of the monarchy was a consequence of its closeness to the ecclesiastical hierarchy, and monarchs assumed the full legal burden with the anointing ceremony, which in fact elevated the king to priestly dignity. In the case of the Carolingian empire, since the emperor was meant to have universal jurisdiction over the temporal realm, the pope, who in turn had universal jurisdiction of the spiritual realm, was supposed to crown him. In this way, the papacy and empire joined forces.

Over time, this also brought with it serious disagreement resulting from each realm's excessive ambition. This happened when the emperor meddled in the legitimate work of the pope—for example, appointing bishops—or when the pope displayed excessive temporal ambition, hoping to extend his jurisdiction beyond the confines of the Papal State. The fourth-century stories of Constantine's caesaropapism and Ambrose's clericalism, mentioned in previous chapters, periodically reemerge in the West.

Charlemagne's empire was an extraordinary, but ultimately ephemeral enterprise, since by the time his grandchildren were in power, it had broken up into German, French, and Italian kingdoms (reflected in the 843 Treaty of Verdun), as well as Flanders, Catalonia, and the Aragonese Pyrenees in the Marca Hispanica. Despite this political disintegration, everything had changed in the West. Charlemagne's restoration of a Latin-Christian empire convinced European sovereigns that the kingdoms in process of formation in the western part of the European continent had a diverse cultural, linguistic, and political heritage from that which had been preserved in Greek-Byzantium and Arabic-Islamic countries in the East.

By the ninth century, these three major areas (Western Christianity, Eastern Christianity, and the Islamic world) were well differentiated. A period of continuity then opened up, starting around the year 800, with the coronation of Charlemagne, and ending around the year 1500. We will explore the question of what happened in Europe during the next seven centuries and, above all, the imprints those societies left for posterity. Most people envision the Middle Ages as a dark and culturally insignificant era of survivors that lacked originality and creativity. This version is easily contradicted when we begin peeling back the layers.

As a western citizen and as a medievalist scholar, it has always been perplexing to me that at an era as brilliant, unique, and imaginative as the Middle Ages still gets popularly discredited as dark by people who take pride in their supposed objectivity. The enlightened eighteenth century held this view of the Middle Ages, projecting their own demons and fears onto it. Given that the discipline of history was underdeveloped at the time, this characterization is not surprising. It is, however, most unfortunate that this vision has penetrated so deeply into society to this day. Yet, accepting this vision of the Middle Ages is equivalent to treating cancer or heart disease nowadays with the medical techniques and procedures available in the eighteenth century.

Of course, I do not intend to present in the next three chapters an idealized image of the Middle Ages. This historical period, like all periods, has its bright spots and shadows, its successes and errors, its advances and setbacks, and, in short, its positive and negative legacies. Given today's economic crises, terrorist attacks, the wars in so many places in Africa and Asia, the multitude of refugees, and the swaths of territories where workers have no rights, it seems preposterous for us to campaign against or try to teach past ages. We must not fall into simplistic generalizations, especially in the case of an era that lasted ten centuries, from the fall of the Roman Empire to the discovery of America. Instead, we should approach the Middle Ages as any other era—with a desire to learn from its successes and avoid its mistakes.

Some have defined the Middle Ages as the adolescence of the West, which is not all together incorrect as long as it is not reduced to a merely preliminary period without its own identity. Yet this long period saw the maturation and consolidation of many of our civilization's values, which I will explore in the next three chapters and whose specific contributions were enormous and for which many have subsequently fought when they have come under threat: the Benedictine *monasteries*, which preserved the classical and Christian cultural traditions; the emergence of the *universities*, an educational model that has spread throughout the world and is still in force today without substantial variations from its medieval origins; the *canonists*, who were able to revitalize Roman law, giving Europe a legal framework essential for the recognition of all citizens' rights; the rationalizing effort of medieval *scholastic* philosophers, who prompted modern science—a real third enlightenment; the *chroniclers*, who began to distinguish between the historical prose of real events and the epic poetry that narrated the heroic deeds of imaginary characters; the art flourishing as in any other era, with the symbolic weight of the *Romanesque* style and the beauty of the *Gothic* style, unique contributions in themselves; medieval *literature*, which expressed chivalrous values that we still understand today as the framework of a decent life; the Mediterranean and Flemish *commercial revolution*, which made the birth of capitalism possible; and the *monarchies*, which reached heights of political stability that had not been seen since the fall of the Roman Empire.

Accordingly, the next three chapters are devoted to the maturation of the Western medieval values during the Middle Ages: first, in the extraordinary territorial and evangelizing expansion, gaining ground on Byzantium in the East, Islam in the South, and the Scandinavian countries in the North (Chapter 6); second, in the peak of the cultural revolution of the twelfth century, which I have called the Axial Shift (Chapter 7), and finally during the phase of intellectual and institutional consolidation of the thirteenth and fourteenth centuries (Chapter 8).

CHAPTER 6

EXPANSION

This chapter is devoted to the first great territorial, military, and evangelizing expansion of the West, from the disintegration of the Carolingian Empire around 870 to the consolidation of European monarchies around 1100. This seemingly difficult period, known to many as the Dark Ages, was in fact the essential phase when the main values of the West as we know them today emerged, and began to develop and mature.

Around 870, Europe experienced the disintegration of the Franco-Carolingian Empire. The change was truly profound. Life in previous centuries had been dominated by rulers who governed territories associated with one or other Germanic ethnic group, such as the Visigoths in Iberia, Ostrogoths in Italy, Franks in Galia, or Vandals in Africa. With the Carolingians, ethnic groups were replaced by lineages, the hereditary system prevailing over the elective. Some of these original lineages founded almost thousand-year dynasties, such as the French one that lasted from the accession of Hugh Capet in 987 to the abdication of Charles X in 1830. Others emphasized continuities despite the diversity of kingdoms, as with the succession of Iberian kings of Asturias, Leon, Castille, and Spain from Pelagius in the eighth century to Philip VI in the twenty-first century. Similarly, the imperial crown won by Otto I featured throughout the whole Middle Ages in the Holy Roman German Empire—which would be anachronistically appropriated by Hitler, though with many dynastic discontinuities.

The dismemberment of the Carolingian kingdom, together with the Viking, Norman, Magyar, and Muslim invasions, turned Europe into a highly unstable locus of crossing paths and peoples in transit. For that reason, the period which began in 850 and lasted until 1100 is the one in Europe that most resembles a *game of thrones*. In spite of these difficulties, from here Europe would begin a period of interrupted growth until the mid-twentieth century, precisely because of the competitiveness of the nations that were born in this period.

This first expansion of the West was carried out jointly by the military and the missionaries, by the knights and the monks—mainly the Benedictines. Until the sixth century, monasticism had been characterized, in both the East and the West, by the desire to remove oneself from the world as much as possible, abandoning any activity that could minimally distract monks from divine contemplation and penitential practice. Christian monks' departure from the world was similar in many ways to that of Hindu monks. However, Benedict of Nursia designed the monastic life as a communitarian life, replacing the individual models put in place by ancient hermits, penitents, and ascetics. Those who resided in these monasteries committed themselves to owning nothing of their own, to remaining unmarried, to taking care of their brothers in the monastery, and to unconditionally obeying the monastery's superior, the abbot.

Benedict believed that penance alone did not adequately fulfill the teachings of Christ, which he thought were more in line with both being and doing good. Thus, together with prayer, monks were called to work: *ora et labora* (pray and work). Benedict founded monasteries where monks lived in community. In some, hundreds of monks gathered and, over time, they began to function as small towns because they occupied very large territories and sought new techniques to improve agricultural yields. These monasteries also decisively contributed to making Europe a society attached to the land, and with a deep-rooted sense of work. From Italy, they first expanded to Ireland and England, and from there to France, Germany, and Spain.

Although they played an essential role in the first territorial and agricultural expansion of the West, the Benedictines are best known for cultivating and transmitting knowledge. In the midst of a difficult period and with scarce resources for culture, monks were alone in preserving Classical Antiquity's ideas, inventions, and discoveries. They organized collections of ancient texts and devoted themselves to copying new manuscripts on parchment; indeed, many ancient texts survive today because of their work. For some centuries, monasteries were the only places in the midst of extensive rural territories concerned with culture and civilization. Some have criticized monasteries with the notion that they did nothing more than monopolize culture, taking advantage of it to expand Christianity. However, given the experience of so many other places where the classical tradition was originally much more rooted there than in Europe such as North Africa, Egypt, Arabia, and Turkey, in which hardly any traces of written classical culture have survived and, we should be very grateful to the Benedictines' work.

Benedictines supported and complemented the expansion promoted by the monarchies that emerged from the disintegration of the Carolingian

Empire such as France, England, and Germany; from the new Centro-European kingdoms such as Poland, Bohemia, Hungary, and Ukraine; from the Scandinavian nations such as Denmark, Sweden, and Norway; and from the kingdoms bordering Islam such as the Iberian and Sicilian territories. The next pages are devoted to the different process of generation, evangelization, and expansion of these territories.

The Capetian kingdom of France was originally of very limited extension. It only occupied the Ille de France: Paris and its surrounding region. But it hoarded a good part of the symbolic capital of the Carolingian legacy, enjoyed a strategic geopolitical situation, and achieved immense cohesion and continuity around its royal lineage. In 986, Louis V died, after the briefest of reigns, leaving the Carolingians in the western kingdom of the Franks without an heir. The candidate was his uncle Charles, Duke of Lower Lorraine, but his rival for the throne, Hugh Capet (987–996), belonged to the prestigious lineage created by Robert the Strong, held several countships (Orleans and Paris among them) and counted the dukes of Anjou, Maine, and Blois among his vassals. Hugo also had the decisive support of the ecclesiastics, headed by the Archbishop of Rheims, primate of the kingdom and anointer of kings. Hugo was eventually elected as king and founded a dynasty that would rule the destiny of France until the mid-nineteenth century.

In contrast to France, the monarchy in England did not arise from an original core that expanded amidst the rivalries of other feudal princes, but rather through resistance to invaders from the north, principally the Vikings and Danes and to assimilation with Norman invaders from the East. Alfred the Great (871–899), King of Wessex, soon stood out among the Anglo-Saxon princes governing the island. He concluded a lasting peace with the Danes, who would in time assimilate to the Anglo-Saxon world and end up converting to Christianity. He established a new system of fortified defenses in anticipation of new Viking attacks, rebuilt several Benedictine monasteries to revive piety, promoted translations of key works of thought from Latin into Anglo-Saxon, and issued a new code of laws. The notable prestige of King Alfred paved the way for the monarchy to become hereditary in England. The development of the island kingdom was not so conditioned by the feudal disintegration that had happened on the continent, above all in France and Germany.

But the island suffered a second wave of Danish invasions in the early eleventh century. In 1016, King Canute II of Denmark reached an agreement with Edmund Ironside to divide up the kingdom, with whoever outlived the other inheriting it whole. Edmund soon died, and Canute became King of England (1016–1035). A Dane among Anglo-Saxons, he did not act as a foreign king but showed respect for the laws and customs established by his predecessors and protected the Church and its monasteries. On his death, the royal office reverted to an Anglo-Saxon, Edward the Confessor (1042–1066), who was able to perform the task of ruling in a relatively conventional manner. However, he could not avoid one of the most momentous events in English—and by extension, European— history: the Norman conquest of England by William the Conqueror at the Battle of Hastings in 1066, which is for many the key date in the foundation of England.

The eastern region of the old Carolingian empire, a good part of which we know today as Germany, pursued a very different historical course from that of France or England. These lands had neither formed part of the Roman empire nor experienced Merovingian rule. Their language had remained Germanic, in contrast to the western region's adoption of Latin. But perhaps what most distinguished it from France and England was the fact that it had hardly known feudalism. The counts were royal officials who simply exercised an administrative function, which relieved them of feudal obligations and servitudes. In such circumstances, the feudal regime did not take root so that most of the land was cultivated by its owners, free men, who were usually not personally tied to their lords. The old tribal areas prior to the Carolingian empire thus reemerged in the eastern part as duchies, specifically known as *Stammesherzogtum*—literally, 'tribal duchies.' They were Saxony, Franconia, Lorraine, Swabia, and Bavaria, to list them north to south. Their dukes based their authority on their own possessions, their military leadership, and their ability to sway their subjects. Bishops and abbots remained outside their jurisdiction. In reality, the dukes functioned as independent units, united only by the figure of the Holy Roman German Emperor from Otto I onward (936–973). The empire not only had a unifying function. It also promoted the expansion toward Italy and the Slavic world and laid the foundations for the birth of a stable civilization in the center of Europe.

The figure of Otto I already operated in a context where hereditary offices had supplanted elective ones and thus generated greater political stability. Around 970, the most energetic military and religious expansionary front arose around the periphery of Europe: to the north, the Scandinavian kingdoms (Denmark, Sweden, and Norway); to the east, the Central European kingdoms (Poland, Bohemia, Hungary, and the Kingdom of Rus); and to the south, the Iberian kingdoms and Sicily.

The appearance of numerous royal and ducal houses in Central Europe made it possible to unify hitherto very dispersed territories and worked in favor of their Christianization. Here we find again the key figure of the 'founding hero': semilegendary personages, heads of lineages, who were the protagonists of historical-genealogical stories. The conversions to Christianity of Mieszko I of

Poland, Wenceslas I of Bohemia (in the present-day Czech Republic), Stephen of Hungary, and Vladimir of the Kievan Rus kingdom (in the present-day Ukraine) had the same emotional and memorial power for their nations as did the conversions of Constantine for Rome and Clovis for the Germanic peoples. From their inception, these four nations inclined toward the Capetian and Ottonian model of centralized monarchy rather than the feudal one of the Anglo-Saxons and Normans. The difference is that these territories had not undergone the Carolingian disintegration, so neither feudalism nor territorial principalities took root. Free of feudal intermediaries, the kings increased their authority.

These four nations would also constitute the West's frontier with the Slavic-Russian world and one of them, Ukraine, would find itself split between the two civilizations, a state of affairs that has generated tensions lasting until this day, with the ignominious Russian invasion of Ukraine in 2022. Indeed, the frontier zone between Poland and Russia was inhabited by Slavs, and gradually swung toward Byzantine Orthodox Christianity. The most influential and lasting of the Slavic Orthodox kingdoms was that of Kievan Rus, forerunner of the modern nations of Russia and Ukraine. The term Russian first appeared in the mid-ninth century in Anglo-Saxon, Byzantine, and Arab sources, referring to the inhabitants of present-day Ukraine. Those documents treat these peoples, indiscriminately, as coming from Scandinavia, and therefore assimilable in their origins to the Normans, or else as the kin of Slavic tribes from the east. This ambiguity about origins, Norman or Slav, marking a tendency to Eurasian equidistance, is present throughout all of Russian history and could explain some of its disengagements. Origins say a great deal about nations as they are today, and this is a fact worth bearing in mind when seeking to understand the actual geopolitical situation, cultural makeup, and religious orientation of present-day Russia.

This Slavic Orthodox tradition was expanding toward the southern Slavs in the Balkans, where there was a somewhat tense encounter between Catholicism and Orthodoxy, among other reasons because of the greater proximity of the two politico-religious centers of each tradition. Croats and Slovenes came under Roman Catholic influence, whereas Serbs and Bulgars under Greek Orthodox. The picture became even more complicated with the increasing Islamization of the Bosnians. Surveying this scene, it is easy to see that the religious loyalties established in this period have been long-standing and given rise to strong political tensions throughout history. These subterranean fault lines erupted to the surface in 1914 with the earthquake caused by the assassination in Sarajevo of the Archduke Franz Ferdinand, heir to the Austro-Hungarian Empire, detonating the Great War, and in the 1990s with the terrible conflict between some South-Slav nations of the Balkans.

Another major front of Christian expansion was Scandinavia. The conversion of the Scandinavian peoples was a slower process than that of the Central Europeans, as they had hardly experienced any previous contact with Christianity. By around 980, Denmark, Sweden, and Norway had been consolidated. These three nations started to assimilate Christianity thanks to the baptism of their respective kings, Harold Blatand, Olaf Skötkonung, and Olaf Trygvesson. Spiritual and political motivations must have coalesced in their decision to embrace the Christian faith. The experiences of their incursions into Britain, Ireland, Brittany, and Normandy had persuaded them of the utility of an ecclesiastical organization for the political stability of their states. But the majority of their subjects still adhered to their pagan beliefs and practices, which is why Christianity struggled to put down roots in a good part of their territory. This phenomenon helps us to understand how Lutheranism took such a strong hold in these lands, because it had an impact on a population where the original Christianity had not left a very deep mark. Lutheranism connected more naturally with the previous pagan substratum than Catholicism.

All of these peoples from the north were known generically as Vikings by their contemporaries. As they advanced south, Norwegians and Danes colonized some areas of Britain and Ireland. The Danes established themselves permanently in some northern islands, especially Iceland, from where they conquered Greenland (which today belongs to Denmark) and it would seem that they went on to North America. Another group of brave warriors—subsequently knowns as Normans—colonized French Brittany where, contrary to their custom, they settled, founding the influential county of Normandy.

The Normans had a massive influence on the following two centuries, especially with their subsequent conquest and settlement of both England and Sicily, and their active politics in France itself. A group of these Normans, together with Swedes (also known as Varangians), expanded across the Baltic sea and conquered Slav lands, coming to form the original nucleus of the proto-Kievan Rus kingdom. Normans all kinds of legendary tales and entered the collective memory of Europeans as an intrepid people, representative of the finest chivalric and feudal tradition: originating from Scandinavia, they ended up with a highly active presence in lands as far flung as England, Normandy, Sicily, and Ukraine (Figure 6.1).

Finally, the Mediterranean front has completely different connotations to those of Central Europe and Scandinavia, as it involved confrontation with a completely different adversary: Islam. The Arab Muslim invaders set about organizing, from their devastating conquest of 711, an autonomous, prosperous, and brilliant state in the center and the south of the Iberian Peninsula, which

FIGURE 6.1 Medieval knight's sword, of uncertain date. © Shutterstock.

they began to call Al-Andalus. That is where their urban mercantile culture sprang up, dynamic and original, as evidenced by the extraordinary vitality and unparalleled beauty of cities such as Cordoba and Medina Azahara. Originally set up as a dependent province of the Umayyad caliphate of Damascus, whose rulers bore the title of emirs, it soon became an independent emirate with its capital in Cordoba. Abd al-Rahman III declared himself independent caliph in 929, taking advantage of the civil war between Fatimids and Abbasids. He revitalized Al-Andalus, but would not be able to subdue the lands dominated by the Christians in the peninsula.

The northern half of the Iberian Peninsula was, by contrast, a dynamic political and military hotbed, where both the geographical and the social borders were constantly shifting. Farmers became soldiers, soldiers became knights, and counts became kings with utmost flexibility. The various Christian territories had been organized into counties and kingdoms in step with their territorial expansion: Asturias (Pelagius, 718), Barcelona (Bera, 801), Navarre (Iñigo Arista, 824), Leon (García I, 910), Aragon (Ramiro I, in 1035), and Castile (Ferdinand I, in 1038). On occasion, when faced with a major challenge, the Christian kings would join forces for the common good, as happened in the great victory of Las Navas de Tolosa (1212). But mostly each of them organized their own border with the Muslims independently and grappled individually with the challenges that arose. As a result of this permanent state of alert, a strong sense of "frontier society" was generated, like that described by Frederick Jackson Turner in his essay on American westward expansion, "The Significance of the Frontier in American History" (1893). An occasional revisiting of the John Ford western, *The Man Who Shot Liberty Valance* (1962), helps to understand, by analogy, how that type of society functioned with such a fluid frontier and so precarious a balance between freedom, order, legality, and violence.

The Christian conquest of the Peninsula, now legitimized by the idea of crusade, intensified during the reigns of Alfonso VI (1065–1109), King of Leon and Castile, and Sancho Ramirez (1063–1094), King of Aragon and Navarre. The accounts of the semilegendary hero, Rodrigo Díaz de Vivar, El Cid

Campeador, come from this period, illustrating how the proximity between Muslims and Christians in the Peninsula, with many centuries of common experience, had left their mark: often coexistence prevailed over confrontation, and commercial exchange over military tension. In 1085, Alfonso VI conquered Toledo, shifting a large part of the border between the two Spains from the Duero to the Tagus. The union of Aragon with the Catalan counties in the mid-twelfth century consolidated the three great Peninsular kingdoms (Portugal, Castile, and the Crown of Aragon), who during the sixteenth century would spearhead one of the most spectacular episodes in universal history with their discoveries and empires.

Naturally, there were areas where *convivencia*—a technical concept coined by recent historiography—between Christians and Muslims was greater. The originality of the culture forged in Toledo stands out as a genuine crucible of Christian, Islamic, and Jewish civilization, notable for its school of translators. The interstices between Mozarabic and Mudejar areas generated some artistic styles that we can still appreciate today when we travel and glimpse their peculiar church towers in the distance, much imitated by nineteenth-century "neo" architectural fashions. The interaction between the three Iberian cultures and religions was dealt with in depth by Américo Castro (*The Structure of Spanish History*, 1954), who pointed out the importance that religiosity, and specifically the Jewish and Muslim minorities, had in Spanish culture. A harder task is to discern whether the Spain of three religions was the near-paradisiacal environment of mutual concord that María Rosa Menocal depicts in her celebrated *The Ornament of the World: How Muslims, Jews, and Christians Created a Culture of Tolerance in Medieval Spain* (2002), or perhaps the more realistic one of Brian Catlos in his *Kingdoms of Faith* (2019). This is a debate with obvious current resonance, especially after the attack on the Twin Towers in 2001, which have provided to medieval Spain with an historiographical interest that would have been unimaginable a few decades ago. The past and the present are in constant interaction through collective memory.

The other great Mediterranean front was the island of Sicily. The Christian recovery of the territory did not come in this case from native forces, but through the action of the ever-restless Norman knights. In the early eleventh century, a group of Norman knights berthed in southern Italy on their way back from a pilgrimage to the Holy Land and realized its potential. Anyone who has visited that island is seduced by its charm, mysteriously attractive despite its aridity. Starting in 1060, Robert Guiscard and his brother Roger expelled Byzantines and Muslims from the island. Roger II (1105–1154) managed to unify it with a centralized and efficient government. On top of that, he received from the Pope the royal dignity for Sicily and for himself as monarch in 1130, becoming one of the most influential princes in the Mediterranean. His charisma is well captured in the famous mosaic of the Church of the Martorana in Palermo, where he is shown being crowned by Jesus Christ Himself.

Sicily became from that time an active multilingual and interreligious cultural center, as it had been under the rule of classical Greece (Magna Graecia). Chancery documents were written in Greek, Latin, and Arabic. Roman and Muslim legal traditions were made compatible with Norman feudal laws. Taxes were administered by two different institutions, two customs: one for taxes received by the king and the other for feudal nobles. Perhaps it is from this—and the chronic impossibility of the island freeing itself from internal meddling for so many centuries—that the quintessential duality of the Sicilians and Neapolitans derives. Over the centuries, an official state-run accounting system has been seen as distinct from another, unofficial one, monopolized by local organizations that have managed to circumvent the administration and tax system of the centralized state. Some of these have degenerated, unfortunately, into the hard-organized crime structures represented by the mafias. The medieval state could at least count on papal protection, seeing as the kingdom had come into being through rendering vassalage to him. The kings were designated permanent legates of the pope, so they enjoyed (and often abused) absolute control over the kingdom's prelates.

As we have seen in this chapter, the West soon ranged from Iberia to Ukraine, and from Sicily to Sweden. Despite its own deep ethnic differences, it appeared to be a cohesive unit by 1100, thanks to the idea of *Universitas Christiana*. It was a transcultural and multiethnic society united by spiritual ties. If up till then it had been lagging behind the China of the Tang, Sung, and Ming dynasties; the Umayyad and Abbasid Islamic world of Damascus, Cordoba, and Baghdad; and the Byzantium of Constantinople, from that moment on, European culture was set on a course of higher development. The twelfth century is therefore considered, and with good reason, an Axial period in the history of the West.

CHAPTER 7

SHIFT

The twelfth century witnessed an intellectual revolution with profound consequences for posterity. Historians like Charles H. Haskins have compared its effects to those of the Renaissance in the sixteenth century. Sociologists like Benjamin Nelson have defined it as the 'axial shift' essential for the consolidation of Western values. Philosophers like Philippe Nemo have termed it an intellectual and legal revolution. Economic historians like Roberto S. López have considered it a real 'commercial revolution,' analogous to the modern industrial revolution. The medievalist Jacques Le Goff has stated that the supposed 'modernity' of the West began in the twelfth and not in the sixteenth century. The most logical approach, therefore, was to consider the period from roughly 1100 to 1800 as a *long modernity*, stretching from the generation of intellectuals associated with Peter Abelard to the French Revolution. The unity of those centuries is greater than that signified by the artificial distinctions of middle, early modern, and modern periods, and they are more aligned with the period of long expansion for Western civilization.

Furthermore, the twelfth century has certain analogies with the Axial Period as postulated by Karl Jaspers for Antiquity. As had happened around the middle of the first millennium BC, in this period, the Christian West maintained greater contact and collaboration with other civilizations, above all with Judaism, the ancient Greek heritage and Byzantium, an expanding Islam and, more marginally, with China through the trips and reports of some Italian merchants—most famously Marco Polo. This brought about some substantial changes in the development of natural theology, speculative philosophy, legal developments, experimental science, and mathematical calculus and statistics as applied to commerce, which stimulated change in mercantile culture, too.

In the early thirteenth century, Islamic science still led in the fields of optics, mathematics, medicine, and astronomy. It was the last occasion when Islamic science was ahead of Western science. With the reception in the West of 'the new Aristotle' and his books on nature via the Islamic translations and their commentators, a new intellectual and scientific agenda swept the intellectual centers and universities throughout Europe, inaugurating a leadership over other civilizations that it would not easily relinquish.

The twelfth century is a fascinating era, full of paradoxes, since it was essentially a dense space hosting a dramatic encounter between past and future, tradition and innovation. On the one hand, it experienced a practice as anti-Western and regressive as the crusades and, on the other, it witnessed a rational revolution—legal, administrative, economic, and political—whose repercussions still register today. Paradoxically, the crusades encouraged political, commercial, cultural, scientific, artistic, and theological exchanges between Western Christianity, Byzantine Christianity, Islam, China, the Jews, and the Mongols that led to intellectual and technical innovations. Christian European translators—especially Castilian and Sicilian ones—facilitated the reception of the Greek philosophical heritage through Arabic and Hebrew texts. Nestorian Christian translators did their best in their translations from Greek into Arabic. Islamic optics, algebra, and medicine were assimilated by European scientists. The compass, new navigation techniques, and paper were imported from China. The Hindu–Arabic numerical system was adopted, along with the mathematical approach to natural philosophy and physics inherited from Aristotle.

But beyond the proliferation of contacts, exchanges, and cultural assimilations between civilizations, the key for the West was the unleashing of political, legal, religious, and economic reforms that are still relevant today, and which established something like version 2.0 of the West, following the adoption and fusion phase of its classical and Christian foundation (West 1.0) and which would enable it to move, from then on, toward modernization, rationalization, industrialization, and universalization of the last three centuries (West 3.0).

Where might the roots of such a revolutionary transformation be found? The starting point was the intellectual debate between Bernard and Abelard in the early twelfth century, which stands as a precise icon of the doctrinal and intellectual changing of the guard taking place in Europe: from the rich Benedictine cultural tradition of the rural cloisters—focused on the tasks of transcription and compilation of classical culture and the church fathers—to the new restless urban intellectual centers, interested primarily in updating and critiquing this tradition through rational speculation and debate, rather than in simply preserving and reproducing it. Bernard was a Benedictine-Cistercian of contemplative rural life, whose aspiration was union with Christ by the mystical way, whereas Abelard was a monk with a passion for logical knowledge, living an active and urban life, whose highest aim was knowledge of God through reason.

But it took a long historical perspective to detect the tectonic shift that was taking place at that time. Things did not seem to smile so much on Abelard during his eventful life. At the end of his existence, misinterpreted, old, and tired of litigation, Abelard decided to settle down and turned to Peter the Venerable, the prestigious abbot of the Cluny. He asked him for asylum in his abbey so that he could be kindly received in the last years of his life. He wanted to rest and reflect on what had been a troubled and tormented existence, full of theological transgressions, logical speculations, intellectual debates, and love affairs. The wise abbot of Cluny, aware that a journey as intellectually fruitful as Abelard's could not be tarnished for later memory by the suspicion of heresy, brought about a meeting between the two great adversaries: Abelard and Bernard. A providential coincidence caused the Abbot of Citeaux, Bernard, to go to Cluny and the two giants—the mystic and the intellectual—were able to reconcile.

It was a singular intellectual encounter with remarkable institutional ramifications, as it implied an embrace between the two great Benedictine abbeys of the time, Cluny and Citeaux. Bernard appeared to be the victor in his day, but the verdict of history was even more magnanimous, as it accords them both the status of greats. Bernard is appreciated as a great Benedictine reformer, the author of some marvelous spiritual works, while Abelard is considered the transgressor who headed an intellectual revolution of gigantic proportions, the most tangible product of which was the scholasticism of the thirteenth century.

The debate between Bernard and Abelard also illustrates the institutional change that was taking place in the centers of knowledge generation, from rural Benedictine monasteries to urban universities. With greater economic development and urban growing, the cultivation of knowledge went beyond monastery walls and spilled over into cities. Aristocrats and, above all, the new bourgeoisie based on the development of trade, began to worry about the cultural, intellectual, and professional formation of their children, usually sending them to educational centers developed around cathedrals (Figure 7.1). Some bishops thus decided to organize specialized centers of knowledge to study the disciplines of theology, philosophy, law, and medicine, and, in the twelfth century, the first universities emerged. They aspired to universal knowledge, for example, the Universities of Paris, Oxford, Bologna, and Salamanca. To understand the ambition and magnanimity of those first university founders, the words of John of Salisbury, which he placed in the mouth of his teacher Bernard of Chartres, are revealing:

> One will more fully perceive and more lucidly explain the charming elegance of the ancient authors in proportion to the breadth and thoroughness of his knowledge of various disciplines. The authors by *diacrisis*, which we may

FIGURE 7.1 Sculptures on the western facade of the Cathedral of Chartres: Matthew, Charlemagne, or Constantine I, and Hildegard of Anglachgau or a queen, ca. twelfth century. © Shutterstock.

translate as 'vivid representation' or 'graphic imagery,' when they would take
the crude materials of history arguments, narratives, and other topics, would
so copiously embellish them by the various branches of knowledge, in such
charming style, with such pleasing ornament, that their finished masterpiece
would seem to image all the arts. Grammar and Poetry are poured without
stint over the length and breadth of their works. Across the field, Logic, which
contributes plausibility by its proofs, waves the golden lightning of its reasons;
while Rhetoric, where persuasion is in order, supplies the silvery luster of its
resplendent eloquence. Following in the path of the foregoing, Mathematics
rides proudly along on the four-wheel chariot of its *Quadrivium*, intermingling
its fascinating demonstration in manifold variety. Physical philosophy, which
explores the secret depths of nature, also brings forth from her copious stores
numerous lovely ornaments of diverse hue. Of all branches of learning,
that which confers the greatest beauty is Ethics, the most excellent part
of philosophy, without which the latter would not even deserve its name.
Carefully examine the works of Vergil or Lucan, and no matter what your
philosophy, you will find therein its seed or seasoning. The fruit of the lecture
on the authors is proportionate both to the capacity of the students and
to the industrious diligence of the teacher. (Quoted by Jacques Le Goff,
Intellectuals in the Middle Ages (Cambridge: Blackwell, 1993), p. 11)

With his appeal to the masters of Antiquity and his enormous
interdisciplinary ambition, Salisbury's words are perfectly applicable to
contemporary academics and would exasperate Enlightened wise men who
considered (or continue to consider) the Middle Ages a dark era.

Founded in the thirteenth century, the university is one of few millennial
institutions still thriving in Europe and beyond. Despite contemporary
universities' aspiration of championing its students' professional training
through the well-known *Bologna* program, a harmonious combination between
knowledge and action was already inscribed in the heart of the university
from its origins in the thirteenth century. Initially, the university primarily
devoted itself to training professionals necessary for the development of five
fundamental aspects in medieval societies, namely the rule of towns through law,
the development of the Church through theology, universal knowledge through
philosophy, better understanding how the human body functions through
medicine, and, finally, the material progress of society through trade. Thus,
universities opened up the possibility of two cultural events of enormous
subsequent influence, namely the recovery of Roman law and the development
of philosophical scholasticism.

The recovery of Roman law slowly developed after the Gregorian Reform promoted by Pope Gregory VII (1073–1085), consolidated by the popes of the twelfth century. It was revolutionary because it attempted to rationalize the episcopal and ecclesiastical government affected by the administrative as well as civil structures of the Church, and implied a reorganization of European society's knowledge, values, laws, and institutions. This reform sought to respond to the progressive feudalization of ecclesiastical positions, which once again led to blending of the temporal and spiritual. In the first place, it decreed that ecclesiastical authorities must appoint all bishops, abbots, and canons, thus removing kings and princes from the temptation to manipulate appointees and increase their power and influence over spiritual authorities. In the second place, it confirmed the practice of celibacy for priests, thus constituting the clergy as an independent social body. Priests no longer had to worry about the fate of their inheritance and could not be manipulated based on it, as well as allowing them to become fully available for their pastoral work. These measures, although not definitive, were an essential step toward a unique part of Western civilization's heritage, namely a separation between politics and religion, between civil and ecclesiastical authorities, and between the temporal and spiritual realms.

Ecclesiastical reforms were also applied through canon law, which systematized them in a way that would not have been otherwise possible. This led to renewed interest in classical Roman law, on which all new universal canonical legislation that drew from the Lateran (1123) and Lyon II (1274) Councils were based. Soon thereafter, a new *Corpus iuris canonici*, known as the Decree of Gratian or *Decretum Gratiani* (1140), was published, which had a similar impact as Justinian's compilation five centuries earlier. All this reordering led to a conceptual unification of ancient Roman law with contemporary canon law, which implied greater humanization of the former and rationalization of the latter. It ultimately promoted the law as such, that is to say, leading the *de facto* practices related to blood revenge, abusive practices of lords, and codes of honor deriving from Germanic or feudal conduct to progressively disappear in favor of a *legal* way, a system based on the application of a more universal, systematic, and civilized understanding of justice.

The intellectual foundation of all these reforms contains the conviction of prioritizing truth over custom, as Thomas Becket, the English archbishop murdered by Henry II's henchmen, explicitly stated. This conviction is also evident in other areas of ecclesiastical activity, such as its attempt to adapt canon law toward consensual marriage (free agreement between spouses). This overcame the practice of regulating marriages for family convenience, inheritance, or influence. In this sense, the medieval Church was progressive, countercultural, and revolutionary, instituting changes that heralded truth over the conservatism that the powerful wielded to preserve their privilege. This evolution clearly contains a nascent rule of law model, which today we proudly refer to as one of Western civilization's greatest achievements. And we owe this to the brave ecclesiastics who revolutionized the medieval Church itself with their reformation.

Regarding the development of philosophy and thinking, monastic theology gave ground to scholastic theology—or in other words, shifted from mystical experience to rational theology. From that moment, the faith structure allowed for the consolidation of rationalized structures of consciousness. New images and horizons of conscience, self, person, society, the cosmos, action, justice, forms or rule, institutions of law, and learning emerged. New logics of rationalization of nature and faith, and new models for explaining natural phenomena by the principles of natural philosophy, replaced the old sacro-magical models of knowledge, ritual, and experience. A new sacramentalized sense of the creation and liturgy was expanded. A new way to express the experience of the self was established. New founding phrases gained sway, such as Bernard of Chartres's "We are like dwarfs on the shoulders of giants, so that we can see more than they … because we are carried high and raised up by their giant size"—the aspiration being to jump on the shoulders of tradition rather than lie at its feet—or Anselm's *Credo ut intelligam* (I believe in order to understand) and *Fides quaerens intellectum* (faith seeks intellect), pithily expressing the idea that faith insistently seeks understanding rather than just passively assuming: from wanting to know in order to believe to wanting to know for the sake of knowing.

That was the norm with the new intellectuals: full confidence in tradition, which they made compatible with an unwavering commitment to the future and the search for the truth, whatever it cost. They were willing to run the risk of climbing up on the shoulders of those giants that had preceded them—and not simply remain sheltered by their long shadow—so that they could see further than their forerunners. They suffered the consequences of their transgression, generally in the form of doctrinal suspicion and institutional cornering, but history has accorded them their rightful place.

Further, new university philosophers and theologians, later known as the scholastics, based their speculations on Greek philosophy. Classical texts came to them in translations and interpretations from Arab sages and new translation schools founded in the most cosmopolitan cities at the time, such as Toledo in Spain and Palermo in Sicily. They thus tried to fit together the rational achievements of classic thinkers like Aristotle with rational discourse on which new philosophical and theological speculation was based. The scholastics started from the idea that some of the most complex Christian dogmas, such as the mystery of the Holy Trinity or the Eucharist, surpassed the sphere of reason, but did not contradict it. All other dogmas, such as the existence of God or the creation of the world, could be demonstrated through rational or speculative methods. Figures like Anselm of Canterbury, Peter Abelard, Peter Lombard, Albert the Great, Thomas Aquinas, Giovanni di Fidanza (Bonaventure), and Duns Scotus must be highlighted here. Philippe Nemo synthesizes this evolution in his essay *What Is the West?*, stating that a new scientific vision of humans finally managed to impose itself, namely one based on a

> compelled recognition of a new scientific vision of humankind, one that revolved around a thorough analysis of human nature and engaged with the moral, political and economic issues of life in the century. Their contribution was a systematic, rational methodology in keeping with the ideals of Aristotle. [...] But as practiced in the universities of the Middle Ages, the scholastic method—an approach involving probing, refining, scrutinizing, and systematically arguing all objections *pro* and *contra*— reawakened the spirit of scientific enquiry so prevalent in antiquity. In doing so, the scholastic method primed researchers for the hypothetical-deductive reasoning of modern science. [...] From this moment on, civilization becomes a synthesis of Athens, Rome and Jerusalem. Scientific and legal reason are, henceforth, in the service of biblical ethics and eschatology. Faith expresses itself through the flowering of human nature. Classical antiquity is fully absorbed into the imagination and identity of Christian peoples everywhere in Europe. This synthesis gives rise to a spirit—to a cultural Form—that is without parallel anywhere in the world. It is called West. (Philippe Nemo, *What Is the West*, Pittsburgh: Duquesne, 2006, pp. 56–58).

Natural philosophy and Christian theology set off on a one-way voyage toward rationalization thanks to the new generation of intellectuals, among the most notable of whom were Roscelin of Compiègne, Peter Abelard, Peter Lombard, Adelard of Bath, Suger of Saint-Denis, Hugo of Saint Victor, Anselm of Canterbury, and John of Salisbury. The development of the logic of Peter Abelard and the natural philosophy of Adelard of Bath laid the foundations for the development, in future centuries, of rational scholastic philosophy and experimental science. The distance between Abelard and Adelard in the twelfth century and Descartes and Galileo in the seventeenth is not as great as has been supposed. The theories elaborated by each one are clearly of their time. But the rational mentality with which they addressed their tasks is identical. The opposition that Abelard, Thomas Aquinas, and Galileo met from the ecclesiastics of their time followed the same pattern: it came from those minds most resistant to change within Catholicism itself, rather than from Catholicism as a whole.

This pattern, consistent with 'guardians of tradition' syndrome, repeats systematically through the ages. In the sixteenth century, Saint Teresa of Jesus suffered the same attacks from supposed orthodoxy, which regarded her as a heretic, as the scientists of the first half of the twentieth century, protagonists of the second scientific revolution who also had to overcome the adverse reactions of some of their contemporaries in seats of authority. But now these critics were not strictly ecclesiastical, in contrast to those that Abelard, Aquinas, Copernicus, and Galileo had to face in their day. Now they were the academics in their respective disciplines, who questioned their hypotheses based not on strictly scientific arguments, but on the transgression of a scientific tradition and some sacrosanct academic forms. Nietzsche launched terrible diatribes against this 'old science,' following the bitter experience he had with his thesis on Greek tragedy. But Ernst Mach, Henri Poincaré, Pierre Duhem, Max Planck, Albert Einstein, and Niels Bohr could say the same.

Despite their best intentions, Bernard of Clairvaux and Walter of St Victor's reaction to the new ideas led to the triumph of logic and dialectics as rational methods for understanding faith, generating greater interest in the assimilation of the pagan philosophical postulates of antiquity, and contributing to their wider dissemination. Walter of St Victor published a polemical treatise titled *Contra quatuor labyrinthos Franciae*, directed against the 'four French labyrinths,' the masters of early scholasticism: Peter Abelard, Gilbert de la Porrée, Peter Lombard, and Peter of Poitiers. It was a caustic attack on the dialectic method as applied to theology, and condemned the use of logic in the comprehension of the mysteries of faith—above all the Incarnation and Trinity. Shortly after his controversy with Walter of St Victor, Peter of Poitiers was promoted to chancellor of the diocese of Paris, and Peter Lombard was recognized as an authority on theology. Their method was adopted by the schools. Their writings were used as a manual and official text for teaching and even commented on by all the great masters, a distinction they kept throughout the whole thirteenth century, until the irruption of Thomistic scholasticism.

Peter Abelard shines among all these intellectuals with a particular splendor. He took part in the great intellectual debate of his time—the quarrel of universals—by developing his conceptualist theory, which involved a radical critique of Augustinian and Neoplatonic naïve realism. His stance, expressed in his *Logica*, marked the first 'linguistic turn' in history. He considered language to be independent of its subject and external reality. Traditionally, universals were conceived as logico-linguistic categories that connect the mental with the physical world and exist as separate entities, whereas for nominalism, as expounded by Abelard, they are arbitrary mental constructs for organizing reality. His logical treatise *Sic et Non* also unleashed a revolution. In a clear anticipation of the scholastic mode of discourse, he used the dialectic method to affirm and deny the same thing in order to find a new truth. Finally, his *History of My Calamities* was conceived as a consolation for an unfortunate friend, but is in reality a pioneering intellectual autobiography that serves to give us an idea of his intense philosophical itinerary and inner suffering arising from his love affair with Heloise.

Abelard is considered by many to be the first intellectual as we conceive of them today. He gave up the profession of arms to embrace the Benedictine rule. But he did not isolate himself in a monastery, surrounded by the peace of the countryside, but rather pursued a hectic life of study in the city. History has undervalued him in reducing his contribution to his transgressive relationship with Heloise, which would provide fodder for nineteenth-century romanticism in its firm commitment to the model of romantic love, hegemonic in the contemporary world. But Abelard has been recognized above all by modern criticism as one of the great promoters and geniuses of logic, one of the key disciplines of the Middle Ages, and which subsequently connected with contemporary Anglo-American analytical philosophy. He is regarded as one of the first 'rationalists' of the new intellectual environment in Europe. He was more of a creator than a compiler. He conceived of theological speculation according to the classical Greek model: a systematic and abstract exposition, in contrast to the linear, historical, and symbolic exegesis of Scripture that had reigned up till then. The new method was also against the millenarian fanaticism that preferred the violent expansion of the crusades to the rational assumption of faith itself. It supported the renewal of Roman law brought about by papal reform. These two pathways—of intellectual and legal rationalization—would not separate again in the West, and would remain one of the most valuable legacies of the medieval age. Without them neither the unfolding of modern science nor the political stability that entailed the consolidation of the State would have been possible.

Abelard died with the maverick stigma that had dogged his entire existence—and which would accompany him in posterity, although now not so much for his commitment to logical rationality as for his creative relationship with Heloise. The following century's generation of scholastics met the same doctrinal resistance, with a synod held in Paris in 1210 under the direction of

Innocent III's legate, Robert de Curzon, prohibiting the study of Aristotle's *Libri Naturalis*. But just few decades later, the Dominicans were encouraging its reading among their university students. It is from there that the figure of Thomas Aquinas, among others, emerged. The new generation of intellectuals, led by Albertus Magnus, Aquinas, Bonaventure, Duns Scotus, and William of Occam, consolidated the logic and dialectic of their predecessors, and sealed the compatibility of theology with rational speculation.

The intellectual parting of the ways between philosophy and thought in the Christian and Islamic worlds is located precisely in this period. While in the West this deep process of philosophical and theological rationalization started, the thirteenth century witnessed the collapse of rationalization in Islamic thought with the triumph of the *ulama*, being the community of guardians, transmitters, and interpreters of religious knowledge in Islam, including Islamic doctrine and law. This made it impossible for any countries with an Islamic tradition to develop rational thought in philosophy, ideas of representation in politics, and the notion of incorporation in commerce or experimental science, all as we know them in the West. In the Jewish sphere, the predominance of the *Halakha*—the collective body of Jewish religious laws derived from the written and oral Torah—had some similar effects by maintaining the prescriptive structures and the Jewish legal framework of the Mishnah and the Talmud.

In the West, the philosophical-speculative innovations soon filtered through to scientific-experimental investigation. Robert Grosseteste of Lincoln is considered to be a pioneering figure in natural philosophy who laid the foundations for rational philosophy and experimental science. But it is rather the mid-thirteenth century generation of scientists who can be credited with a rigorous and systematic method of experimentation that gave rise to modern science: Roger Bacon and Thomas Bradwardine in physics, Petrus Peregrinus in magnetism, and the Pole Vitello in optics.

Another substantial element in this axial shift by the West is the emergence of subjectivity and self-consciousness in Western individuals. From a spiritual point of view, the embedding of the ritual of sacramental confession and the emphasis on personal conscience rather than just on external criteria implied a switch from sacro-magical structures to faith structures, and then to rationalized structures. Abelard laid special emphasis on the matter of *conscientia* as it already existed in Antiquity thanks to the works of Seneca and Cicero, among others. His new logical perspective allowed for more reflective analysis of the possibilities of conscience. Conscience sought to make itself more viable and operative, meaningful and fruitful in myriad ways. Whereas the pre-Abelardian conscience is outward-looking, the post-Abelardian is introspective. What is really new is that everyone in society, without exception—including nobles, kings, and popes—has a personal conscience to which they are answerable. The figure of the spiritual director—and confession—emerged as a consequence as one of the key means of salvation. Even the pope and the king have their confessors. All of them are answerable for their own acts. Conscience is an equalizing dimension for the whole of society.

The obligatory annual confession established by the Fourth Lateran Council of 1215 acted simultaneously as a passive reflection of the situation and its active trigger. It entailed the proliferation of moral theology, which established cases of conscience to contribute to a considered examination of the conscience by the faithful. There thus arose, perhaps as an unintended consequence, a proliferation of indexes of prohibited books and excommunicated people that fell short of the moral criteria established by the moralists. The apogee of these practices came during the theocracy of Pope Innocent III (1197–1216), especially with the figures of cardinals Stephen Langton of Canterbury and Robert de Curzon, who also went into the moral consequences of usury. By that stage, however, this intolerance was no longer a reflection of the majority view among actual ecclesiastics, but rather a minority and countercultural trend.

With the transformation of the structures of conscience, the scholars of the new universities were better equipped to defend certain philosophical and scientific propositions against the fideistic objections of the ecclesiastical hierarchy. That was the case with Abelard and Thomas Aquinas in their pioneering commitment to rational logic and the reception of pagan philosophy, but history repeated itself some centuries later with the 'Galileo affair,' in the properly scientific-experimental sphere. In reality, these cases demonstrate that the opposition of the Church was concentrated in particular groups of ecclesiastics who were resistant to any doctrinal openness. But their swift rehabilitation shows that conditions were ever more propitious for the development of a rational philosophy and science in Europe.

Another major area of the twelfth-century revolution was legal reform, initiated in the papal curia but soon extended to the whole of Europe. Jurisdictional reform had effects in feudal, manorial, urban, commercial, and royal areas. The new legal order generated the idea of the *corporation*: the legal and political principle (and fiction) of treating collective actors as a single entity. The new corporate actors had some very considerable effects in the most diverse political, economic, and social fields. They fostered the proliferation of new forms of political, civic, and economic associations that were unheard of in other contemporary advanced civilizations such as the Chinese and Islamic.

They laid down new organizational principles that allowed for the beginnings of constitutional governments, parliamentary practices, consensus in decision-making centers, the right to legal and political representation, the power of adjudication, jurisdictional delegation, and the power of autonomous legislation.

The new autonomous legislation of the political, cultural, and economic corporations allowed for the conceptual and legal legitimization of key new institutional forms such as city councils, the huge charitable organizations sponsored by the Hospitaller orders and the cities themselves, the universities, the merchant guilds, and the new artisanal occupations. It also made possible the diversification and specialization of the new urban professions in handicrafts, manufacture, trade, and shipping, with organized groups of artisans, merchants, moneylenders, financiers, professional philosophers, lawyers, doctors, notaries, and mathematicians. It enabled the creation of specific rules, regulations, penal systems, and specific recruitment processes for each of these socio-professional groups.

The cities generated their own fiscal systems, a task made easier by the geographical limits clearly marked by their walls. They also created their organs of political representation, their specific modes of election, and their legal systems and penal processes. They implemented their legislative and legal autonomy, usually through complex pacts established with the relevant monarchs, as if their very existence depended on it. All this generated a legal autonomy, a plurality of institutions and, consequently, a density in civil society that was unprecedented in the West and unknown to other historical traditions such as the Hindu, Chinese, and Islamic.

One of the keys to the extraordinary political institutionalization, social stability, material growth, and territorial expansion of the West was based on the consolidation of the corporations. The theory of corporations existed as far back as in Roman law, but was not applied on a large scale until the twelfth century in the West, generating a great multitude of political and economic institutions. They were collective undertakings possessing legal rights different from those of the individuals that had created, financed, and served them. This permitted a distinction between the property, assets, debts, and liabilities of the corporation and those of its individual members. A major constraint on economic growth in late antiquity and the early medieval period, its glass ceiling, had been that anyone undertaking a business venture had to guarantee the initial investment with their personal fortune. In the event of bankruptcy or ruin, the investors had to surrender their assets or those of their nearest and dearest to meet the demands of creditors, putting up their own lives as collateral. Many violent racist policies of the Middle Ages, especially anti-Jewish ones, were a consequence of the *personalization* of business, a state of affairs that was remedied by its subsequent corporatization. The new corporations, in contrast to what had gone before, generated collective rather personal responsibilities and separated the debts of individuals from those of the corporation. They could assume commitments and pursue legal claims on their own account, independently of their constituent members. They had the capacity to establish consensus without every one of their members having to adhere to it. They outlived their founders. Their owners could be different from those who were empowered to adjudicate for the corporation.

Corporate theories and practices also contributed to recovering the key distinction between public and private spheres of conduct and responsibility that was so typical of Roman society and law. All of this had a massive influence in the political and economic realms. In politics, the idea of the corporation allowed for the assumption of political premises that made the emergence of the modern state possible—a corporation in its own right. In economics, the corporate system involved the consolidation of the collective ownership of companies and the proliferation of commercial contracts, two basic conditions for the stability of the economic system and its eventual expansion. These reforms would obviously form part of the foundations of the future industrial revolution.

The theory of corporations, allied with its large-scale implementation in Europe, definitively set Western civilization apart from its Hindu, Chinese, and Islamic counterparts, where no such institution existed. This would explain in large measure the West's march toward modernization, in contrast to these other civilizations. Based on this reality, Max Weber argued that the rigidity of bureaucratic and hereditary societies like India and China prevented the formalization of justice, the rationalization of knowledge, and the development of technical innovation, viewed as threats to established power and tradition. Timur Kuran synthesizes the differences between the West and Islam in terms of the sociological significance of the corporate form of legal autonomy:

> In the nineteenth century, financial reforms in the Middle East included the legalization of interest, the establishment of secular courts, and banking regulations, all based on Western models. Islamic law blocked evolutionary paths that might have generated financial modernization through indigenous means. Sources of rigidity included: (1) the Islamic law of commercial partnerships, which limited enterprise continuity, (2) the Islamic law of inheritance system, which restrained capital accumulation, (3) the waqf system which inhibited resources pooling.

To all these reforms was added the firm commitment of the reforming popes to distinguish between areas of authority in the spiritual and temporal spheres, from Gregory VII onward. The twelfth century papal reforms had a galvanizing effect, since the clarification on the separation between the temporal and spiritual, and the radical reforms to the legal ecclesiastical system, altered and consolidated the foundations of virtually all social, political, and economic relationships. In politics and society, individuated persons are bearers of rights and rationalized universals become the focal points of governing norms. Dialogue and dialectic replace the established logics of authority and tradition. Such essential metaphors as *universitas*, *civitas*, *communitas*, *persona*, *libertas*, *conscienctia*, *aequitas* (equity), and *machina* came into being—or were recovered. The world is seen as a machine rather than chaos, which is why so many works are dedicated to exploring the evidence and stamp of divine artifice in the world of nature: Robert Grosseteste's *De Machina Universitatis* distinguishes the 'book of creation,' the 'book of nature,' and the 'book of conscience.' Roger Bacon was the first to speak of 'laws of nature,' in his triple capacity as theologian, philosopher, and scientist.

All of this also contributed to a fundamental change in the customs, values, and priorities of the West. Until that point, the society of the Christian West had privileged the nexuses and bonds inspired by *amicitia*—friendship: a sort of 'spiritual fraternity'—and trust in the tradition passed on from parents to children. This type of bond was more familiar, affective, and private than professional, legal, and universal. *Traditional* feudal relationships were dominated by ties of trust and loyalty. In a typical feudal context, individuals were tied by bonds that obliged them even to put their own lives at risk to defend the rights of the other party or to come to their aid in the continuous conflicts that arose, in the absence of a universal legal order. The friend–enemy relationship was thus key for the development of feudal societies. As a result, relations between political and religious communities were very polarized, which explains the radical nature of some military and spiritual expressions. Among friends, everything was held in common, especially enemies. This also explains the dense solidarity relationships from a 'horizontal' perspective: between nobles themselves and between members of the same religious community, for example, within the Benedictine monastery system. This fraternity was sublimated in the figure of Jesus Christ, 'the great friend': "Greater love hath no man tan he lay down his life for a friend" (John, xv: 13). Notions of 'fraternity' and 'community' were therefore essential for the functioning of feudal societies, but would soon prove inadequate for an urban society, asserting the universality of its legal and social order.

From the twelfth century onward, the processes of philosophical rationalization and legal universalization were an effective solvent of the most pernicious effects the touchstones of kinship, clan, caste, tribe, or race had as powerfully formative elements of public life. Those institutions, made absolute, block universality and promote arbitrariness, corruption, despotism, and cronyism. They are core institutions, worth preserving and cultivating, but they must not impede the growth of the plural unions and associations necessary for the development of civil and public life—the most efficacious antidote to tyranny. When there is a vigorous civil society, universal rights prevail, because sectarian criteria based on clan, class, or race cease to be hegemonic.

These new urban context and values were compatible with the emergence of a chivalric spirit, especially among nobles and knights. Chivalry is an aspect of medieval culture that should perhaps be better known, recognized, and practiced in their most elegant manifestations. The development of hierarchical feudalism and an eminently masculine and warrior society is not, of course, counted among the most positive facets of the Middle Ages. Yet, it contributed to the development of knightly values that we now identify with a good education and that, as Ernst Gombrich explained in chapter 23 in his *A Little History of the World*, make us all more human:

> And if it seems natural to you today to let a lady go through a door first, or to bend down and pick up something she has dropped, it's because inside you there is a remnant of the thinking of those knights of old who believed that it is a gentleman's duty to protect the weak and honour women.

These codes of conduct, may at first glance appear to be mere protocols or simple questions of courtesy, but they refer to values that are essential to the harmonious development of persons and societies. Keeping one's word, for whose fulfillment gentlemen were willing to give their lives, is essential for the development of public life based on reality, fair politics, a viable economy, and a more equitable society free from corruption. The development of *courtly love* does not come close to the advances that have been made toward the equality of the sexes, but it is an antidote to frivolity when it comes to sentimental relationships or sexist mistreatment. The duty to unsheathe one's sword only when strictly necessary and to avoid humiliating or mistreating a defeated adversary are two lessons that, were they well assimilated, would spare us many wars and humanitarian tragedies and would bolster respect for international conventions regarding the treatment of prisoners of war or the use of chemical weapons and those of mass destruction. Another lesson whose effects are all too relevant to our time involves the moral obligation of the powerful to protect the weak, destitute, refugees, and pilgrims. The Middle Ages are full of literary examples that reflect these values, for example, the texts around the legend of the English *King Arthur*, the Spanish *The Poem of the Cid*, or the German *The Song of the Nibelungs*.

The period after the Middle Ages recognized the enormously positive moral weight of these values, which Miguel de Cervantes and William Shakespeare made eternal in the sixteenth century. Even today, we still use the terms 'chivalrous,' 'lady,' and 'gentleman' to describe a person who acts in this way since he acts, more or less unconsciously, according to the ideals of a medieval knight. Chivalry, of course, did not always win out, and stories of cruelty and brutality also survive from the Middle Ages. Even still, this period left us a legacy of chivalric values that we would do well to review from time to time, and the study of these should be obligatory for anyone who intends to devote themselves to politics or hold public office. Medieval chivalry was actually enriched by early modern courtesy—the enhancement of manners in the context of royal courts—and modern civility, linked to the new manners developed in the cities. The development of chivalry, courtesy, and civility may seem to refer just to formal manners, but they actually improve our own humanity, our personal dignity, and our social lives.

As a counterpart, above all in urban areas, institutions fostering fraternity and fellowship, such as brotherhoods or religious communities, began to be founded. The cities were bulwarks against the old prescriptive rules laid down by the ecclesiastical and temporal powers, especially through feudal structures. The watchword of the cities, originating in a German proverb, was "city air makes free." New mercantile and artisanal professions were asserting themselves. The universities, a typically urban institution, were the setting for burgeoning debate and dialogue, where dialectic logic and scholastic speculation arose.

All of this leads to the conclusion that the scientific revolution of the seventeenth century did not arise out of nowhere, agreeing in all essentials with what the historian of science Thomas Kuhn maintained: the most significant and lasting advances in science occur when there is the right balance between tradition and innovation. As William and Martha Kneale have argued in their work *The Development of Logic*,

> it is arguable that the exercises of the medieval universities prepared the way for modern science by sharpening men's wits and leading them to think about the methods of acquiring knowledge. For it is certainly a mistake to suppose that all the philosophers of the Middle Ages believed in systems of

deductive metaphysics, and that experimental science began quite suddenly when Galileo or some other Renaissance worthy made an observation for the purpose of refuting a generalization of Aristotle or Galen, just as it is wrong to suppose that Luther was the first to suggest reform of the Church.

The social, intellectual, and institutional changing of the guard was concomitant and contemporary—at once cause and effect—of the transition from an essentially rural to an urban society, from feudal to monarchical, from monastic to scholastic, from cloistered to courtly, from Benedictine to mendicant, and from compilatory to creative. The new societies replaced the old world—hierarchical, paternalistic, feudal, and seigniorial. Resistance to change on the part of those holding spiritual authority—say Bernard of Clairvaux or Walter of St Victor—was stubborn and well intentioned, but always on the wane. Faith structures gave way to rationalized ones. As Benjamin Nelson diagnosed, "the cracks of the medieval structure came from two sides—the routinization of the charismatic and the sacralization of the profane" (the old prophecy and charisma versus the new routine, institutionalization, and rationalization). Finally, the reforms initiated in the twelfth century implied the creation of the basic conditions for innovation, which took shape in the emergence of representative politics, the creation of new economic actors and techniques, and the development of new institutions and rules for scientific research. Nothing would ever be the same again in the West, starting by the transitional (and unique) exuberant figures of Dante and Giotto, as the next chapter shows.

CHAPTER 8

EXUBERANCE

When underneath us was the stairway all
Run o'er, and we were on the highest step,
Virgil fastened upon me his eyes,

And said: "The temporal fire and the eternal,
Son, thou hast seen, and to a place art come
Where of myself no farther I discern.

By intellect and art I here have brought thee;
Take thine own pleasure for thy guide henceforth;
Beyond the steep ways and the narrow art thou.

Behold the sun, that shines upon thy forehead;
Behold the grass, the flowerets, and the shrubs
Which of itself alone this land produces.

Until rejoicing come the beauteous eyes
Which weeping caused me to come unto thee,
Thou canst sit down, and thou canst walk among them.

Expect no more or word or sign from me;
Free and upright and sound is thy free-will,
And error were it not to do its bidding;

Thee o'er thyself I therefore crown and mitre!"

Dante, Divine Comedy, Purgatory, Canto 27

We already know this scene from the *Purgatorio* of Dante's *Divine Comedy* because I have chosen it as the image for the cover of this book, and I have commented it in the Introduction. The scene also confirms that, beyond the medieval poets' appreciation of the classics, there is still an impassable wall between Christianity and paganism. Virgil must remain in the delightful and bucolic limbo prepared for the classical sages, along with Aristotle and Plato. The duality between paganism and Christianity is reissued in the equidistance of Dante's double coronation: the crown of the temporal and the miter of the spiritual. Dante must equip himself with both in order to act on his own judgment on his journey to paradise. The essential tension between the political and the religious that the West have suffered from Constantine remained intact for thousand years. In another of his works, *On Monarchy*, Dante clearly favors the autonomy of temporal power, arguing that if the rulers of the world were to agree that one of them should have authority over the others, he would accumulate so much power that he could not fall into greed, and peace would return to the world. Dante had suffered greatly from the displacement of the pope's power into the temporal realm, through his possessions in the Papal States.

Exiled from Florence in 1302, we imagine him wandering from city to city with the manuscript of his Comedy under his arm, slowly composing thousands of chained tercets that make up this sublime work, until his death in 1321. The Comedy is not only a perfect image of the architecture of the ideas prevailing in the late Middle Ages, with an impeccable sense of geometry, symbol, hierarchy, and justice. It is also one of the most enduring literary works in history, and it lives up to that inscription on his tomb in the church of Santa Croce in Florence, which still awaits his remains to be repatriated from Ravenna: "Honor the highest poet." Frankly, I do not know how it is possible that a supposedly dark age like the Middle Ages could have welcomed a poet as sublime as Dante, almost as heavenly as his own Comedy.

Dante based the plot of his Comedy on his admiration for a lady, Beatrice, a position that, according to the feudal code so familiar to the aristocracy of his time, ennobled the knight. But he had the genius to sublimate that relationship by turning it into an allegory of divine love. The narrative takes the form of the journey or road, another of the classic themes of world literature as an allegory of life itself, as Ulysses' Odyssey. It is also a cosmovision of the entire Christian universe, and of the place of the person in that world, but giving a poetic explanation rather than a theological or philosophical one.

The work is imaginatively autobiographical. At the beginning of the poem, Dante falls into a deep dream in the middle of his life (Nel mezzo del cammin de la mia vita). He then embarks on an initiatory journey that begins in hell, enters purgatory, and culminates in paradise. The author narrates his encounters with personalities of the present and the past, whom he places in each part of this universe (hell, purgatory, heaven), according to the morality of their acts. From paradise, once he has said goodbye to Virgil, he is guided by his idolized Beatrice, who clearly appears as an allegory of the divine light of Christian revelation.

The poetics of the Divine Comedy represents a graphic counterpart to the intellectualistic rationality of Thomas Aquinas' *Summa Theologica*. Literature allows us to enter the complex world of human thought and action in a different light than that of theological speculation and logical reasoning. Dante chose his characters for their historical notoriety, present or past, but all of them acquire a suggestive symbolic—that is, exemplary and universal—dimension through the categorization of their actions. Realism and allegory are reflected in the same story, which is a good part of the charm of the poem, for having been able to combine particularism and essentialism.

Dante materializes a real changing of the guard in European culture. This change of style is manifested in the idealized naturalism of painting (Giotto), the new models in literature (Geoffrey Chaucer's *Canterbury Tales*), the preeminence of nominalism and conciliarism against essentialism and the first formulation of human rights (William of Ockham), the emergence of secular political thought (Marsilius of Padua), the inauguration of the eclectic path of philosophy (Ramon Llull), the combination of theology and mysticism (Meister Eckhart), and the flourishing of civil architecture (Palazzo Vecchio in Florence). They materialize this attitude, so typical of the great intellectuals and artists of the West, who are capable of combining the preservation of the best of their tradition with the break-up of part of it. All these authors and works mark new trends that will be imposed in Europe and will dominate the cultural, artistic, and philosophical scene until the Renaissance.

Perhaps the greatest of them, after Dante, is Giotto. Because of this unpleasant tendency the *moderns* have of robbing the Middle Ages of what is proper to them, Giotto has been assigned the label of being "one of the forerunners of the Renaissance movement in Italy" or "the first of the modern painters," as can be read, for example, in his Wikipedia entry. But Giotto is a distinctly medieval author, and this should not be a slight, but simply the recognition of a historical reality. His mastery of symbolism and schematic pictorial language is admirable. The expressiveness of his characters is not based on the pictorial realism that would be imposed with the Renaissance, but on simple and rectilinear strokes that—if we are to label them—are much more similar to the French modernism of the late nineteenth century than to the Renaissance of the sixteenth century.

Giotto enriches the Byzantine heritage of medieval Italy, endowing his frescoes with an unusual naturalism. The spiritual parallels with St. Francis are obvious. His figures are sober but solid, delineated with simplicity, but with a deep dramatic, theatrical, and expressive sense. His style is very personal, immediately recognizable. He favored narrative frescoes, highlighting the scenes of the life of St. Francis in the Basilica of Assisi and those of the Scrovegni Chapel in Padua and the Church of the Holy Cross in Florence (Figure 8.1).

FIGURE 8.1 Basilica of St. Francis of Assisi (Italy). © Shutterstock.

It seems obvious that Giotto's work inspired many later Italian painters, already in the fifteenth and sixteenth centuries, true geniuses such as Botticelli, Leonardo, Raphael, and Michelangelo, who added a greater presence of perspective, chiaroscuro, and human anatomy. But along the way they lost much of the richness of symbolism and simplicity of the medieval ones: to each his own. Once again, it is necessary to avoid the unpleasant obsession of the moderns to conceive history as a linear progressive process, where the modern is always superior to the medieval. This is an ugly vice, inherited from the eighteenth-century enlightenment and nineteenth-century positivism, which we should eradicate once and for all. History is a complex reality of comings and goings, of chiaroscuro and ups and downs, rather than an ascending line where the present is superior. At this point, I invite readers to stop reading for a moment and google the images of Giotto and the painters of his generation (Cimabue, Duccio, Simone Martini, and Ambrogio Lorenzetti), all of them from Siena and Florence, and active around 1300. They are marvelous works, to which we usually try to artificially fit the label of Pre-Renaissance, when in fact they are simply and plainly artists of the trecento, gothic, or however you prefer to label them, but always within the framework of 'the medieval'—to great honor.

Yet they broke with the tradition received within the Middle Ages itself. They innovated in their idealized naturalism. Their figures adopt more natural and realistic gestures, especially noticeable in the expressiveness of their figures, which reflect pain, pleasure, sweetness, and tenderness without the mannerist or baroque excess. They filled their scenes with a narrative sense and made historical paintings fashionable, such as Giotto's Life of St. Francis. They also humanized the themes, from the sublime Romanesque Pantocrator (who is not overwhelmed by the welcoming majesty of the Christ of Taüll) to other more dramatic ones such as the Crucifixion, the Pietà (the Virgin with the deceased Christ in her arms), the Virgin and Child communicating with their eyes and smiles, the most diverse scenes from the life of the saints, and the representation of the landscape as a frame for their works. The techniques also change, adapting to the desire to capture the chiaroscuro and a greater perspective. They also introduce the portrait as a genre, as Giotto did to his admired Dante.

Geoffrey Chaucer joins Dante in his commitment to an alternative narrative to the classic chivalric tales. His *Canterbury Tales* were as influential in the consolidation of English as the *Divine Comedy* was for the Tuscan. They relate the lives and experiences of pilgrims to Canterbury, and deftly depict the lives of the various characters, from poor beggars to rich knights. Their versatility in themes and genres is proverbial, from chivalric romance to courtly love, from hurtful satire to passionate lyric. The characters are masterfully constructed and the stories are far from predictable. It remains a highly recommended reading, which has entered the Pantheon of literary classics in its own right, and is considered one of the greatest works in the English language, with Shakespeare's permission.

Marsilius and Ockham are two of the most influential political thinkers of the West. Their parallelism is based on the reformist nature of their work. With his *Defensor Pacis*, Marsilius advocated the sovereignty of the people, something that would become a constant in political thought until the French Revolution. The community should be the basis for the election of political representatives and the development of laws. This applies both to the state and to the government of the Church, whose sovereignty resides in the body of believers and in the gathering of ecclesiastical representatives in a general council. In view of the centuries, the firmness with which Marsilius defended some lay positions that contravened the whole ecclesiastical tradition is impressive:

> We say, then, in accordance with the truth and opinion of Aristotle in the *Politics*, book III, chapter VI, that the legislator or the first and efficient cause of law is the people, by election or will expressed by words

in the general assembly of citizens, who command that something be done or omitted with respect to human civil acts under threat of a temporary penalty or punishment.

Although he did not see it put into practice, it is obvious that his approach began to catch on among the rulers of his time. Marsilius is also a pioneer in the development of the concept of state, a word he mentions repeatedly in his writings, giving it a natural and not divine origin, and defining it as a plurality of cities and provinces subject to a single and exclusive power.

Ockham, for his part, defended the precedence of the gathering of bishops, formalized in the ecumenical (universal) councils, over the authority of the pope. He postulated, as opposed to the essentialists, that only the individual exists. Universals are a pure product of the imagination, which requires abstractions and generalizations to understand, but which in this case are based on arbitrary inferences. Therefore, contrary to what the whole Platonic tradition had defended, universals have no existence outside the human mind. These ideas, apparently limited to theoretical debate, acquired a decisive influence in practice. In philosophy, they laid the foundations for the later development of rationalism in the Modern Age, and the decline of scholastic speculation based on the philosophy of being. In politics, they legitimized parliamentarism, promoted conciliarism, and reaffirmed the anti-universalism of the nascent nations in the face of the universal power of the empire, three very typical and transcendental movements of the fourteenth century, with a decisive later influence, as is evident.

Ockham belongs to the post-scholastic generation, which privileged voluntarism over intellectualism. He enjoyed the travel companion of another of the most renowned medieval philosophers: Duns Scotus—not to be confused with the Neoplatonic Carolingian Scotus Erigena. He thus confronted the firm tradition of the previous two centuries, from Abelard's "to investigate in order to know the truth" and Anselm's "to understand in order to believe" to Thomas Aquinas' "Grace perfects nature." Ockham's ideas had a corrosive effect on the religious sphere, since they led to the disintegration of the syntheses between reason and faith that had been postulated by the scholastic philosophers. His opposition to the institutionally considered Church connects with his radical Franciscanism. His religious skepticism hardly had any real effect in his time, although he would later link up with some Protestant ideas. On the other hand, his philosophical nominalism soon became hegemonic in the universities, or at least remained in open debate with scholasticism. He also contributed to the development of experimental science by favoring concrete and specific phenomena (verifiable by inductive investigation) over universal and essential concepts (verifiable by deductive speculation).

Last but not least, Ockham has been considered the promotor of the first formulation of the concept of *subjective* human rights. This concept would be the foundation of today's liberation movements, since Ockham articulated it as the antithesis of the traditional *ius naturale*, which privileged the natural or objective. Ockham, by siding with a radical nominalism, privileged the individual over the collective, and the subjective over the objective, which naturally led him to an individualistic political theory. He also imposed a semantic revolution by associating, for the first time, the concepts of *ius* and *potestas*, of right and power.

However, it is also obvious that Ockham drew on the legal revolution that had taken place in the twelfth century, as I have examined in the chapter on the Axial Shift. The emphasis placed on the individual person—individual intention in assessing guilt, the personal responsibility, the individual consent in marriage, the individual conscientious scrutiny, and personal confession of sins—contributed decisively to an early assertion of the idea of individual rights as they were articulated after World War II. Yet Ockham, in his argument against the Pope, also recovered the idea of natural rights as articulated by twelfth-century canonists. To define the limits of papal *potestas* he argued that all just governments existed for the common good, but he privileged the individual natural rights of the subjects—the rights and liberties conceded by God and nature. This was probably the first time that the idea of natural rights had been used to challenge the claims of absolutist power. This idea would be retaken by the influential theologian Jean Bergson, who defined the right as "a faculty or power belonging to anyone according to right reason." This concept justified the natural right of self-defense against a tyrannical authority and a natural right of liberty through which a Christian could seek his own salvation even in a corrupt Church.

These ideas were brought into play with the discovery of the New World. Suddenly, abstract scholastic discourse became relevant to a major new historical problem facing humanity: the justification of colonialism and the rights of indigenous peoples. Both problems, which would be extraordinarily recurrent in the following centuries, deserved the attention of the most prestigious Castilian jurists of the time, especially those of the School of Salamanca: Francisco de Victoria and Bartolomé de las Casas. They revised the restriction that Aristotle had made on slaves based on the theorizing of the medieval canonists and nominalists. Las Casas declared unambiguously that "all the races of humankind are one," thereby defending the concept of universal human rights and, in particular, the right to freedom, property, self-defense, and the right to organize one's own government. Displaying a modernity that astonishes today, Las Casas argued that when a natural right was at stake, the consensus of the majority could not prejudice the right of a minority of individuals. In case of conflict, the right of the dissenting minority must prevail. Although some intellectuals of his time, especially Juan Ginés de Sepúlveda, opposed Las Casas' ideas, he continued to argue against the Aristotelian doctrine of the natural origin of slavery.

Finally, the ideas of the Iberian neo-scholastics of the sixteenth century revitalized the old idea of the natural rights of the canonists of the twelfth century and the individual rights of the nominalists of the fourteenth century. With the subsequent historical contingencies—especially the new colonization processes led by other European nations, particularly Great Britain— the enthusiasm for the idea of human rights declined. The solution was aggravated in the nineteenth century by the emergence of legal positivism, cultural relativism, and strong ideologies such as Marxism and Fascism. But after World War II, there was a remarkable revival of the concept of universal human rights, perhaps because of the pain caused by the atrocities suffered during the war. But this is a story that already connects with what is developed in Chapter 17.

The last topic to be considered in this chapter is the increasingly relevant role that women played in Europe in the Middle Ages. Beyond the postmodern clichés that attribute to other periods a misogynistic tendency that was not always as pronounced as has been pretended, women also emerged in this period as essential actors in the political, religious, and cultural fabric. The French-Italian intellectual Christine de Pizan wrote around the year 1400,

> If it were customary to send girls to school and then make them learn the sciences, as is done with boys, they would learn to perfection and understand the subtleties of all the arts and sciences as well as they do, for although as women they have a more delicate body than men, weaker and less skilled to do some things, so much more acute and free they have the understanding when they apply it. (Christine de Pizan, *The City of Ladies*, chapter 27)

Born in Venice in 1364, Christine de Pizan was fortunate to be able to devote herself to study and writing since the transfer of her father, an astrologer, from the court of Venice to that of King Charles V of France. Her life was not, however, a path of roses in the midst of an ivory tower that preserved her passion for knowledge. In 1390, her husband, Étienne, also a courtier, died and she was left with the care of her three children and a meager inheritance. But she decided to get by as best she could with her work as a writer, until she finally found the patronage of the Dukes of Burgundy and the kings of France. In addition to her famous *The City of Ladies*—a collection of heroines of the past that gave her the opportunity to develop her own ideas on the role of women in society, she disserted on the politics of her time (*Epistle to Queen Isabella*), gave her opinion on military policy (*Book of the Deeds of Arms and Chivalry*), innovated with his own autobiography (*Christine's Vision*), rebelled against the courtly customs of his time with respect to amorous practices (*Epistle to the God of Love*), and dedicated an ode to one of the women of his time whom he most admired, Joan of Arc: Song in honor of Joan of Arc. In 1418, she moved to live in the monastery of Poissy, where she died around 1430, sexagenarian.

Pizan looks immensely like the forerunner of Western modern feminism, five centuries before its emergence. But, once again, it seems unfair to label her simply as a 'precursor,' as has been done with Giotto for the Renaissance or with Dante for humanism. The reading of her great work, *The City of Ladies*, is more than enough to consider her in itself an advocate of the role of women in the society of her time, without the need to limit her to the role of predecessor. The quote just referred is an impressive testimony to the intelligence of her proposal: she advocated equal education for men and women as a basic strategy of female rehabilitation. Christine was convinced that "the greatest is he or she who has the most merit. The superiority or inferiority of people does not reside in their body, according to their sex, but in the perfection of their habits and qualities."

Moreover, he argued without any fear or prejudice. He went so far as to identify the beginning of the evils of the Church in the condescension with which some hierarchs accepted the gifts of the civil powers:

> Now let us speak of the popes and men of the Church, who would have to attain greater perfection than the rest of mortals. During the early times of the Church they did reach holiness, but since Constantine endowed the Church with wealth and strong income, what is left of holiness. What am I going to tell you? You only have to go to the history books.

Once again, the parallelism between other notable women of that time, such as Catherine of Siena, Bridget of Sweden, and Joan of Arc, in their courageous denunciation of the corruption of the ecclesiastics is striking, with enormous courage and firm determination, even though they knew the possible consequences of their acts and words. Pizan's commitment to progress and her detachment from tradition, when it impedes progress, are also incorruptible: "There are many things that are accepted for a long time, until one day they end up being debated and rejected." These quotations suffice to show that Pizan's contributions should not be reduced to a pioneer of feminism, but also go into the broad field of social criticism that undoubtedly contributed to improving the situation of her world. This brave woman represents the best of the medieval tradition, which many consider mistakenly a dark era, but the reality is very different. Without intellectuals like her, it would not have been possible the outbreak of modernity, a topic to be analyzed in the next chapters.

PART III

DEVELOPMENTS

CHAPTER 9

MODERNITY

Toward the middle of the fifteenth century, the West began to experience the cultural shift which we have inherited and which we now broadly refer to as modernity. Beyond its diverse origins, geographical specificities, and chronological variations—all of them analyzed in this chapter, modernity truly converged and began toward the second half of the fifteenth century. Yet there is a clear distinction between early modernity, analyzed in Chapters 9–14, and the late modernity beginning in the late eighteenth century with the French and Industrial Revolutions, analyzed in Chapters 15–18.

To us, 'modern' signifies the novelty, progress, and adaptation that allow us to elide entrapment in impoverished traditions, and look to the future with hope. The adjective 'modern' is certainly much more favorably regarded than 'medieval.' This chapter goes beyond these inadequate labels—inadequate because history is never truly understood from the context of comparative moralizing generalizations or ideological reductionisms. It analyzes what we understand by modernity, as well as examines the essential imprints of the future that derived from European values starting at the dawn of modernity.

When historians observe a seismic change in the past, they first inquire about geography and chronology: the where and the when. Yet, in this case, modernity was a heterogeneous and variable phenomenon in space scopes and time rhythms. The diverse regions of Europe became 'modern' at different times and in different ways. Italy is characterized by an idealization of the classical world so that it is difficult to find a very marked transition between the Middle Ages and modernity there. In the Netherlands, modernity also arrived very early because of extraordinary economic development and an appreciation for a humanistic culture. Spain, Portugal, France, and England developed earlier politically, rather than economically or culturally, based on the earlier development of their authoritarian monarchies. Germany was quickly subject to

Italian cultural influence, although their modernity manifested itself especially in religion, alongside the Protestant Reformation.

Chronologically, the conquest of Constantinople by the Turks in 1453, the invention of the printing press in 1455, and the discovery of America in 1492 are some of the milestones of the transition to modernity. Yet, other tectonic transformations are experienced during the second half of the fifteenth century. In economics, the model of the French bourgeois Jacques Coeur is replaced by the financial profile of the German Jacob Fugger. In religion, Europe experiences the outbreak of Lutheran Protestantism. In science, the fronts of the discoveries related to navigation promoted by Henry the Navigator and the inductive investigations initiated by Copernicus are very active. In art, the brilliant last generation of the Flemish medieval artists such as Jan van Eyck and Roger van der Weyden is replaced by that of the three great Renaissance Italian masters Leonardo, Michelangelo, and Raphael, together with the sublime Botticelli.

Historians' second question, after the 'where and when,' tends to be the 'who.' A list of characters considered especially representative of a historical phenomenon is helpful, and even more when the consequences for posterity have been so vast. Early modernity's list includes Leonardo da Vinci (humanism), Lorenzo Valla (literary criticism), Michelangelo Buonarroti (the Renaissance), Lorenzo the Magnificent (patronage), William Shakespeare and Miguel de Cervantes (literature), Christopher Columbus (exploration), Martin Luther (the Protestant Reformation), Gutenberg (technical invention), Teresa de Avila (the Catholic Reformation), Phillip II (the state), Jakob Fugger (capitalism), and Galileo Galilei (science). All of them were born during the second half of the fifteenth century. This necessarily limited list includes a representative from every clearly 'modern' field; each of these individuals broke with a firmly established tradition to a greater or lesser extent. Authorities of the day even pointedly scrutinized some of them, such as Columbus, Galileo, or Teresa, whose ideas clearly transgressed the established order.

The third question pertains to the causes that led to such profound change. From the political point of view, the monarchy initiated the origin of a state with more means at its disposal for implementing a truly effective administration, a stable tax regime, greater government specialization, and a fixed military structure. From the economic point of view, mercantile growth generated so many benefits that the bourgeoisie decided to use them as capital, although producers shared in ownership (corporations) and were separated from the results of production (work). From the social point of view, a thriving mercantile group grew between two traditionally dominant social groups (the nobility and the clergy), destabilizing the previously established social order (the three-order society: those who prayed, those who fought, and those who labored). This group established a new mode of social promotion based on having (work) rather than being (birth) and rose to power through the growth of new wealth creation centers (cities). Culturally, the new bourgeoisie understood the interconnection between power and knowledge, leading them to share in a significant intellectual and artistic project with the Church. They contributed to the proliferation of lay art along with sacred art, generalized the system of art promotion started by medieval patrons such as the Duke of Berry (patronage), and stimulated humanistic studies, as well as revitalized classical studies.

While the Christian God was at the center of all things in the Middle Ages, modern human tends to replace him. This is, of course, a generalization—something that historians detest—but it helps understand European culture's shift during the Renaissance. Perhaps it would be more accurate to say that the person became the center of all things along with God, because Western society remained essentially Christian, and that Western citizens became more aware of their possibilities.

All this materialized with the idea of humanism. By the year 1400, Florence was the closest thing to classical Athens as a bourgeoisie republic protective of its autonomous government and its sublime taste. Merchants eager for novelty and luxury replaced the nobles. Its citizenry was more concerned with carving out an exclusively self-dependent future than on preserving any inherited tradition. People were valued for their ability to create, do, and think rather than for their military skill, submission to received tradition, or fidelity to faith. They preferred to reference Classical Antiquity when referring to tradition, thus skipping the intermediate period (the Middle Ages) that stood between them and the ancient Greeks.

This fascination with Classical Antiquity was encouraged by the rise of cities, making the urban past seem more relevant, in contrast with the dominant rural context of previous centuries. This attraction emerged through knowledge, science, beauty, and art. This included accessing Greek and Latin texts, leading to a revival of classical language learning. The development of literary criticism (Lorenzo Valla) made it possible to retrieve texts from the past and reinterpret them. The elite insisted on the revival of classical culture, which they saw as having perished with the arrival of Germanic barbarians, through the recovery and analysis of original texts. Intellectual curiosity seemed universal at the time. Humanists who wanted to understand everything through knowledge emerged. Some, like Leonardo da Vinci, appeared to achieve this (Figure 9.1). A sublime painter and unrelenting scientist, da Vinci became interested in human anatomy, animals, nature, flight mechanics, fluid dynamics, and planetary motion, leading him to build new devices and machines that permitted flight and extended underwater submersion, among others.

FIGURE 9.1 Drawings by Leonardo da Vinci for the anatomical study of the hand. © Shutterstock.

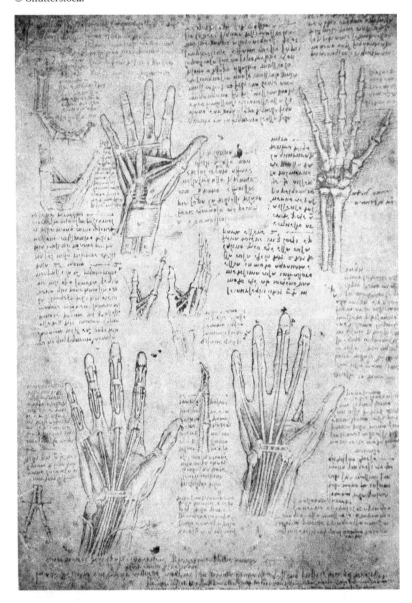

This classical recovery also witnessed the development of a new aesthetic movement we now call Renaissance art. Artists imitated classical architectural and sculptural models. New themes emerged, creating new functions and renewing old ways. Columns from the classical period were readapted to new civil and religious buildings. Artists, such as Botticelli, Michelangelo, Brunelleschi, Bernini, and Caravaggio, seemed to imitate nature in their incredibly beautiful creations, generating a healthy competition among rich Italian cities to see which was capable of creating more and better things of beauty. Florence's pioneering work was soon imitated in Rome with more artistic activity of a religious nature, promoted by the Church, and soon after that in Naples and Venice. This humanistic and artistic spirit also spread throughout Europe, especially to port cities in France, England, Flanders, and Germany.

Both humanistic knowledge and Renaissance art would have been nearly impossible without the emergence of a patronage system. The bourgeois, eager for architectural, sculptural, and painted splendor, devoted enormous amounts of their surplus to promoting art, meaning that the Church was not the only institution that invested in artistic development. Thus, lay art arose and distinguished itself from religious art in its design, function, and themes. Public buildings competed with cathedrals. Indeed, some municipal ordinances, for example, in Milan, stipulated that no civil building could exceed the *Duomo's* highest point. Sumptuous bourgeois palaces that still stand in Italian and Flemish cities began to house works of art. Yet, nobody was as generous as Lorenzo de' Medici, rightly called the Magnificent. The Medici family, merchants and bankers, aspired to govern fifteenth-century Florence as Pericles had done in Athens twenty centuries before. The streets of Florence still attest today to the "magnificent" proportions of this aspiration.

The expansion of the spirit through humanism and Renaissance art also furthered geographical expansion, thanks to the expansion to the New World. At that time, the 'known world'—that is, the world known to Europeans—stretched from the *finis terrae* in Santiago de Compostela to the Indies (as territories in Southeast Asia were known) and from the Scandinavian countries to the Sahara Desert. We inaccurately apply to that time the theory that the earth was flat and that, therefore, venturing out beyond Spain and England brought one to an endless precipice. In fact, Nordic sailors, known as the Vikings, had already reached lands west of their borders, but they retreated because they found no sign of civilization or possibilities for trade. The most ignorant and superstitious believed legendary stories of sailors being swallowed up by the sea upon arrival to the West Indies. The more educated maintained a fear of the unknown based on ignorance of how much distance lay between them and the West Indies, but they believed that the western itinerary was possible. They were sure though that this route would free merchants from the considerable work and danger involved in the route to Indian markets in the East.

Like other times in history, a visionary emerged who changed the course of things. Christopher Columbus was a Genoese adventurer who spent his life enthusiastically analyzing both ancient legends and new descriptions of the Earth, wondering what would happen if he tried to reach the West Indies. While studying ancient texts, in particular from the Egyptian–Ptolemaic age, he found claims that the earth was not flat, but rather round. Thus, it became a matter of following the same course west until finally reaching the Indies. In addition, he had in his possession for the first time the compass, a new invention from China that reliably marked the north. The Chinese had perfected it in their incursions through the Asian steppes. The Arabs imported it for orientation in the desert and it reached the West via the Crusaders.

Columbus' initial motivations were strictly economic—another case in which material ambition led to discoveries and inventions. His desire to reach China and the Indies by sea alone was based on avoiding the enormous difficulties that Alexander the Great had experienced, as well as those experienced by the mercantile caravans of his time with Chinese silk and Indian spices, which obtained huge profits through trade with Europe. Columbus began to look for a wealthy merchant in Italy to pay for his trip to the West Indies, and turned to France and Portugal too, but no one trusted his instincts. He then went to Spain where, after several ventures, Queen Isabella of Castile agreed to support his journey. Columbus sensed that he would find something more than the already-known territories of China and the Indies and he negotiated with the queen that if his trip was successful he would receive the title of noble, he would be the representative of the king in all newly expanded lands, and would receive a tenth of the taxes from those lands. Isabel must have thought that, in short, she did not have much to lose since the two ships she planned to lend him were an insignificant part of her assets. Columbus had to obtain the third ship himself. She must have been convinced by Columbus' threat to present his project to the rival French crown.

The subsequent events form part of the global history. Columbus arrived to a Caribbean island on October 12, 1492, and remained persuaded for a long time that those lands were an Indian part of Asia. He claimed them for the kingdom of Castile and the crown of Aragon, united after the marriage of the Catholic Monarchs, Isabella and Ferdinand. Despite this geographic inaccuracy, nothing would be the same in the world again. Shortly thereafter, this territorial expansion began to have enormous consequences for Western geopolitics. The Mediterranean ceased to be the center of the known world, a shift that had already started after the Turks' 1453 conquest of Constantinople. The North Atlantic began to lead the international market, and port cities in England, the Netherlands, Germany, Poland, and even Russia benefitted from this. Perhaps the future will witness the Pacific's dominance, given China's enormous growth, but to date, the Atlantic's centrality and the Mediterranean's decadence have been in force for half a millennium.

During that first venture, and those immediately following, Iberian sailors capable of leading military expansion, such as the legendary Hernán Cortés, Francisco Pizarro, and Juan Sebastián Elcano, captained the ships. Priests and merchants soon joined them, verifying the peculiar politic-economic-religious agreement so distinctive of Western colonial expeditions and expansions. This raised serious problems for evangelization resulting from the imposition of a specific culture, as in the case of the Spanish. In fact, this was nothing new for the monarchies of the Iberian Peninsula, which had spent seven centuries conquering the lands they believed to be theirs (in a process known as the *Reconquista*). They had never distinguished between military expansion, colonization, urban settlement, commercial establishment, and evangelization of native populations. After all, the Romans created this model of expansion (Romanization), which contemporary powers then reproduced, known by a name based on the original Genoese discoverer: colonization. This process involved the imposition of a culture and a specific civilization (Roman and western) in which religion was also inscribed (pagan for the Romans, Catholic for the Iberians, and Protestant for the British). Spanish colonization in America was supported by a very strong desire to evangelize, and the results are still visible today.

In the case of the Spaniards and Portuguese, clerical elites, led by friar Bartolomé de las Casas, and the prestigious University of Salamanca, promoted an internal critique of the methods employed in the colonization of America, an unprecedented reflection for the time. Cruelty in the Spanish conquest was appalling, although almost certainly no worse than that of other empires that had existed until then, from the Babylonians of Nebuchadnezzar in Antiquity to the Mongols of Genghis Khan in the eighteenth century. However, this was the first time an empire's colonizing efforts were subject to such strong internal critique.

We have already considered essential concepts that arise from modernity's origins, including intellectual humanism, artistic renaissance, geographical expansion, technological innovations, and religious reform. But there is another key concept that took shape and materialized in a branch of philosophical thought that was extremely influential thereafter, that is, rationalism. Rene Descartes was the first to systematize this doctrine, which prioritizes rational thought over the submission of faith: "I think, therefore I am." Rationalism promotes an eminently deductive form of thinking, centered on philosophical speculation or mathematical reflection, as Baruch Spinoza, Blaise Pascal, or Gottfried Leibniz made clear, rather than strictly on research and experimentation. It developed mainly in French-speaking areas and was an immediate guide for the Enlightenment. French deductive rationalism had its counterpart in inductive English empiricism, with thinkers like David Hume, whose effects were noted above all in science and technological exploration. A progressive separation between a continental philosophy, oriented to speculation and rationalization, and Anglo-Saxon philosophy, privileging analytical exploration, is probably the clearest manifestation of these divergent cultural and scientific directions.

Beyond its appearance in the history of philosophy, starting from modernity, this approach led to an attempt to rationalize all processes, be they political, economic, cognitive, or religious. Thus, modernity gave the West four models, each of which refers to areas of reality and whose hegemony lasted from the fifteenth through the twenty-first centuries, including the state in politics (Chapter 10), capitalism in economics (Chapter 11), science in knowledge (Chapter 12), and reform attitude in religion (Chapter 13). Experience throughout the intervening six centuries has shown that each of these systems and values have their limitations, especially when left to their own devices and free from an ability to moderate or rein them in, from a healthy orientation toward the public good or from basic moral restrictions. Free of these commitments and regulations, the danger of losing control becomes more real, as in the expansion of the Nazi state, the crash of the Lehman Brothers and subprime mortgage capitalism, the invention of the atomic bomb, and experimentation with human embryos. However, they are also the four aspects of modernity that, for better or for worse, continue to be the most present in our lives. For this reason, and because we still have not found viable alternatives, we cannot consider them as solely belonging to the past. Thus, each of them deserves careful reflection.

CHAPTER 10

STATE

When we were in the school, the teachers showed us the political maps, which were distinguished from physical maps in that they were filled with a multicolored symphony of lines. Each area represented a particular country, which were represented in a different color. Today, we assume the existence of entities with well-defined geographical boundaries that are fully autonomous in their political design, legal system, and administrative organization. But it has not always been so. These units, which respond to a political reality known as the state, emerged at the dawn of the Modern Age.

Max Weber defined the modern state as an association of domination with an institutional character that monopolizes legitimate physical violence within a territory. To this end, it gathers all material means in the hands of its sovereign, expropriates part of the private properties, through an extractive fiscal regime,, and create its own legitimate hierarchies. This definition includes the basic notion of the state as we know it today. The state is an association arrived at by more or less explicit consensus. Historical, cultural, linguistic, and religious common heritage weighs heavily on our understanding of this institution. The fact that it is an institution assures a continuity beyond the members at any given time, including leaders. Its effectiveness is based on domination, which implies that some rulers emerge from the mass of citizens and exercise that sovereignty. It is endowed with a monopoly on violence, an essential idea that other classical philosophers, such as Thomas Hobbes and Carl Schmitt have noted. Its territory has well-established borders, as evidenced in maps' colored areas. It relies on the rationalization of government action, that is, on the ability to plan means in order to achieve an end, in this case the domination of subjects. Finally, it establishes a body of officials or civil servants who ensure the state's proper functioning.

The state has justified itself from the beginning with a myth, rather than with rational argument, consisting in the construction of certain stories about human nature and its tendency toward conflict and disorder when it comes to social organization. This implies the need for an instrument when conflict emerges, or that simply eschews conflict with its intimidating presence. Thus, myths about the providential state, the redeeming state, and the messianic state all emerged to ensure humanity's salvation from divisions and conflicts. Yet, unfortunately, most of the time it degenerates into a miserable *police state*, turning the paradise they were supposed to create into a hell on earth.

To achieve this harmony, the state is endowed with abstract and centralized power, maintained through a monopoly on physical coercion within a geographically defined territory. It is also constituted as a social body, a metaphor that founding theorists of the modern state made explicit, especially in the figure of the Leviathan, which also appeared in the first edition of Hobbes's book of the same name (Figure 10.1). Hobbes explained the meaning of this image in these terms: the Leviathan's soul represents state sovereignty; the magistrates are its limbs; compensation and punishment are its nerves; and covenants and agreements, by means of which the parts of this body politic were originally created and then united, resemble God's fiat in creating humans.

FIGURE 10.1 Illustration of the cover of Hobbes' Leviathan. © Shutterstock.

The body subordinates the parts of the whole organism to its general functioning. An entity that exists beyond its individual parts, the state also provides each of its citizens with a specific function that, in turn, ensures the organism's proper functioning.

This was the original justification for the modern state. But where did it come from historically? What previous experiences influenced it? The first seed of the state was constituted by feudal monarchies that arose from the disintegration of Germanic kingdoms in the eleventh and twelfth centuries. Kings came on the scene as protectors of peace that the feudal order was unable to impose, as well as defenders of peasants and the bourgeois against the arbitrariness of lords. The royal order sought to supplant the feudal order, but kept its rigid hierarchy intact with the king as its apex. This is the case of William the Conqueror in England, Louis VI the Fat of France, and Alfonso II the Troubadour of Aragon. However, these kings were the head of a feudal hierarchy rather than proper sovereigns of a kingdom, thus they were still conditioned by the feudal system's lord–vassal pacts.

In the thirteenth and fourteenth centuries, feudal monarchies began the transformation process into territorial monarchies. Their sovereignty was directly linked to a territory, which they expanded through military conquest and matrimonial strategies. Such was the case of Iberian kings who expanded into lands dominated by Islam, for example, James I the Conqueror of Aragon and Ferdinand III the Saint of Castile, as well as Philip Augustus the Conqueror of France and the legendary Frederick II Hohenstaufen, the conqueror of Jerusalem. Territorial monarchies were a step closer to the model of the modern state because the king became directly linked to a kingdom, which corresponded to borders that, although still unstable, were recognized from the outside. Yet, the king was still seen as a military leader rather than a governor of his kingdom. The court was still a place of representation and ennoblement rather than the kingdom's seat of government. Governmental structure contained nothing like a body of specialized officials. However, the model of the wise king, a good ruler capable of directing all his operations from a fixed headquarters, in place of the errant conquering king from previous centuries, represented significant evolution, which Machiavelli masterfully reflected on in *The Prince*.

During the second half of the fifteenth century, the seeds of authoritarian monarchy were planted, which became hegemonic during the next two centuries, and which reflects the modern state clearly. Three characteristic examples of this kind of monarchy are found in Henry VIII of England, Philip II of Spain, and Louis XIV of France. All these kings were meticulous rulers, acting as a kind of prime minister rather than the first among the kingdom's warriors, carefully choosing their collaborators who resided at the court and who held specialized responsibilities, such as the Chancellor, Minister of War, or Minister of Finance. Louis XIV was particularly popular and given the honorific epithet of the Sun King, a title expressive of his greatness and authority. He is credited with the phrase, "L'état, c'est moi" [I am the state], which plainly reveals the absolutism that authoritarian kings sought.

During the early modernity, the king aspired to authoritarianism because it allowed him a more effective government, beyond from the objections of nobles and ecclesiastics. These aspirations were certainly hindered by the same social agents the kings aimed to control, so that the theory of royal authoritarianism led to its weaker practice. Yet, beyond these difficulties, authoritarianism has become synonymous with modernity, and was practiced by the kings of France, Spain, and England, which explains why they were the great powers at the moment. This also justifies the authoritarian kings' obsession with fighting anything that could threaten the unity of their kingdoms. At that time, many considered religious issues to be the weakest link in the chain that united a kingdom, which is why Ferdinand the Catholic began the Inquisition in the Crown of Aragon in the late fifteenth century, an unfortunate but effective instrument for the kingdom's unity and political control that other modern European sovereigns, whether Catholic or Protestant, imitated. Indeed, the Inquisition's original motivation was political, not religious, although some Catholic and Protestant ecclesiastics took advantage of it to justify their excesses.

In this authoritarian race, Spain and France were ahead of England. The Magna Carta of 1215 forced English monarchs to consult the Parliament on their most important decisions. One king, Charles I of England, bypassed this rule and was deposed and beheaded in 1649 on the basis of a popular rebellion led by Oliver Cromwell, who even assumed sovereignty for a time before being substituted by the next king. England perhaps delayed its incorporation into the world's elite power circles due to its monarch's lack of complete authority. Yet, in the long term, this agreement was extraordinarily beneficial and formed the basis of the powerful British Empire between the eighteenth and nineteenth centuries. This new model of expansion was founded on a pact among empire, capitalism, and science—that is, the three major emerging forces of early modernity.

Sometimes we make the mistake of thinking that kingdoms like England or the Crown of Aragon, characterized by the early establishment of representative bodies, like parliaments or *cortes*, were more democratic than others. We all tend to project contemporary realities onto the past, which distorts an objective view of it. Elite medieval parliaments clearly served as a model for American and French revolutionaries in the late eighteenth century, when the first truly representative meetings were being constituted, but their purpose and operations were not at all the same as those of medieval bodies. They were composed entirely of members who belonged to exclusive noble circles, who, over time, were joined by the wealthy bourgeois in mercantile cities. Thus, these forums did not fully represent the people, nor were they democratic, since they emerged from scrupulously maintained lists that were very difficult to get on to. The wealthiest bourgeois managed to get on them when they married their sons to nobles' daughters. The second generation held a noble title that gave them access to elite circles and seats in parliament. The nobles, in their turn, won money in the interchange. This is the classical transaction between symbolic and material capital, as highlighted by the sociologist Pierre Bourdieu.

The next step, closer still to the state as we know it, came with the absolutist despots that emerged from eighteenth-century Europe's enlightened milieu. They included Frederick II the Great of Prussia, Catherine II of Russia, Joseph II of Austria, and Charles III of Spain, for whom Madrid residents still show great affection with the saying, "The best mayor, the king." Whether they know it or not, the *Madrileños* are applying to their king a phrase used by Lope de Vega, one of the key figures of the Spanish Golden Age of Baroque literature, as a title of one of his works, one century earlier. These monarchs were skillful administrators as they organize for the first time departments with specialized officials. They and exemplify the newly enlightened kings. Well educated and capable of attracting intellectuals as councilors in their courts, they felt they were the state's main official—not its owner, as previous generations of kings such as Henry VIII of England, Philippe II of Spain, and Louis XIV of France tend to think and act—so that they fell under the new general current of enlightened despotism or enlightened absolutism. At the beginning of eighteenth century, Frederick the Great of Prussiaorganized an extraordinary army trained with the latest combat techniques which was the basis for Germany's subsequent supremacy on European battlefields. He is an excellent model for this generation of enlightened kings, who based their government on the rationalization of processes rather than on just authoritarian decisions.

Two momentous events changed the modern state's course and are considered efficient causes in the emergence of the liberal state. In 1776, the United States of America declared itself independent of England and enacted a constitution that guaranteed the sacred human rights of freedom and equality for all its citizens. The monarchy was abolished and replaced by a presidential system with four-year term limits, giving rise to a paradigmatic example of liberal democracy and, more properly, of republicanism. Tocqueville certainly aimed to popularize the idea of democracy in America. However, the founding fathers of the new republic were modeled on the Roman Republic and the central objective was not to center sovereignty in the people, but to establish a political regime that would fragment power. They put the emphasis on avoiding despotism or the centralization of power in the hands of any particular group or social stratum.

Few years later, in 1789, the French Revolution broke out, which resulted in the abolition of the French monarchy and the establishment of a republic that exalts the values of freedom, equality, and fraternity. There, the people, represented by delegates, were given the power to govern. Revolutionaries executed King Louis XVI by guillotine. This was not a random act, as Charles I of England had been beheaded in 1649 during the English Civil War between Parliamentarians and Royalists. Masters of symbolic language, these revolutionaries had extraordinary empathy with the public. Cutting off the king's head symbolized a radical break with tradition given that previous political practice was based on the idea that sovereignty came from above, that is, from the divine, which corresponds to the so-called 'descending theory of government.' By cutting off the king's head, the noblest part of the body, where the crown was placed, the monarchy was seen as out of date and lacking direct communication with the divine. An 'ascending theory of government' materialized, which holds that sovereignty comes from below; that is, it resides in the people and they transmit it to representatives, a theory that still dominates today.

The American and French Revolutions gave intellectuals like Alexis de Tocqueville and Montesquieu, and leaders like Thomas Jefferson and Benjamin Franklin, much to think about and learn. Their works, based on classic thinkers such as Hobbes, Locke, Smith, and Rousseau, shaped the currents of liberalism with two very clear upshots, namely 'liberal democracy,' a theory of state that has dominated the world in the last two centuries, and 'liberal economics,' a theory and practice that, together with capitalism, also prevails today.

The liberal state was gradually imposed in nineteenth-century Europe. However, its implementation was not in the least simple. The Napoleon era—whose mission was to expand revolutionary ideas—shook many European leaders of the time, who sought to reestablish (*Restauration*) the old absolutist order with the 1815 Congress of Vienna. Ultimately, and especially during the second half of the nineteenth century, the idea of a liberal democratic state was imposed. Some countries, such as Great Britain and Spain, retained a more traditional state form with Constitutional Monarchies. Therein, the king submits to a constitution—a higher law—like all citizens. Other countries opted for the state form that revolutionaries implemented shortly after cutting off the king's head, which they called a republic in honor of how the Romans ousted monarchy in their days. These republics developed very different governing styles because some, like the United States, have a presidential system in which the president is vested with significant authority. Others, such as the Italian, French, or German systems, prefer duality between the president of the republic, who acts as head of state, and a president of the government who exercises mostly executive functions. The president of the republic usually takes on all representative activity and international projection.

The core of all these liberal regimes is a representative body democratically elected by the people. Parliament, as it is called in many places, is the source of sovereignty and holds legislative power. For this reason, these regimes are often known as parliamentary democracies. Once laws are set, leaders execute them (which is why governors, presidents, or prime ministers are often described as 'executives') and judges ensure compliance through the imposition of penalties on those who fail to comply. The separation of these three powers—the legislative, the executive, and the judicial branches—as writers such as Tocqueville and Montesquieu ably explained is standard to any liberal democratic system. Certainly, the boundaries between these three areas are not always clear, which is why leaders must act prudently and honestly so that the system does not fail in guaranteeing justice for its citizens.

The consolidation of the liberal state, concomitant with the spread of romantic ideas, also brought with it the idea of the nation. This concept etymologically refers to 'birth' (*nasci* in Latin) and is therefore loaded with connotations associated with common origins, a collective identity, shared traditions and values. In the nineteenth century, notions such as country, kingdom, state, and nation, which until then had been used more or less synonymously, began to acquire diverse meanings. The concept of country took on a more neutral meaning; it now hardly has ideological connotations and is thus most frequently used. Kingdom was used generically for a long time—but today it is restricted to traditional monarchies—although kings everywhere no longer possess the absolute sovereignty previously ascribed to them. State is, in fact, used as a synonym of country, but it has a more restricted meaning because it refers to the political structure that gives a certain society its "body" and is therefore more neutral in terms of identity. Finally, nation refers both to the *given* place of birth and to the *constructed* cultural values that provoke a feeling of belonging to a social body, and therefore goes beyond the political consensus that institutes a state. Cohesive national values are diverse, but they often emphasize history, tradition, customs, folklore, and a common language, as well as the collective recognition of *us* versus *the other*. Experts often, and rightly, point to the constructed or imaginary nature of nations, but they sometimes forget that the feeling that accompanies it is real and inspired by awareness of experiences shared with other members of a group to which one feels linked.

The distinction between state and nation is key for understanding many of the conflicts that erupted in Europe starting in the second half of the nineteenth century: from the wars of unification in Germany and Italy, the World Wars, to the multiple fronts opened in Africa and Asia, often as a consequence of mismanaged postcolonial processes. This is explained by the fact that many consider the 'nation' an authentic 'religion' (or, rather, a substitute for it), which can turn its defense or expansion into an irrational matter with unpleasant consequences all around. Religion in itself has a specific rationality, or rather its own suprarational scope. When it is truly spiritual, and therefore avoids mixing with political parties and matters, it does not degenerate into irrationality. The political, on the other hand, also has its own rationality, which must be respected, based on a general consensus that adapts society's ends toward achieving collective objectives. Yet, certain nationalisms toss off their specifically political nature by presenting themselves as messianic responses, skillfully exploiting citizens' patriotic feelings to the exclusion of the *other*. Monstrosities can then arise, as seen in European nations' disproportionate competitiveness at the root of World War I, or German nationalism during the interwar period that degenerated into Nazism.

Western countries have perceived and experienced the concept of 'nation' very differently according to each one's diverse historical experience. In the United States, Poland, and Ireland, and in other countries that fought for their independence, the idea of nation emerged in a context of struggle for the very recognition of their existence, which generated a strong sense of belonging and cohesion around a common project. In Spain, the nation arose as a survival instinct when faced with an external enemy, in this case Napoleonic invasion, which made subsequent debate on what kind of state the nation needed should be founded: traditional or liberal.

Three particularly opposed ideas of statehood are the pragmatic in England, the plebiscitary in France and the ethnic in Germany. In England, during the Victorian era and the extraordinary expansion of the British Empire, a pragmatic vision of the nation flourished, which enabled its assimilation of varied traditions and ethnicities, making its language universal and allowing it to expand its culture all over the world without fear of losing its own national identity. However, this English pragmatic view also resulted in a progressive breakdown of its original core (such as in the cases of Northern Ireland and Scotland). It also promoted an unstable behavior that lacks principles when engaging in supranational organizations, as the Brexit process has confirmed. In France, the idea of the nation as a daily plebiscite predominates. Adhesion to the nation is the result of cultural bonds rather than of ethnic origins. Leaders are constantly tasked with arousing their citizens' enthusiasm for a common national project of which they can be proud. Ideas of grandeur naturally materialize, as do popular demonstrations to strengthen patriotic sentiment, which are promoted with great zeal. In Germany, however, the idea of the nation was perceived—especially after the growth of Romanticism—in terms of race given by nature itself and therefore demanding of complete, instantaneous, and sentimental adhesion above any plebiscite and that therefore far beyond favorable or unfavorable circumstances. Nazism skillfully exploited this tendency and led it to its worse consequences.

This connects with totalitarianism, the penultimate form of state experienced during the twentieth century in Mussolini's Italy, Hitler's Germany, and Stalin's Russia and, secondarily, in Fidel Castro's Cuba and Chávez's Venezuela. Its closest model is Napoleon's France. Visionary leaders, who skillfully take advantage of conflictive historical circumstances to launch a messianic message and seize absolute power, create totalitarian states. Their rhetoric is usually associated with a dynamic of territorial expansion that some geopolitical situation opens up. Its effectiveness is based on a skillful link among national fervor, ideology, and imperial expansion. This artificially constructed ideology (fascism in Italy, Nazism in Germany, communism in Russia, populism in Venezuela) attempts to substitute religion, which is emptied of all its suprarational elements and becomes, in fact, irrational. Historical experience has shown that these systems inevitably lead to dead ends and discredit themselves. Even so, we have often failed to learn from history and continue to repeat these past mistakes.

The modern secular state had to face from the beginning the challenge of maintaining peace among quarrelsome religious factions during the wars of religion. The secular state arbitrated those conflicts, supposedly acting as a neutral agent, and religion was moved to the private sphere and excluded from public space. However, historical reality has failed to bear out this redeeming and messianic vision of the modern state. The state is incapable of being a neutral reality since real people with their own political ideas govern it. Thus, it is naive to think that the state spontaneously and neutrally performs its role as arbitrator. Public schools, for example, guarantee free compulsory education, which is in itself important for the defense of basic rights. But teachers and educational administrators have certain convictions, values, and ideas, and they are generally incapable of complete neutrality. This is neither good nor bad in itself but rather a fact that must be recognized as such. In addition, historical experience has shown that when sovereigns want to exempt themselves from any higher authority (which in traditional societies was the Christian God and in contemporary societies is the constitution or natural ethics), the state tends to automatically occupy their position, generally turning itself into a cruel and unjust god, and ultimately a substitute for religion outside of its proper context. In fact, at critical moments, many subjects have come to see the most infamous dictators (e.g., Napoleon, Stalin, Hitler) as religious and messianic leaders rather than as merely state administrators. The establishment of constitutions during the nineteenth century mitigated part of this problem. A constitution, despite its limitations, is superior law, which prevents tyrannical appropriation of sovereignty. It also resides outside of the continuous ideological and governmental shifts that all political action entails. It can certainly be manipulated, as dictators from Hitler to Chávez have done, to justify tyranny, but today it plays an essential role in the maintenance of a previously agreed-upon order.

Finally, the last system in this sequence is the liberal-democratic structure, which currently predominates. We must face the question of how our system will be judged in the future. We certainly see it as the fairest, and it probably is, after contrasting it with the previous systems examined in the previous paragrpahs. Francis Fukuyama explained the idea of the liberal democratic state's superiority in his 1992 book *The End of History and the Last Man*. His idea of 'the end of history' was not apocalyptic. Rather, he intended to emphasize that, with the Cold War concluded, liberal ideology achieved absolute hegemony. The West had accomplished such political and economic progress and stability that it was no longer a question of looking for another formula but rather of perfecting the one we already have. Although his perspective is based on flagrant triumphalism, Fukuyama's optimism is partly justified since no viable alternative to the current political system has been presented to date. But there is one gaining more and more acceptance and looking for justification: authoritarianism. Robert Kagan has recently argued that among the geopolitical transformations confronting the liberal democratic, the one for which we are least prepared—and appears to be more justified—is the ideological and strategic resurgence of authoritarianism. We are not used to thinking of authoritarianism as a distinct worldview that offers a real alternative to liberalism. Trumpism and other similar movements are reflections of the search for order and the reestablishment of old hierarchies, moral, sexual, and political values. The liberal system still shows some notable shortcomings, especially the increasing gulf it has produced between politicians and citizens, which is today very worrying, and the apparently insuperable rulers' tendency to corruption. The future will judge.

It goes without saying that although these imperfections are real and significant, no alternative currently exists. The new populisms have tried to improve the system with its juxtaposition between a corrupt elite against an idealized people. Yet, despite its efforts to demonstrate the opposite on theory, the practice is failing: the assembly system that populism advocates may function for governing local meetings (and even then sometimes fails) but has actually proved to be devastating for administering an entire country. The representative system leaks in many places, but we do not seem to have found a direct formula that is more advantageous, especially since it does not usually pass politics' final test, namely *possibilism* (i.e., what *can* really happen, not just one *would like* to happen). Still, the assembly system and other populist proposals are presented as alternatives. Populism has made a comeback in Europe and America in recent decades thanks to striking rhetoric based on binary simplification of reality, demagoguery, and some of its leaders' eloquence. But real life is more complex than a text or a speech. As the popular maxim puts it, "everything holds up in paper." We must continue looking for a truly viable alternative to substitute the current system, but getting rid of something without a better substitute never turned out well.

One viable alternative is perhaps found in the post–World War II emergence of supranational organizations such as the United Nations (UN), the North Atlantic Treaty Organization (NATO), and the European Union (EU). These organizations are a clearly recognizable result of globalization, which can be positive from a political perspective. The modern state guarantees countries' full autonomy, presented as preventing unfair external interference. However, these supranational political organizations—and their jurisdictional derivations, such as The Hague's Human Rights Tribunal—are a valuable aid for countries that face political difficulty, social instability, and economic crises. Some readers of this book will certainly recognize the objectively beneficial effect that membership in a supranational body like the EU has had in Southern-European countries like Portugal, Greece, and Spain. Perhaps their collective memory begins to fail, but entry into the EU assured these three countries unprecedented political, social, and economic stability, which make possible the prolongation of their welfare states, protected them from the authoritarian tendencies long experienced in the past, and constituted a highly valuable framework for cultural exchange.

While the state has been the West's central political institution since the dawn of modernity, capitalism has been its predominant economic system and science its most lucrative cultural achievement. The three share a close relationship, as reflected in the fact that they emerged at the same time during the early modern period. The state and capitalism seem to constitute two sides of the same coin because one needs the other. Commercial development required a particular security context that only the modern state could guarantee. Medieval political structures, arising in a military rather than commercial context, and more mobile than sedentary, were insufficient to guarantee new mercantile and financial activities that emerged in an unmatched qualitative and quantitative scale. The novelty of capitalism, in turn, provided the state and the science with the economic means for its consolidation and expansion. Thus, the state and capitalism formed a feedback loop as they launched at the dawn of the Modern Age, and both are increasingly and incessantly legitimized by scientific and technological achievements.

CHAPTER 11

CAPITALISM

Beginning in early modernity, the wealthier merchants began to be recognized as capitalists. Until that point, merchants, the main agents in the medieval economic system, had traditionally been recognized for their primary activity: trade. They gradually began to gain recognition for the surpluses their work produced, that is, capital, rather than for the work itself. The economy's essential element shifted from the activity that produced profit, and the agents that carried out the jobs associated with it, to the profit itself. This change led to a profound transformation in modern European economics and in the history of the West and the entire world.

Capitalism arose at the end of the Middle Ages in the context of the need to rationalize the administration of substantial economic surpluses that mercantile activity began to generate. Approaching the emergence and development of capitalism necessarily includes an examination of the connections among the three elements that make it up, namely, the individual, work, and capital. This relationship was relatively harmonious in medieval societies since few merchants (such as Marco Polo and Francesco Datini of Prato) stood out as extraordinarily successful. The individual saw the fruit of his labor immediately (agricultural, livestock, craft, or commerce) since he himself collected the capital generated, which provided enough profit for subsistence. Large profits were generally absorbed by stifling taxation or monopolized by the sovereign or feudal lords. Immensely wealthy individuals who made personal use of surpluses only very rarely exist. The few that emerged did so based on extensive agricultural properties, as in the case of some of the most prominent feudal lords. These surpluses were usually reinvested in internal activities, such as maintaining slaves and servants, paying day laborers, purchasing tools, and constructing or maintaining a castle from which to rule the land. These rich people were nevertheless so few and far between that their activity was unable to constitute anything like a new system.

The feudal system began changing with the commercial revolution and Europe's urban growth in the twelfth century, especially in the axis between Italy and Flanders. Cities like Florence, Pisa, Genoa, Milan, Venice, Bruges, Ghent, Antwerp, and Amsterdam accumulated immense mercantile flows that soon began to be known as *capital*, that is, the surpluses that exceeded the narrowly conceived relationship between a worker and the immediate benefits of his or her work. Other cities, such as London, Paris, Marseille, Lisbon, Barcelona, Valencia, Seville, Prague, Cologne, Augsburg, Danzig, Krakow, and Stockholm, were also protagonists in this profound economic transformation but they grew under the enormous influence of the English, French, Castilian, Aragonese, German, Portuguese, and Swedish monarchies.

Over time, these cities became powerful financial centers capable of completely transforming the economic system to the point of creating a real alternative to the reigning feudal-seigniorial system. Trade surpluses reached exorbitant heights and their owners formed part of a new social group called the mercantile bourgeoisie, who perfectly assimilated to the new economic dynamic—they were in search of profit for the sake of profit, wealth for the sake of wealth. While this dynamic today seems completely normal, at the sixteenth century it implied a radical break with tradition. The bourgeoisie did not have the moral restrictions of ecclesiastics or religious vows that limited their lifestyle to evangelical-inspired poverty, nor did they have the conceptual restrictions proper to nobles. They were used to spending all they earned, and rarely considered that their abundant surplus might have another function outside of being reinvested in their own businesses or immediately spent on their own welfare and the consolidation of social privileges. Once again, economic change stimulated a social transformation and vice versa.

The expansion of this new bourgeois and mercantile mentality would have been unthinkable without the work of the Catholic mendicant orders—particularly Franciscans and Dominicans. . From the fourth century on, St. Benedict had provided the West with a positive sense of work by considering it inseparable from contemplative activity, as one of Benedictine order's founding principles highlights: *Ora et labora* ('pray and work'). Yet, beginning in the thirteenth century, Saint Francis of Assisi, the son of wealthy merchants, founded a new Order that moved Benedictine values from the rural to the urban world and legitimate the mercantile activity, whose professional practices had hitherto been considered sinful by the churchuntil then . Society most often saw merchants as usurers, as individuals who disproportionately obtained profit from their work. Some, like bankers, simply waited patiently for time to pass ('time is money') and collected interest on their loans. However, in the fourteenth century, the Catalan Franciscan Francesc d'Eiximenis dared to argue as follows:

Merchants are the life of the public realm; they are the life of our earth; they are a treasure for public life; without merchants, communities fall, princes become tyrants, young people are lost, the poor weep; merchants are favored by God, in death and in life for the benefits they bequeath to public life, for the great hardships they endure on land and at sea, and for the great losses they frequently suffer: all public entities should always pray for merchants (*Regiment de la cosa pública*) [Government of the Republic], chapter 33).

With the help of this and other testimonies, society accepted mercantile work as merely another activity that citizens engage in and are susceptible, like all others, to morally reprehensible activities. The new bourgeois began to consider the possibility of reinvesting their commercial surpluses (capital) beyond the expansion of their business in specifically financial businesses through speculation and credit. While some Jewish businessmen practiced this before (since they could exercise usury with Christians), they had always employed it as a complementary mode of profit and never as a standalone economic activity. The founding of the first banks (*montes de piedad* in Italy, *mesas de cambio* in Castile, and *taules de canvi* in Catalonia) provided capital to merchants for the establishment or consolidation of their businesses, while enriching bankers with profit from the interest their debtors paid (Figure 11.1).

Thus, some merchants began to devote themselves almost exclusively to finance, a phenomenon that first emerged in Genoa, Florence, Venice, Augsburg, Antwerp, and Bruges. Another source of enormous profit also emerged with the provision of huge sums of credit to the new authoritarian monarchs of Spain, France, and England, who needed large amounts of capital to finance their military enterprises. Not even all the gold in the colonies, which at that time was pouring into Spain, was enough to cover the costs associated with an extensive empire whose roof always sprung some leak and whose financing demanded constant credit. This new financial business also merged with the immense credit that large urban political centers, such as Paris, London, Barcelona, Palermo, Marseille or Naples, needed. Their public debt grew so much that ordinary tax revenue was no longer enough to pay even the interest on their outstanding credits. History repeats itself.

During the first modern centuries, credit activity was not considered a business. Both creditors and debtors' mentalities remained founded on the fact that the request for credit is a lesser evil in the face of a pressing need

FIGURE 11.1 A young merchant working on his beads, with coins and an open book in his hands. Pieter Gerritsz van Heemskerck, 1529, Dutch painting, oil on panel. © Shutterstock.

or the desire to invest capital in a new mercantile enterprise. This transaction carried with it an implicit agreement that the credit would be paid off as soon as possible. Thus, the banking business was based on the principle that credit should be repaid in the short or medium term. When this principle was not respected, and no other remedy remained, a life-long or even perpetual financial interest was applied. However, huge credit requests from monarchs during the last decades of the seventeenth century led to the establishment of a long-term debt trend based on paying interest alone. Enormous sums were invested in the Netherland's expansion to Indonesia, in a new model of economic-capitalist expansion which replaced the Spanish military model. This situation came about while England was thriving in the second half of the eighteenth century, fully immersed in its first industrialization wave and a mercantile expansion that was on the verge of going global. English financiers then began to lend credit as an investment opportunity. They were interested in attracting large companies or governments as debtors without the prospect of return in the short or medium term. They intended to secure fixed capital inflows through the collection of fixed annual interest, which allowed them to provide new loans that, in turn, would yield new interest.

This led to the problem of countries with pressing credit needs accumulating enormous debt, as was the case of early modern Spain. The great Genoese and Flemish merchants financed the bulk of Charles V and Philip II's military campaigns, assuring their subsistence in the short term, but also shackling them with an economic dependence on their lenders that greatly weakened their imperial project.

Given this panorama, it is easy to see why currency soon became an indispensable mechanism for economic activity. Certainly, currency existed in late medieval and medieval Europe since mercantile cities never stopped using it; however, a dual economy—using both currency and bartering—prevailed. In this new context, it quickly became clear that only the monetary economy would survive because it was the only one capable of supplying the system with necessary versatility demanded by an extraordinary variety of exchanges associated with the establishment of new economic practices. States monopolized currency minting in order to control the value of money and could devalue it when certain economic situations called for it.

Along with this monetarization process, and the practical disappearance of bartering, other procedures and techniques developed that made the material presence of currency unnecessary. Merchants ran high risks at sea and sometimes lost all the profits of a careful commercial operation because of shipwreck or piracy. The provision of new deferred payment techniques enabled them to carry minimal amounts of money during their travels. To disburse large amounts at the set place of exchange, they began using documents to ensure that this amount could be collected at one of the new banking establishments, or a guarantee that it would be paid in the future. A bill of exchange was used to verify these transactions, the origin of which can be dated to the twelfth century and is still used today in the form of checks and other supporting documents.

All this leads to trust, which new mercantile agents began to cultivate and covet as the basis of the whole capitalist system. Beyond the penalties that could arise from the breakdown of pacts established in business, a conviction prevailed that virtues such as trust, loyalty, and honesty are essential for the smooth running of the economy generally considered. For this reason, corrupt behaviors were especially punished although clearly this problem continues to exist in our own societies.

In addition to the relevance of the trust, the emergence of capitalism led to the confirmation that compliance with the rules benefits the whole society, even if these benefits might not be perceived in the short term. This mentality mainly prevailed in countries of Germanic and Anglo-Saxon roots, such as Germany, Great Britain, and the United States, as well as in the Scandinavian countries, and from there spread to Central European countries and, with greater reluctance, to the Latin world. When rules are not respected, the power of violence prevails over the law. Then, it usually damages the values of constant work, intelligence, and innovation in favor of the law of the strongest. This is especially important in economic matters because they require political stability and legal guaranties. The breakdown thereof threatens the entire system and initiates a degenerative dynamic. A society accustomed to breaking the rules—an attitude that starts with the example of the rulers—or in which corruption is unpunished, risks turning its economic system into a mafia. There, the work of honest people, which is what actually moves countries forward, is neither socially recognized nor properly paid. Civic responsibility largely guarantees societies' harmonious development, equal opportunities, and the eradication of corruption, which is a true cancer for many underdeveloped and developing countries.

Logically, even if a society tries to live out these civic values, there will always be lawsuits between commercial agents. In the origins of capitalism, ordinary justice resolved these litigations to the extent that it was implemented in medieval cities. But commercial agents soon realized that their cases were so specific that they decided to separate and settle them with judges specialized in mercantile cases. Thus, specific mercantile legal institutions were born, which have survived today mainly for business cases, but have retained their original nomenclature: commercial law. A Consulate of the Sea in Mediterranean cities such as Barcelona, Valencia, and Mallorca, which began as early as the thirteenth century, are exemplary in this regard. Commercial law began to gain autonomy over the sovereign's reach, begetting a clear area of economic autonomy that capitalism skillfully exploited (and not always in pursuit of a more just society). Debates surrounding market regulations have become more necessary than ever, seemingly a norm with common sense on its side as long as it does not stifle entrepreneurs' freedom for initiative.

Most disputes settled in court had to do with bankruptcy and companies' subsequent inability to pay their creditors. To resolve these problems, traditional societies had resorted to unfair, if not flagrantly unjust, means that meant taking justice into one's hands. Some resolutions were even concealed as ethnic or religious cleansing—for example, the massacre of Jews in the Middle Ages had much more to do with debt relief than with religious zeal or ethnic purity. Further, capitalism reached more civilized outlets, the most important of which came in the form of insurance companies. At first, commercial agents insured commercial trips with their own capital and agreed with various parties involved (suppliers, sailors, merchants) to distribute the losses in the case of shipwreck, fraud, piracy, or other unexpected circumstances. Over time, companies emerged with enough financial means to dedicate themselves exclusively to the task of protecting commercial transaction. Insurance companies, as we know them today, date back to the late Middle Ages.

This new modern capitalist spirit was perhaps most clearly embodied in the great Dutch and English mercantile companies in the seventeenth century. The era of discovery and the first steps toward globalization made commercial activity global as well. Dutch and English merchants were the first to design trading companies capable of operating all over the world, from the shores of the North Sea to the rich cities of the Indian Ocean, passing through the ports of southern Africa. Each commercial company had a specific geographical scope of action based on its commercial activity or experience in a certain place. The organization and structure of these large companies, true forerunners of contemporary multinationals, required unprecedented levels of capital investment. Individual contributions were no longer enough to provide the capital necessary for the foundation of these companies, or for their subsequent growth and consolidation. They thus decided to issue shares—designations of company ownership—that entailed periodic returns. These shares were supposed to carry the name of their owners, but shareholders were soon so numerous in some of the largest companies that, in fact, it was impossible to pin down all their identities.

And so corporations began, an essential practice for the consolidation and subsistence of the capitalist system. Corporations concealed darker characteristics that developed over time and led to harsh practices that continue to this today. These societies were based on the depersonalization of company ownership, as its name Public Limited Company indicates. Before the foundation of this system, bankruptcy could lead not only to the ruin of its investors but also to harsh physical and criminal penalties. Clearly, such a system could not work in the long term. The system has been perfected in this direction such that bankruptcy of a company does not necessarily lead to investors' personal bankruptcy. However, the process of making companies anonymous also brought with it a radical loss of responsibility in that it psychologically separates investors from the people who carry out the jobs that they finance—artificially splitting the people who work and the work which generates the capital from the capital itself.

Over time, some of the economic practices generated by the early capitalism became perverted, becoming the main argument of the current critique of capitalism. In my opinion, there are three main problems that deserve special attention and claim to be revised: the *anonymization* of the economy as the capital has become the hegemonic actor of the economy; the enormous power acquired by some multinationals, some of them more powerful than the states; and the increasing economic inequality among countries, and even within the countries.

The first problem—the anonymization of the economy—grew over time, especially during the processes of transition from traditional economy to industrialization during the nineteenth century, and received serious and merited critique in the Marxist reading of capitalism. Marx developed his theory in London during the early period of industrialization, where terrible conditions for workers developed, in large part, based on radical separation between the three agents involved in economic activity, namely, persons, work, and capital. Industrialization heightened this problem because workers began to perform more mechanical and specialized, rather than creative and comprehensive, work, leading to a loss of global vision of the production process. Workers tightened the screws but did not see the fruits of their labor, as Chaplin reflected in *Modern Times* (1936). In addition, workers also lost all reference to the benefits that their activity generated (capital) since they received a salary, but did not intervene in the process of distribution of dividends, what Marx called surplus value.

It is easy to foresee the vicious circle that this situation produced since employers' search for greater profit (also known as owners, patrons, capitalists, or shareholders) exclusively relied on exerting greater pressure on workers by either extending the workday or decreasing salaries. In the end, this proto-industrial system had a lot in common with the former slave systems of Antiquity and the serf–vassal relationship in the feudal system of the Middle Ages. This situation began to improve only when authorities realized that some regulations were necessary to alleviate the effects of the exploitation of workers. Unions were then formed to ensure those rights, to denounce bad practices, and to set up an institutional platform from which to negotiate with owners and politicians.

These advances were evident and, in some way, providential, since they not only improved working conditions, giving workers back their dignity, but also made capitalism's continuance possible. Marx denounced practices that certainly should be corrected, and the effects of this denunciation were perhaps Marxism's greatest benefit in guaranteeing the working class's progress. However, his solutions were never going to be entirely effective since they promoted a constant state of struggle between classes, where hatred as a concept and violence as a strategy are the only criteria for social improvement. Perhaps from having witnessed the deplorable situation of workers in mid-nineteenth-century English cities, Marx was simply unable to formulate any other solution. But his followers, later known as communists, were mistaken in projecting all his ideas onto societies such as Czarist Russia, countries integrated in the USSR and its satellites, post-Hispanic Cuba, Vietnam, or North Korea after the World War, all of which did not share the same circumstances as London in the process of industrialization.

The second perverse somewhat unexpected consequence of capitalism is that over time, Public Limited Companies, especially the larger ones, became multinationals. Some managed economies greater than those of many countries. This distorted the global panorama because decisions taken by these big businesses, which affect scores of people from around the globe at the same time, are based on economic motivations and often from outside the places they will affect—delocalization of the companies. The economy is a very noble and necessary activity for our sustenance, but it should never be left exclusively to its own internal logic and dynamic since it easily spirals into profit for the sake of profit, becoming inhumane, regardless of the material and spiritual damage caused along the way. This has increasingly occurred in the last century as speculation with respect to production dramatically rises. Mercantile agents and Fund Companies make economic transactions completely apart from the contexts that their decisions will affect. This has occurred especially in recent decades when companies are created with the sole aim of speculating not only on the actions of companies but also on companies themselves, and investing all their capital to it. A family company in Porto, whose workers always felt relatively close to the owners and therefore important decisions between shareholders and workers could be more easily agreed upon, can now be bought overnight by a colossal speculative foreign insurance company. The family business becomes a tiny cog in a huge machine, and these new owners make decisions without considering the people those financial operations will affect. This is perhaps the penultimate link in the chain of depersonalization to which the savage version of capitalism, abandoned to its own fate, can lead because its logic is solely commercial and, therefore, inhuman.

The third problem is inequality and is being severely criticized by some economists nowadays, most notably the work of Thomas Piketty, especially in this *Capital in the Twenty-First Century* (2014) and *Capital and Ideology* (2020). There is certainly a lot of demagogy in some current critical approaches to capitalism, since on many occasions the alternative to these inequalities proposed by the new visionaries would have been the impoverishment of all. Capitalism has objectively generated greater wealth, which has manifested itself in the eradication of poverty in many places, the construction of the welfare state, and the generation of a vigorous and extensive middle class—certainly today in danger of disappearing. But it is also evident that some of the poorest countries are shackled by paying off high sums of debt that, based on confused historical origins, often they themselves did not even sign on to. Most of these public debts were often originate in the complex processes of colonization, decolonization, and independence of which these countries were victims rather than beneficiaries of the greed of the powers that now function as implacable creditors. In developing countries, the poorest experience degrading working conditions, while the privileged few concentrate in residential areas whose security measures cut off communication with the city's poorer areas, a process that desensitizes young people.

Once the three major problems of capitalism have been diagnosed, what are the solutions? The first adjustment in order relates to true market regulation. This possible line of action would at least prevent certain financial and speculative practices that completely distort and dehumanize the system. Perhaps the medieval sages were on to something with their reluctance regarding usury. Credit is clearly indispensable for the functioning of the economy and material progress, and it is logical that institutions focus on this. However, when the separation between the person and capital becomes an abyss, and those who make important decisions ignore the consequences, something needs to be fixed. For example, much of recent employment regulation has come up in reaction to US financial multinationals' purchase of foreign companies, a purchase that is nothing more than a number in their accounting books, and the hundreds of families that survive thanks to the work there are irrelevant to them.

Experience has shown that direct relationships between owners or employers and employees heighten solidarity and production.

To reverse this situation, greater market regulation is needed, especially regarding purely financial and speculative matters. But for some reason, lessons from the great financial crises of our time seem to be absorbed only in theory and not in practice, as the successive economic and financial crises of 1929, 1973, and 2007 have dramatically demonstrated. Despite the tumult, and the severity of the last of these crashes, we are no more immune than before and keep delaying the precise measures needed to prevent future instability. Implementing effective regulatory systems could help improve and readjust the capitalist system in its entirety, which would signify a true breakthrough.

The second adjustment relates to policy progress regarding the education of local elites in developing countries through systematic theoretical and practical training. This does not just involve providing scholarships for them to study at the best European and American universities to then bring back and apply what they learned to their countries of origin. It is also important that they experience, through practical training, what they intend to promote in their countries of origin, namely a culture of respect for the rules, meritocracy, and business practices free from corruption. This kind of *from within* training is much more effective than direct aid policies, which are necessary at first, but that, when they last too long, go from volunteering to voluntarism and fall into paternalistic attitudes that are not entirely helpful, when not directly harmful, in that they can engender a sense of dependency on the donor. Obviously, there are times when pressing needs require humanitarian aid, but it is not a medium- or long-term solution. This idea is aptly synthesized in the proverb, "Give a man a fish and you feed him for a day; teach a man to fish and you feed him for a lifetime." Simply giving 'fish' to developing countries instead of teaching them to fish generates a paralyzing and submissive mentality, which in turn leads to dependence on stronger powers, if not an ingrained sense of victimhood that usually degenerates, paradoxically, into violent reaction against donor countries—and usually into civil wars.

Training from within is also the only way for the capitalist system to adapt to local traditions and culture, which often vary widely. Experience reveals that a certain type of capitalism (for example, the American brand) is not easily literally transplanted to other areas, for example, when artificially implanted in Muslim countries or in most of Africa. Some Asian countries, such as China and Japan with their Asian equivalents of the Protestant Ethic, have managed to establish independent capitalist systems. They are compatible with their own traditions with very positive results—for example, the so-called

Four Asian Tigers—that is, South Korea, Hong Kong, Singapore, and Taiwan. Ultimately, the question remains as to whether nations with cultural traditions that significantly differ from the West can maintain their specific cultures while adapting to something as foreign as Western capitalism. The case of Japan showcases the tensions at stake; there, little balance has been achieved between the population's dedication to work and its attention to other values such as family, social relationships, and spiritual life.

Finally, the capitalist economy should balance itself out with a gift economy, that is, a logic that is not strictly mercantile (the search for material profit at all costs). This involves believing that some human values are above commercial transactions, and that people are more important than capital. When these values are ignored, capitalism systematically degenerates into avarice, which (paradoxically) distorts the capitalist system itself, as the crises of 1929, 1973, and 2007 clearly demonstrated.

In sum, after analyzing the problems, and challenges of capitalism, the conclusion is that the solution does not seem to be found in demolishing the capitalist system all at once. A balanced examination of world history teaches us that utopian and messianic solutions produce many more injustices than the ones they attempt to resolve. This is very much the case of the two experiments that, to date, have been presented as alternatives to capitalism, namely communism and populism. History has clearly demonstrated the failure of both these systems, on a practical level. It thus seems more reasonable to focus on improving the system instead of demolishing it, at least until we find other alternative solutions that are truly viable. Capitalism, like all human creations, has its bright spots and shadows, its positive and negative aspects. When seen in perspective, since its foundation at the dawn of the Modern Age, one is amazed by the material progress that the West has achieved. Capitalism is—perhaps together with the state and universities—one of the three Western institutions that have shown astonishing resistance over time and have most influenced other civilizations around the world.

CHAPTER 12

SCIENCE

One of the most fascinating aspects of Western history and legacy is found in the development of science and technology. Science is to knowledge as technology is to application. Early modern European scientists soon realized that theory and practice, knowledge and action, culture and skills, are all complementary. Europe's material development starting in modernity is very much based on mutual feedback between science and technology, theoretical knowledge and practical application. This was made possible because of the realization of the benefits of knowledge for knowledge's sake, since it paradoxically but systematically leads to practical application. It is thus fruitless to raise the question of the supremacy of science over technology, or vice versa, since each is meaningless without the other. It would be like trying to settle if the West's mentality is based more on Greek philosophers' speculation or Roman engineers' technology and jurists' applications. Transforming the world with technology is impossible without previous knowledge of that world, in the same way that medicine could not have advanced without detailed anatomical knowledge. At the same time, the results of scientific knowledge would not make much sense if they were never practically applied. Even reading a literary classic has enormous practical meaning, perhaps the most practical of all, since it lends meaning to our existence, and prevents it from devolving into a trivial and directionless pursuit.

All civilizations are concerned, in one way or another, with satiating their curiosity about the essential questions of human existence, including the meaning of life, the creation of the world, how nature works, the immensity of the universe, the origin and the end of life, the hereafter, and the existence of God. Ancient civilizations had extraordinary astrologers, the forerunners to modern astronomers. Until the dawn of modernity, the most relevant inventions in the West (paper, gunpowder, printing) originated in China. Europe also inherited, rather than invented, its two most important means of knowledge transmission (alphabetic script and Arabic numerals) from other civilizations, namely the Phoenicians, Hindus, and Arabs. Egyptian cosmology, Greek physics, Chinese techniques, Indian mathematics, and Arabic astronomy were developed before the birth of modern science in the West.

So, the question is: why did the scientific revolution take place in Europe and not in China, India, or in the Islamic world, considering that some of them were scientific and technologically superior to the West prior to the sixteenth century? To understand why modern science arose in the West, it is essential to study not only the technical aspects of scientific thought but also the religious, legal, and institutional arrangements that either opened the doors for enquiry or restricted scientific investigations. So the answer may lie in the nature of Western educational institutions and in the structure of Western law. The European legal, jurisdictional, ecclesiastical, and political revolution rose in the axial shift and the newly invented universities at the thirteenth centuries (see Chapters 7 and 8) created a neutral space that gave birth to the scientific revolution.

First, the West was always more open to *learn* from other civilizations. Numerous Islamic, Hindu, and Chinese scientific discoveries and technical inventions ended up in the West, including the numeral system, the magnetic compass, the gunpowder, the compass, the paper, the printing, and the mechanical clock. The Islamic world also acted as an intermediary with classical culture, through the invaluable work of Jewish intellectuals such as Maimonides or Islamic intellectuals such as Averroes and Avicenna. When these innovations, transactions, and inventions reached Europe, they had a great impact on social life transforming Feudalism into Capitalism, revolutionized the sociopolitical system, increased the political competition, helped to stimulate the economy, and stimulated the Scientific Revolution. By the end of the fifteenth century, Europe was actively financing scientific discoveries and nautical exploration (Figure 12.1).

What happened, then, with the Islam and China? The former was left behind in scientific exploration in the thirteenth century because religion invaded the field that, in China and in the West, had been autonomously occupied by intellectual and scientific innovation. The latter could not take benefit from its own vanguardism, since its sociopolitical system was not affected by its own inventions. Unlike the West, it did not have a structure in which merchants could profit off of their inventions.

The paradox of this was that Europe surpassed China in scientific innovations, using Chinese technologies and it surpassed the Islam using Islamic ideas. During the late Middle Ages, Europe imported Islamic ideas and Chinese technical innovations when it was needed. During the early modernity, China and the Islam did not import European innovations when

FIGURE 12.1 The cartographer Gerardus Mercator, on a commemorative gold coin. © Shutterstock.

it was needed. This was especially highlighted by the failed attempts of the Jesuits—who played an essential role in the cultural and scientific encounter of Chinese and Western civilizations in early modernity—to implant a Western regime in China. One of those pioneering Jesuit missionaries, Mateo Ricci, wrote around 1590 that "no people esteem mathematics as highly as the Chinese," but immediately clarified the differences in the fundamentals of both civilizations: "in their method of teaching, they propose all kinds of propositions but without demonstrations." The consequence was that the flourishing of modern science in the seventieth century and its main fields such as astronomy, physics, and optics had no comparison with that of other civilizations such as the Chinese, the Hindu, or the Islamic.

The reason for this extraordinary development is the West's capacity to harmonize science and technology in a continuous interaction. Humanity's most prodigious intellects have much in common, including Aristotle, Thomas Aquinas, Leonardo da Vinci, Copernicus, Galileo, Newton, Kepler, Descartes, Pascal, Leibniz, Alexander von Humboldt, and Einstein, to offer an abbreviated list. All of them are characterized by their remarkable capacity for philosophical speculation, fruit of their profound humanistic education, to which they united extraordinary scientific knowledge, and the result of intellectual curiosity. It was precisely the combination of these two fields, philosophy and science, that gave them the necessary intuition to produce great inventions. Most of the comforts we enjoy today originated, more or less directly, in Aristotle and Thomas Aquinas's inductive-rational argumentation, in da Vinci's development of geometric calculations and perspective, in Galileo and Newton's dedication to modern physics, in Copernicus's foundation of modern astronomy that replaced esoteric and superstitious astrology from the ancient and medieval worlds, in Descartes, Pascal, Newton, and Leibniz's development of modern mathematics and infinitesimal calculus, in Einstein's theory of relativity, and in Niels Bohr's quantum theory.

Ultimately, all of these scientific advances were based on the rationalization of knowledge and experimentation, just as the formation of the state and the development of capitalism are based on the rationalization of politics and economics. Both were possible thanks to scholasticism's rationalization of religion (due in turn to the holy fathers' first enlightenment in late Antiquity in their dialogue with their contemporary intellectual tendencies), making the Christian faith compatible with rational thought. Commentators agree that the theological–philosophical synthesis of late medieval scholasticism, led by authors such as Peter Abelard, Thomas Aquinas, Albert the Great, Bonaventura, Roger Bacon, Ramon Llull, Duns Scotus, and William of Ockham, made modernity's scientific-technological progress possible. Their conviction that no investigation into nature that was truly rational could threaten the Christian faith inaugurated modern science. The Christian faith was viewed as suprarational, but never irrational or anti-rational. This argument tapered the interference of irrational and superstitious beliefs in research on humans and nature, which was ancient and medieval research's greatest obstacle, and which still lingered in modern Western society and differentiated it from Islamic tradition.

Once late medieval philosophers and theologians legitimized rational investigation of nature, the first philosophers of nature emerged, a peculiar hybrid between speculative-theological and experimental-scientific discipline that notably influenced the later establishment and development of modern science.

In England, Roger Bacon inaugurated a line of inductive thought that was very influential in the development of experimental science, which emphasized the primacy of the individual versus the universal and argued in favor of the physical homogeneity of the cosmos. Bacon directly observed physical reality using systematic and rigorous mathematical analysis, thus setting up the conditions for a truly experimental methodology. The following words, written in the mid-thirteenth century, give us a glimpse of the extent to which supposedly 'medieval' thinkers were already laying the foundations for modern experimental science:

> For the things of this world cannot be made known without experience. Reasoning draws a conclusion, but does not make the conclusion certain, unless the mind discovers it by the path of experience. (Roger Bacon, *Opus Majus*, Part VI, Chapter 1)

These lines feature in part the path modern science took. The motor of all scientific knowledge is universal curiosity, which is not satisfied with the contemplation of truth, but requires experimentation. Rational speculation and experimental knowledge must complement one another, although Bacon clearly took the side of experimentation. This preference remained intact throughout the entire English and Scottish inductive tradition, which ran parallel to the more rationalist French tradition expressed in Descartes famous phrase, "I think, therefore I am." However, the dichotomy between British experimentation and a more continental speculation deserves clarification since Descartes, himself a mathematician, intended to extend his rationalist reductionism to all areas of knowledge, both inductive and deductive.

The development of the experimental sciences, based primarily on the study of nature, progressed during the thirteenth and fourteenth centuries, especially based on the work of philosophers and theologians who studied and taught at the Universities of Paris and Oxford, for example, Robert Grosseteste and Albert the Great. William of Ockham was also an important link in this chain of research based on his inductive and empirical style. Also trained at Oxford, his logical-linguistic analysis of reality and his intuitive speculation enabled the development of mechanics. His nominalist approach, opposed to the essentialism of classical scholasticism, led to a functional, rather than speculative, analysis of fundamental concepts like space, time, and movement. Indeed, Ockham was not as interested in their meaning, philosophical entity, nature, or causality as he was in the conditions that govern them, their movement, speed, operations, and how they relate to one another.

Along with Ockham, Thomas Bradwardine, William of Heytesbury, and Francis of Marchia produced kinematic, gravitational, and inertial studies in the fourteenth century at Oxford, as well as similar studies from Albert of Saxony, Jean Buridan, and Nicolas Oresme in Paris. This mechanical turn triggered the replacement of the former philosophers of nature, and had an evident influence on Galileo and Newton's modern experimental physics. Thus, the absolute character of universal knowledge, as Aristotle had proposed and as Islamic tradition and Christian scholasticism had assumed, was replaced by empirical and logical knowledge of the relationships among things. Yet, this rise of institutionalization of experiment surely derived from the practice of artisans as well as from the ideas of philosophers.

During the Italian Renaissance, between the fifteenth and sixteenth centuries, these scientific advances, developed till then mostly between Oxford and Paris, began to spread. In the classical style of Western symbiosis, the values related to Renaissance humanism that developed on the continent merged with those of England's experimental sciences. The Renaissance's interest in the investigation of nature and human body was more motivated by an aesthetic, rather than a properly speculative, approach. But the results were the same. After all, both motivations (aesthetic and cognitive) respond to two values, namely beauty (art) and intelligibility (science) that—together with unity and goodness—correspond to classical philosophy's transcendentals. It is hard to forget the way the pioneers Bill Gates and Steve Jobs stressed the relevance of *taste* in the design of the first phones and computers[1]—a resonance of the Dostoyevsky's idea that: "beauty will save the world" (*The Idiot*, chapter 5). The first modern humanists, Renaissance artists, and scientists' curiosity and aesthetic sense of existence led them to contemplate nature naively, with a sense of novelty and free from prejudice. They represented things as they are—with clarity and accuracy— in all their splendor, beauty, and simplicity, abandoning the conceptual symbolism of the Romanesque or Gothic periods. Perhaps it was they who best embodied the idea that beauty would save the world. This aesthetic impulse also led to a cognitive impulse because they wanted to understand the beauty they represented.

Leonardo da Vinci best embodies this initial aesthetic impulse that became an insatiable interest in rational knowledge of existence and the world. He also first modeled the figure of the classical humanist that influenced the likes of Galileo,

---

1 https://www.youtube.com/watch?v=oBISzVRmYIM and https://www.youtube.com/watch?v=W1wP6v4maL0.

Newton, Descartes, and Einstein. This humanism, on which the material progress of Western civilization rests, is tri-dimensional—that is, aesthetic, scientific, and technological. Da Vinci was known above all for his art, in which he represented the perfection of human anatomy and facial expressiveness. He wanted his portraits to be so realistic that he began dissecting corpses to study anatomy. He also inquired after the anatomical basis and weather conditions that allow birds to fly, and wondered if humans could achieve something similar, leading him to design the first flying machine in history in the style of an artificial bird. Once he applied experimental knowledge to the land-based animals, his interest turned to the seas. Da Vinci explored the possibility of humans sailing underwater, but decided not to make his designs public "because of the evil nature of men who would practice assassination at the bottom of the sea." (quoted in Kenneth D. Keele, *Leonardo Da Vinci's Elements of the Science of Man*, New York, Academic Press, 1983, p. 184). We are fortunate enough to have access to many of da Vinci's drawings and observations from his notebooks, some of which survived the ages. His annotations reveal ideas about planetary movement that clearly foretell later discoveries of the universe's natural and universal laws. What had started with a pure aesthetic impulse resulted in the research of nature and technical exploration.

When da Vinci died in 1519, the world was undergoing rapid change. In addition to the studies of mechanics and kinetics at Oxford, calculus also provided another key for modern science's development. This occurred, to a large extent, through the implementation of commercial techniques referred to in the previous chapter, although the systematization of formulas and mathematical operations using calculus as a method is usually dated to the second half of the seventeenth century. Merchants needed more accurate instruments to calculate their increasingly complex financial operations and to understand the viability of their investments. These calculations were applied to knowledge surrounding the laws of nature, including the laws of pendulum motion, weight and velocity, and binary star motion. Maritime dynamics were more and more dominated by the first Spanish and Portuguese global explorers. This decisively contributed to the consolidation of da Vinci's idea that nature never breaks her own laws. Thus, understanding nature's logic materialized when its operations were understood to function based on systematic laws that could be discerned rationally rather than on mysterious forces driven by a magical hand. Once a law was deciphered, it could be applied universally because it systematically repeats itself when the originally described conditions are met. Knowledge of formulas for calculating these laws became a new kind of alchemy that allowed for vast knowledge.

Galileo Galilei developed the mathematical study of nature. After many years of study, he became persuaded that the earth and the other planets revolved around the sun, rather than the other way around. Galileo based his findings on the Polish scholar Copernicus and his studies published half a century earlier, around 1543. Nobody believed Copernicus then, perhaps because of the fear of reprisal from Catholic and Protestant ecclesiastics who did not like the idea because it overturned ancient tradition and seemed to contradict the Bible. Galileo tried to retract his theories about the movement of the stars. He retracted because he was a man of faith, but legend has it that after signing the act of recantation, he muttered under his breath: *Eppur si muove* ("And yet it moves")—a wonderful image of the first pioneers Western scientists' mentality, reported by Giuseppe Baretti in his book *The Italian Library*. In reality, Galileo never uttered his famous words at his trial. But just as the Italians like to say about stories that cannot be verified, "se non è vero, è ben trovato" ("even if the story is not true, it is ingenious").

The 'Galileo affair,' as it has been popularly transmitted, contains substantial fabrication and exaggeration, but also great lessons. Given its resolution, the process could not have been as terrible as sometimes reported. But one of this story's clearest lesson is that truth (be it religious, philosophical, historical, or scientific) eventually wins out. In fact, all eras devise mechanisms to control theology, philosophy, history, and science. Not all have necessarily been as attention grabbing as the Inquisition Courts, but many have brought about the same, or even more, physical or psychological cruelty.

The seventeenth century, that is, a generation after Galileo, witnessed the modern scientific revolution led by Isaac Newton. To him we owe the theory of gravity, which led to countless scientific advances and technical applications. This principle postulates that all bodies are attracted to each other with a force proportional to the mass of each and inversely proportional to the square of the relative distance between them. At great distances, both the weight and the acceleration of a fall are reduced, but they never reach zero. The Sun's gravity is extraordinary because it attracts planets that are at astronomical distances. Since these laws of gravity are universally applicable, they apply not just to planetary motion but also to that of the seas with their constant ebb and flow. Newton also confirmed with his theories that since natural reality is uniform, the most incomprehensible and difficult questions can be deciphered by figuring out their principles, and may be understood through general laws.

The Renaissance humanist was able to combine philosophy, science, and technology, a description that certainly applies to Newton. He devoted his life to the experimental investigation of nature, but he also spent hours upon hours discussing theology with John Locke, another of the great English thinkers of the time. Locke, a medical doctor, had just concluded his influential treatise, *An Essay Concerning Human Understanding* (1690), and found in Newton a close friend and respected colleague. Together, they spread the values of rationality, empiricism, and tolerance, convincing others of their importance for science and development. Their friendship illustrates their wide multidisciplinary reach, both having education based on broad knowledge of theology, philosophy, and many of the scientific disciplines in existence. Newton did not just leave his theory of gravity for posterity; he also established a practical and completely open research program. At the end of his life, he asserted that his program remained incomplete, and that much more work was required, with calculations to complete and theories to verify.

We owe an enormous debt to thinkers and scientists like Leonardo, Galileo, and Newton, and to so many others who promoted science in early modernity. When studying the history of science, we must realize that not everything that appears as evident today was perceived with the same clarity in earlier periods. In this way, we can assess scientific advances well and value what it meant for their authors to break with certain inertias in knowledge, which are by far the most difficult to overcome. Political and economic changes take time, but they are usually implemented on their own with the onset of urgent problems, for example, when reacting to an economic crisis, a political problem, of defending oneself against a foreign military attack. However, advances in knowledge do not usually come about through favorable external factors, but rather through certain visionaries' restlessness, courage, and intellectual honesty.

At the beginning of the eighteenth century, science had developed many theories on nature, even those without much practical application. From then on, it began to drive the inventions and technology that society increasingly demanded during the early days of industrialization. In the eighteenth and nineteenth centuries, modern science continued to advance, but there were no new qualitative leaps until the development of Einstein's theories of relativity at the beginning of the twentieth century. During that time, which not by chance happened around the time of the industrial revolution, the expansion of technology took the lead, particularly in the development of new machinery. The previously established scientific ideas enabled technicians to take greater advantage of the natural forces, controlling them and putting them in the service of human comfort and material progress.

Technology developed as a way to harness nature in search of material benefit and human comfort. If science is mainly based on discoveries, technology is based on invention, the creation of a new object. The concept of machine best reflects the spirit of invention, which made extraordinary material progress possible in eighteenth- and nineteenth-century Western society. The first came in the form of the steam engine, patented by Watt in 1769, which made the first steamboat run in 1807, and the steam locomotive in 1814. The expansion of the railroad, in turn, stimulated the use of iron and other materials for improving industrial performance. These inventions also led to a progressive rationalization of the energy sources needed for machines to function. Oil replaced coal, since it accelerated the automobile industry in the early twentieth century. More effective substitutes for oil, like gas and atomic energy, subsequently emerged in the next periods.

Endless inventive activity aimed, to a large extent, to reduce (and even entirely substitute) human labor by rationally manipulating the forces of nature. Spinning and weaving machines proliferated, industrial application of which occurred in 1825, together with the mechanical loom, as well as other kinds of industrial machinery that freed up a lot of labor in traditional, mostly unchanged, workshops. Rigid hierarchical professional structures associated with traditional guilds and businesses maintained since the Middle Ages collapsed in the blink of an eye. New inventions brought with them the important question of the relationship between humans and technology, between humans and their own inventions. Unlike their makers, machines do not need sleep or rest, but, in the early days of industrialization, machines rather than people set the pace, soon making working conditions unbearable, as explained in the previous chapter. Twentieth-century science fiction movies developed to engage the new relationships between humans and the machines they create, including, *2001: A Space Odyssey* (Stanley Kubrick, 1968), *Blade Runner* (Ridley Scott, 1982), *Terminator* (James Cameron, 1984), and *The Matrix* (Lilly and Lana Wachowski, 1999).

Inventions related to land and maritime transportation—a characteristically Western obsession—occurred around the same time as advances in telegraphic communication. In 1837, Morse sent his first telegram. Telecommunications continued to expand throughout the world; the telephone was invented in the twentieth century and the Internet in the twenty-first century, which has today become the main means for the transmission of ideas.

James Clerk Maxwell's development of electromagnetism (the branch of physics that unified electric and magnetic phenomena into a single theory) at the end of the nineteenth century generated, and continues to generate, enormous practical applications. An interesting and contemporary line of historical research called the "history of technology" analyzes the relationship between technical advances and cultural development. Its scholars agree that the discoveries that had the greatest influence on Western culture include alphabetic writing, Arabic numerals, and printing. Many of them also argue that the development of the Internet is another great milestone that has contributed so much to cultural transformation, the limits of which we have not yet reached.

Experimental science, on the other hand, appeared to recover all of its original energy at the beginning of the twentieth century with the development of Albert Einstein's theory of relativity (1905) and quantum theory from Niels Bohr and Werner Heisenberg (1920), who took advantage of Max Planck's pioneering work. Copernicus, Galileo, and Newton's spirits were thus revived with the uncovering of theories that explain the natural functioning of the world. These scientists sought to decipher a mathematical relationship that would give them access to a unified theory of the world. They did not find this great theory, but they made possible considerable advances in science exploring the universe with the theory of relativity and the the atom with quantum laws. This great scope, from the largest to the smallest in the world, has led to our current focus on uncovering the great enigmas of the universe and on biochemical research with medical applications, and admirable technical advances have been promoted by space and atom exploration. The invention of the atomic weapons is the dark side of this evolution.

Clearly, these scientific and technological developments have contributed to an overall improvement of material conditions. They have also freed up much energy that can now be devoted to more intellectual, professional, and cultural development. In addition, they have raised general healthcare standards to levels that would have been unthinkable a few centuries ago. Yet, they have also shown that their flawed use, especially when it comes to medical and military research, can lead to self-destruction. Ultimately, humanistic and scientific knowledge is to technology as the soul is to the body. Historical experience proves that progress focused solely on material development entails a loss of meaning that dismisses human spirituality as useless and leads the world into decadence and self-destruction. But no one can deny that modern science and technology have definitely improved our lives and will continue to do so thanks to the scientists and technicians' brave effort.

CHAPTER 13

REFORMS

The expansion into the New World coincided with dramatic divisions in Christianity. As Spain and Portugal divided up the world, Italy and Germany were still territorially dispersed. Italy eased its own disorganization with its cities' enormous commercial strength, which functioned, in fact, as Greek city-states and therefore had their own political and administrative structures—and their own sublime art. But the situation in Germany was more complex with the loss of the Holy Roman-Germanic Empire (and the imperial crown's transfer to Spain with Charles V), which left the country mired in an enormous variety of political structures that ranged from autonomous cities to diverse regions controlled by an earl, duke, or king. In this context, the flame of religious dissent that the Augustinian friar Martin Luther ignited spread with unusual force. Shocked by the collection of indulgences to finance St. Peter's Basilica in Rome, he began to preach a new Christian confession that prioritized faith and in which the ecclesiastical hierarchy, beginning with the Pope, was superfluous—although his followers soon came to believe in the need for pastors. He saw each person as called to freely interpret, according to his conscience, the Sacred Scriptures. The sacraments were not in fact signs that grant a specific grace, but simply symbols that each person could understand.

Luther's reform might have ended in an inquisitorial process, like that of other dissidents from previous centuries, such as Joachim de Fiore, Jan Huss, Girolamo Savonarola, or Giordano Bruno, but Luther and his supporters benefited from the printing press, which had been imported from China and subject to Gutenberg's 1453 efficient redesign. His mastery of simplified language, effective rhetoric, and skilled use of the printing press allowed dissidents to spread their ideas with a speed unknown until then. When papal reaction arrived, many of Luther's associates had already adopted his ideas, and the Reformation expanded like a fire across a Mediterranean pine forest.

As has happened so many times throughout history, the diffusion of a new technology concurred with the spread of new ideas. Significant examples in history oblige us to consider the question of whether the Protestant Reformation would have prevailed in the absence of the printing press, or if it would have had a much smaller impact without expansion to neighboring countries such as Switzerland, France, or England. The same kind of question applies, for example, to the invention of the contraceptive pill, which was massively distributed at the beginning of the 1968 Revolution, and to contemporary radical Islamism's skillful use of Internet-based technologies. These tendencies all share the blending of political motivations or economic interests with religious beliefs and ideological convictions, but its own expansion greatly benefited from, if not made possible, technical innovations.

In the end, Luther and his supporters ultimately separated from the Church around 1518 and were joined by German princes eager to achieve greater political autonomy from Rome. However, Protestantism was also deeply divided almost from the beginning. Iconoclastic movements re-emerged, such as the Zwinglians, in Switzerland and part of Germany, and the Calvinists, in France and The Netherlands, because they feared idolatry. Anabaptists, who taught that it was wrong to baptize children since each person must freely decide with their use of reason, were another prominent group. Other branches of Protestantism emerged in Zurich, led by the parish priest Zwingli, and in Geneva, guided by the scholar John Calvin, whose doctrine of predestination decisively contributed to the expansion of radical ideas and capitalist practices. In France, Protestants, known as the Huguenots, never established supremacy over traditional Catholicism. In England, King Henry VIII established Anglicanism, an authentic model of civil power's hegemony and domination over ecclesiastic power (Figure 13.1).

The Church that remained faithful to Rome during the Protestant turbulence decided to reorganize, reforming as needed and emerging strengthened from this crisis. This movement is commonly known as the Counter-Reformation, although perhaps the name Catholic Reformation might be more representative, since it was much more than a simple reaction—but both concepts might work. The Council of Trent (1545–1563) became a fundamental milestone for the Catholic Church's internal reflection. There, traditional doctrine was revised, the practice of priestly celibacy was reaffirmed, and the entire doctrine associated with the sacraments was confirmed. Trent had a lasting influence since no ecumenical council was called until more than three centuries later with Vatican Council I (1870).

FIGURE 13.1 Statue of King Henry VIII, King's College, Cambridge (England). © Shutterstock.

Two Spanish characters represent the long-lasting spirit of Trent, namely Saint Ignatius of Loyola and Saint Teresa of Avila. Saint Ignatius stands out for founding the Jesuit order, an army of priests who received profound intellectual training to embark on the evangelizing challenges that geographical expansion inspired. Saint Teresa reactivated female religious life through multiple programs. Her sublime autobiography (*El libro de su vida*, circa 1568) has become part of world literature.

As a woman who developed her work in a male-dominated civil and ecclesiastical world, we cannot exaggerate the extraordinary nature of her spiritual profundity, brave personality, and literary achievements.

Yet the break between Catholics and Protestants in the sixteenth century was not only religious but also political. Luther and the Lutheran Reformation became mortal enemies of the Spanish-Habsburg Emperor Charles V since he was recognized as the protector of Christianity and particularly of the Pope, as was his predecessor Charlemagne seven centuries earlier. Besides, he saw this new heresy as possibly inspiring rebellion in Germany, of which he was the sovereign emperor. He was not, of course, clueless. Basic political ambitions were united, once again, with spiritual aspirations since political unity in the Modern Age demanded a unity of creed. Overall, it was bad business. The political-religious tensions inaugurated in 1521, the year in which Luther definitively separated from Rome, were projected onto conflict among the Spanish Empire against Germany, the Netherlands, and the French and English monarchies.

The so-called Thirty Years War (1618–1648) was the first major European civil war, with clear parallelisms—although very different motivations—from that other period of European civil war in the twentieth century during the two World Wars (1914–1945)—considered by some historians as a 'Second Thirty Years War.' A tragic, violent, and self-destructive affair, it at least had the distinction of being Europe's last expansive 'wars of religion.' After the Peace of Westphalia (1648), Europe was left definitively divided into nations that would battle from then on to achieve power and glory. The competition even seemed lucrative for Europe at first, because it encouraged economic growth and drove a universal expansion that culminated in the carving up of the globe by the European powers with the colonization of the nineteenth century.

Later, other European struggles, such as the World War II, were exacerbated by a clash of ideologies that certainly contained eschatological and messianic dimensions (e.g., fascism and communism), but they did not present themselves to their respective peoples and their enemies as true religions in the spiritual sense. The events of the Reformation and its subsequent projection on the battlefield had at least one positive result, namely, the conviction that politics and religion should run their course separately.

Yet, beyond the doctrinal and religious-political upheavals that this split entailed, an essential debate for Western civilization is the extent to which Protestantism injected the West with a greater dose of rationalizing, modernizing, and innovative power in the face of Catholic traditionalism. Protestantism challenged the political, social, economic, and scientific tradition of the West, a rupture that was reinforced by the Enlightenment and the initial impact of the Industrial Revolution. There are some obvious manifestations of the rationalization that was supposedly promoted and accelerated by Protestantism: the emergence of the state in politics, the promotion of a capitalist ethic in the economy, the bureaucratization of the different forms of social life, the secularization of worldviews, the development of modern science, and the subsequent passion for technology. All of these resulted in an evident disenchantment, a secularization that the West would not relinquish, but which was at root more of a 'substitution'—the sublimation of the temporal in place of the spiritual—than an alternative. As Carl Schmitt famously stated in his conceptualization of the *political theology* as methodology of analysis, "all significant concepts of the modern theory of the state are secularized theological concepts not only because of their historical development but also because of their systematic structure."

Protestantism encouraged the ability to think with and in the world, a kind of inner-worldly asceticism that allowed its adherents to enter into more of a dialogue with *that* world, even if it was from the cloister. Here, Protestantism connected with the old Benedictine tradition, in which the monks also developed an ethic of inner-worldly asceticism. The monastic emphasis on the methodical life, disciplined under one rule—a day-to-day existence based on a community standardized by the daily rhythm of liturgical time—constitutes the original core of what Weber later defined as the 'Protestant ethic,' so essential for the origin, development, and consolidation of the modern world.

Protestantism reacted against the forum of conscience that had been instituted in Europe from the papal reform of the twelfth century. As an alternative, it encouraged its adherents to be guided by the subjective inner light that God had made shine in their hearts, without the need to compare it with an external objective authority. The Protestant Reformation was based on a critique of the medieval integration of conscience, casuistry, and spiritual direction, which finally coalesced in the judgment of one's own conscience. The fundamental role of the confessor and the spiritual director had been essential since the catechetical conversion processes in early Christianity, as Michel Foucault made clear in his essay *The Government of the Living* (1974). However, the critique of medieval casuistry and probabilism was questioned, in early modernity, by both Catholic and Protestant authors, notably Luther, Calvin, Galileo, Descartes, and Pascal. They presented as an alternative the study of natural laws, from which every moral rule was derived and thus had universal scope, to be discerned in each specific case by personal conscience. These reforms therefore had most influence on spiritual matters and questions of conscience, without entailing significant innovation in the philosophical, scientific, juridical, civil, ecclesiastical, and religious institutions, which had already been reformed during the axial shift of the twelfth century.

But no one can deny the profound shock that Luther's emphasis on his mission as a 'liberator of conscience' delivered to all Europe, and by extension to Western civilization, in his first years as a reformer. In carrying out this mission, he railed against the *Corpus juris canonici* and certain medieval treatises on cases of conscience. He reacted against the medieval organization of moral and religious life, and in particular its tendency toward control of the conscience by means of the triad conscience–casuistry–cure of souls. Having proclaimed his maxim, and especially after his reflection on St Paul's *Epistle to the Romans*, he proclaimed the triumph of faith and penitence over works. The sacramental confession and mediating function of priests in administering the sacrament of penance was thus no longer valid. He also discredited the tendency of medieval morality to make conscience operative through a casuistry that steered souls toward rigidism and vigorous asceticism. Luther therefore tended toward an anti-Pelagianism that simply sought union with Christ, through imitation and mystical union. It all went against spiritual direction and external control of the conscience as it had been conceived and designed in the medieval age. The Protestant cultures fostered subjectivism and individualism, a context in which confessors, counselors, casuists, moralists, regulators, and spiritual directors had little room for maneuver.

In accordance with the subjectivization of the conscience, Protestantism postulated direct access to Scriptures—*sola scriptura*—with the Augustinian Luther's own specialization in the study of the Scriptures thus counting for a great deal. The only source of authority was hearing the voice of God, without any institutional intervention. The three traditional sources of Christian revelation— Scripture, tradition, magisterium—were reduced to the first as the sole normative source, so that subjectivism, intimism, and religious feeling gained a great deal of importance in the final interpretation. The doctrine of justification came to be the universal principle of Protestantism, its critical and dynamic source of realization. Stemming from the principle of *sola scriptura* are those of *sola fide* and *sola gratia*, too, though always as a consequence of it. Based on the passage of St Paul in Romans 3:27, in which it is said that the Christian is justified "by the law of faith," Luther declared that the Christian is saved simply through the free grace of God—from *sola fide* to *sola gratia*. The shift from justification by works to justification by faith left the market of indulgences administered by the Church in desuetude, delegitimizing the Church's monopoly as a depository of faith (*depositum fidei*) and sole administrator of the seven sacraments.

Beyond these theological differences, the bifurcation between Catholicism and Protestantism made itself felt far more in the question of conscience than in any other area. Yet Protestantism's commitment to individuality and the liberation of the conscience has not proved a solution in itself, as it has required their *substitution* by new forms of subjectivity, especially from the nineteenth century onwards. Paul Tillich defined this new phenomenon, so characteristic of the contemporary world, as a new spirituality: "the religion of the transcendental self, the transmoral self beyond conscience." Literature and philosophy have been especially sensitive to this tendency. The inner journeys of Rousseau, considered by many to be the first autobiography as such, Goethe, and Fichte were pioneers in this direction. But in their wake can be traced the existentialist phenomenologies of Hegel, Kierkegaard, Nietzsche, Heidegger, and Foucault, and the tormented spiritual paths of Charles Baudelaire, Arthur Rimbaud, Marcel Proust, Joseph Conrad, Thomas Mann, James Joyce, and Frank Kafka. The sublimation of this new religion of the transcendental self arrived with Freud and psychoanalysis, and his massive influence in the West during the last century. Benjamín Nelson concludes, "when Freud's *Interpretation of Dreams* was ended, there was little life left in the gallery of guises—Byronism, Prometheanism, Parnassianism, dandyism, diabolism, pietism, scientism, moralism and so many others—assumed by the philosophies and substitute religious of the modern era."

Protestantism eventually prevailed as the major religious force centered on the self, just as psychoanalysis did as a substitute for religion as such–or maybe more accurately, by making a religion of itself. And yet, the paradox of this pairing is that psychoanalysis did not emerge in a Protestant context, but rather was created by a Jew in Catholic Vienna. The confession that brought spiritual direction into disrepute now yielded to *another* type of guidance, but external guidance all the same: the direction of the therapist. A new era in spiritual direction was thus initiated with Freud. Carl Gustav Jung exposed this substitution, in books such as *Modern Man in Search of a Soul* and *The Undiscovered Self*. The dissolution of the traditional religions in the West during the nineteenth century, whether Catholic or Protestant, demanded the emergence of certain symbolic archetypes in the collective unconscious that would provide guidance for many tormented spirits with the loss of external points of doctrinal reference.

In addition to all these spiritual implications, the expansion of Protestantism had many economic implications. Weber's essay *The Protestant Ethic and the Spirit of Capitalism* (1905) offers some insights into how the emergence of capitalism influenced the West. But it is not so clear that the two terms boldly expressed in the title (Protestant Ethic/Spirit of Capitalism) operate as cause and effect, among other reasons, because they are not expounded as such in the text, and nor did Weber take too much trouble to shed light on the matter. What is clearer is that capitalism did not originate historically in lands that would subsequently adopt Protestantism, but rather in the very Catholic regions of Tuscany, Catalonia, and the Low Countries. The constraints on usury that had been experienced in the Middle Ages had already been overcome in the fourteenth century, two centuries before Protestantism would irrupt, thanks above all to the charismatic efforts of the Franciscans. Weber convincingly argued that the diverse forms of Protestantism—Calvinism, Pietism, Methodism, Anabaptism—drove a rationalization of the world that encouraged capitalism. But there are many doubts as to their true role in its emergence, real scope, and subsequent consolidation.

These doubts emerge when we consider that the notions of rationalization and modernization cover more ground than that of Protestant ethic. The problem is that Weber, as befitted the age in which he lived, conceived his theories about rationalization in terms of linear progress rather than cyclical or simultaneous progressions. He posited a mechanical succession, clearly influenced by Comtean positivism, in which other-worldly mysticism gave way to inner-worldly asceticism and irrepressible impulses gave way to rationalization of conduct, charisma to institutionalization, magic to science. But all these processes of rationalization, intensified from the sixteenth century onwards, were driven, simultaneously, by both Catholic and Protestant monks, intellectuals, and scientists. Luther and Copernicus, respectively Protestant and Catholic, were the leaders of modernity's religious and scientific revolutions. They illustrate perfectly the *changing of the guard* in the West that begins with modernity.

The combination between Catholicism and Protestantism went on into succeeding generations, with the figures of Calvin, Galileo, Descartes, Newton, Leibniz, and Pascal, not to mention the new spirit brought by the Spanish Jesuits and French Jansenists. They all agreed with the critique of medieval morality's casuistry and probabilism as they were resolutely committed to rationalization in its processes.But at the same time, they had respect for received tradition since a good part of them remained Catholics.

This peculiar combination between tradition and innovation challenges the idea that Catholicism was a brake on scientific investigation and Protestantism a stimulus to it. Copernicus, Descartes, Galileo, Pascal, and other philosophical and scientific innovators developed their work in countries with a Catholic tradition and culture. The greatest innovators in philosophical method, experimental design, mathematical formalization, and technical transformation did not require the intervention of the so-called Protestant ethic or inner-worldly asceticism. Copernicus and Kepler reacted against this fictionalism, the 'hypotheses saving the phenomena' that had prevailed or so long in astronomy, while Descartes, Galileo, and Pascal tackled probabilism—a move that sought to overcome the casuistry of the professors of logic and of the philosophical and theological morality prevalent since the late Middle Ages, but which in reality ended up entangling them in its web. Their critique of probabilism was highly effective, as that was soon left out of intellectual discussion, displaced by the dramatic irruption of the scientific method, with its search for verifiable truths and rejection as a mere game of what it considered a rhetorical debate about probable opinions. It is paradoxical that Blaise Pascal made his critique of probabilism compatible with the development of one of the first approaches to the calculation of probabilities, while at the same time trying to create a logical formula to affirm that belief in God constitutes the safest moral option.

All this points to exercising caution when it comes to marking a radical rupture between Protestantism and Catholicism, not so much in specifically religious terms—where the rift is clear—but more as regards the general values of the West. The ideas of Luther and Calvin were more decisive in their assumption of a new type of conscience—rational, self-critic, and autonomous rather than fideistic, submissive, and objective—than in their new rationalist or capitalist visions. The Franciscan movement and late medieval economic ethics had already assumed many of the ethical consequences—the tolerance of usury among them—long before a supposed 'Protestant ethic' made its appearance in the thirteenth century. The theologian Ernst Troeltsch had already stated in his book *Protestantism and Progress* (1906) that the Reformation and the early Protestantism remained profoundly indebted to medieval concepts of order. Therefore, as Hans Joas has argued, "we must be extremely cautious about crediting Protestantism with the authorship of every positive achievement of modernity". Friedrich Wilhelm Graf concludes that "the Reformation and early Protestantism remained profoundly indebted to the medieval concept of order and their religious impulses toward freedom with their inherent critique of tradition contributed to the achievement of political and social freedom only in a multiply fractured way, through extremely complex processes of mediation". So the 'Protestant ethics' of Ernst Troeltsch and Max Weber, and their ideas about the birth of capitalism, have their limitations, though no one can deny that they have analytical potential for an intellectual approach concerning the nonreligious consequences of religious faith, thought, and action.

Also inherent in Protestantism from its origins was the seed of expansion, as it was in original Christianity and Western civilization in general. Its major expansion in Asia, Latin America, and Africa was concomitant with the colonization of the nineteenth century, in which Protestant missionaries played a role that cannot be underestimated. By the twentieth century, it saw division into new confessions and churches. The Pentecostal churches, emerging from Methodism after 1906, particularly stood out. All the Pentecostal groups, having expanded throughout Latin America especially, show impressive growth rates, high charisma ratings, and in some cases even the beginnings of bureaucratization. Their effectiveness lies in their embracing and adapting to the local cultures, in true indigenization processes that diversify them still further among the different branches and raise doubts about their viability as religions, seeing as they often end up actually dissolved into their respective indigenous cultures. The North American variations of Pietism, Puritanism, Methodism, and the American Awakenings revival movement have invigorated Protestantism, without substantially altering its course.

Today, the borders of Protestantism, both inward- and outward facing, are blurred. The Anglican front is more flexible, with the peculiar phenomenon of high-Catholic Anglicans, and the continuous processes of conversion to Roman Catholicism. The Protestant family grows and divides still further. Every movement or sect traces its genealogy and seeks out its origins in the Protestant movements of the sixteenth century, but generates its own exclusive legitimization and particular descent. In any case, they have all developed the practice of self-reflexivity or self-examination that is so common in the West. The famous Protestant theologian Friedrich Schleiermacher, in *The Christian Faith* (1922), expressed the division between Protestantism and Catholicism in this simplified formula: "the former makes the individual's relation to the Church dependent on his relation to Christ, while the latter contrariwise makes the individual's relation to Christ dependent on his relation to the Church".

In conclusion, the function of Protestantism in the formation of the West and in the processes of modernization acts as one factor among many. Protestantism contributed to the deepening of the processes of rationalization experienced by the West over the course of its history and eventually found concrete expression in an incorruptible legal mentality, logic in thought, the state in politics, capitalism in the economy, the scientific revolution, the mass processes of industrialization, and relentless technological development. Protestantism as a modernizing and westernizing agent cannot be judged in isolation, but only as part of a whole from which, if any part breaks off, becomes distorted, and loses its effectiveness.

CHAPTER 14

ENLIGHTENMENTS

The aspects of modernity examined in the five previous chapters (Chapters 9 to 13) developed most notably during the sixteenth and seventeenth centuries. Yet, at the beginning of the eighteenth century, some of the European elites began to experience a certain euphoria based on the political, economic, cultural, and artistic advances it had achieved since the Renaissance. This environment was ripe for the spread of a kind of intoxication with rationality, such that they defined their era as a luminous age (*lumières*, in French, *Aufklärung*, in German, *ilustración*, in Spanish) in contrast to what now seemed to them as the previous gloomier and dark eras. The golden age of the Enlightenment extended from 1715, the year in which its most influential intellectuals coincide, to the French Revolution in 1789.

Given the history covered in the previous chapters and taking a long-term view, the first thing to clarify is that the eighteenth century coincides with the West's *fourth* Enlightenment. The three previous Enlightenments occurred in classical Greece (rationalization of pagan thought), the Christian patristic era in late Antiquity (assimilation of pagan rational philosophy with Christianity), and medieval scholasticism (harmony between the Christian faith's philosophical and theological argumentation and that of the secular realm). In the eighteenth century, several Enlightenments postulated the primacy of rationalization processes over religious beliefs and the value of sentiment. As is often the case in such cases, they argued that they were the first to put forward a true rational enlightenment, but this was not the case. Yet, in its most radical version, the Enlightenment was an attempt at unconditional rationalization that sought to overcome everything sacred by substitution and analogy. Overcome by rationalization and secularization, and having exiled the Christian God, many attempts arose to fill in the vast symbolic gap that resulted. Enlightened reason became a pagan goddess, whose revolutionary iconography was taken from traditional images of the Virgin Mary. The *people* burst forth as a new social and political category, investing themselves in the traditional absolute sovereignty of sacralized kings of traditional societies. The Enlightenment thus emerged as a secularized age that saw itself as at its peak and verifiably superior to everything sacred. The effects of this Enlightenment are still very palpable and its values are fully in line with modernity.

The original name of this movement arose in France and Germany. In French, it appeared in plural, *lumières*, emphasizing the source of light, and in German in the singular *Aufklärung*, placing more emphasis on the process of illumination. In any case, it refers to the concept of light, whose powerful symbolism we have seen before, for example, surrounding the conversion of the Emperor Constantine. This concept has profound implications both for paganism—many of whose doctrines were based on the theme of light—and for Christianity, for which Christ is *lux mundi*, the light of the world, as reflected in the beginning of the fourth Gospel and represented in enormous images of Christ the king of the universe (*pantocrator*) in many medieval churches. The Enlightened set referred more to the legend of the Platonic cave where light flooding in from the outside liberates humans from ignorance and allows them to access knowledge free from prejudice and fabrication.

The Enlightened modeled themselves after English philosophers and scientists who, in the previous century, had contributed to the establishment of inductive and experimental knowledge, for example Francis Bacon, Isaac Newton, and John Locke, as well after continental rationalist philosophers, such as René Descartes, Baruch Spinoza, and Gottfried Leibniz. These thinkers paved the way for the rationalization of knowledge and human action, from which there was no turning back. The Enlightened added to this process of rationalization a process of secularization or desacralization. These ideals persist to this day because the Enlightenment was not simply a historical moment that gathered a few rationalist intellectual tendencies; rather, it is a philosophy, a kind of new religion, which had (and continues to have) a devout following.

Obviously, the Enlightenment did not arise *ex nihilio*. Paul Hazard defined the period that preceded it with a phrase that also titles his book, published in 1935, *The Crisis of European Mind (1680–1715)*. Scholars generally talk about this transitional period by highlighting four influential intellectuals. A Dutch Jew of Sephardic and Portuguese origin, Baruch Spinoza argued that the Bible is a book of sacred history and a source of universal knowledge, but that knowledge of religion and interpretation of the truths of faith result purely from intellect and reason, rather than from any received scriptural heritage. The French Huguenot Pierre Bayle fervently sought to do away with all forms of idolatry because he believed that they preclude rational knowledge, making it preferable to be an atheist rather than indulge in superstitious knowledge. The English physician and thinker John Locke was one of the founders of classical liberalism. The Irishman John Toland, a republican and adventurer, served as a model for eclectic thinkers who resist being pigeonholed into any position regarding religion, ideology, and politics. He also postulated deistic ideas, denying the presence and provident activity of God in the world.

Giambattista Vico, the great philosopher of history from Naples, could be added to this list. In his book, *The New Science*, he proposed a scientific method based on the recognition of poetry and myth for understanding societies. This method was soon recognized as an extraordinary and imaginative contribution to the humanities. Vico also inaugurated a kind of rational history, although he was still very much influenced by traditional ways of writing history that rely on the impact of divine providence. In fact, he defined his work as a "rational civil theology of divine providence," in a description characteristic of Enlightenment thinkers. By assuming the autonomy of the social sphere with regard to nature and grace, Vico's work also serves as a precursor to social sciences such as social psychology, sociology, and anthropology, whose influence spread starting in the beginning of the twentieth century with the pioneering work of Max Weber and Émile Durkheim.

Given these forerunners, who were the key characters of the Enlightenment? First in line are French philosophers who, for the first time, assumed a role that, over time, gave rise to the concept of public intellectuals. These thinkers not only committed themselves to the rational presentation of certain ideas but also to the improvement and transformation of the world through the application of these ideas in the public sphere. Men like Bayle, Voltaire, Diderot, d'Alembert, Montesquieu, and Condorcet took up the gauntlet. Clearly they were not illiterate townspeople but rather were born into the social and intellectual elite— except Diderot, who was the son of an artisan—which gave rise to another of the Enlightenment's key concepts, namely 'enlightened despotism.' This notion belies any attempt to 'democratize' or 'popularize' the Enlightenment. Enlightened European kings applied enlightened despotism exactingly, for example, Frederick II of Prussia, Catherine II of Russia, Charles III of Spain, and Joseph II of Austria, who surrounded themselves with Enlightened thinkers, a move that cannot be said to demonstrate any closeness or empathy, intellectual or demagogic, with the people.

Among them, Voltaire is usually distinguished as the most representative Enlightenment thinker, the author of texts that became very popular in his lifetime, such as *Candide* and the *Treatise on Tolerance*. His most historical work, *Essay on the Manner and Spirit of Nations*, published in 1756, left no doubt that enlightened tolerance extended to everyone except to those who opposed its ideas and morals. That is, Enlightenment thinkers did not intend to attach themselves to a descriptive analysis of reality but rather wanted to change personal and public morality, which implied imposing models for judgment and action. They inaugurated the difference between intellectuals who read the world and ideologists who change it. Marx described this attitude later in his *Theses on Feuerbach*: "The philosophers have only interpreted the world, in various ways. The point, however, is to change it." This point is important because the Enlightenment emerged as the first systematic intellectual movement configured, in fact, as a substitute for religion. Paradoxically, by appearing as an anti-religious movement, it was immune from the criticism that it launched against confessions with a minimum of doctrinal and moral coherence, such as Catholicism and the most consistent Protestant confessions.

The Enlightenment thus appeared as the first ideology, i.e., a set of doctrines designed not only to convince intellectually but also designed to bind the will, usually through an appeal to sentiment. For this reason, both the Enlightenment and other ideologies, such as fascism, communism, liberalism, and populism, function at a certain level and under certain circumstances as 'secularized religions' or 'political religions' that, significantly, lack a transcendent objective. In any case, the ideologies inaugurated with the Enlightenment later unleashed great conflicts in the nineteenth and twentieth centuries, which Chapter 15 will address.

According to the European political evolution, and the increasing strength of the states in the international context, the Enlightenment developed some specific national cultural traditions. The German, British, American, and the already mentioned French, were the most influential, not only in its time but in the future. The German Enlightenment had a perhaps more theoretical and properly philosophical dimension than that of French thinkers and activists, but it also left an important imprint on the future of the West. It was strongly influenced by the previous generation of rationalists, particularly by Leibniz. Immanuel Kant, for example, conceived of the Enlightenment as the freedom to make public the personal use of reason with the aim of freeing humanity from its self-imposed immaturity (Figure 14.1). Moses Mendelssohn conceived the Enlightenment as an essential milestone in the enculturation and education of the people. Cristian Wolff and Gothold Ephraim Lessing respond to the humanists of this period, approaching almost every scholarly subject of their time, from theology to mathematics, and from esthetics to literature. Finally, Johann Wolfgang Goethe, poet, philosopher, and scientist, presented

FIGURE 14.1 Fragment of a monument to Immanuel Kant against the background of the sky. Kaliningrad (Russia). © Shutterstock.

German Classicism and Romanticism as a potential source of spiritual authority for Europe, privileging the spontaneous dynamism of the nature over its mathematical interpretation, and favoring poetic and intuitive observation over rationalistic speculation.

The British Enlightenment was also active and profoundly influential in the medium and long terms. In his *The Natural History of Religion*, David Hume delved into one of the key concepts of the Enlightenment: progress. Persuaded of the "natural progress of human thought," Hume also helped shape scientific empiricism, which, as explained in Chapter 13, bore its first fruits in the great discoveries of modern physics to which Hume himself was a witness. The great theorist of mercantilism and liberal economics, Adam Smith, monopolized the economic side of the Enlightenment. We will refer to him a little later since his work must be placed in the context of liberalism. Finally, Edward Gibbon defended civil history against more traditional stories that blend the sacred with the worldly, and he did so through a work that definitively influenced his field, namely *The History of the Decline and Fall of the Roman Empire* (1776). Enlightenment historians laid the foundations for the secularization of history, an activity that is vitally important from the point of view of the transmission of ideas. This work came to full fruition a century later with the great Germanic historicism movement, led by Leopold von Ranke, which signified history's emergence as a scientific discipline.

American culture also resonated with the Enlightenment because its 1776 Declaration of Independence owed much to ideas that were brewing at the time in Europe. The American Revolution and its subsequent influence was, in large part, the work of Enlightenment statesmen like John Adams, Benjamin Franklin, Alexander Hamilton, John Jay, Thomas Jefferson, James Madison, and George Washington. They are known, in fact, as the Founding Fathers of the United States, whose progress and achievements were immortalized a few decades later in Alexis de Tocqueville's influential text, *Democracy in America*, which very effectively contributed to the establishment of contemporary democracy.

Enlightenment ideals are most distinguishable for their confidence in the power of reason and their desire to make religion disappear from the public square. Both ideals are intimately connected because Enlightenment thinkers considered religion an irrational impulse, an illogical confidence in the supernatural, which was, in turn, identified with the magical and superstitious. The French Enlightenment's real enemy was the Catholic Church, rather than religion in general or Protestantism and other confessions, although, paradoxically enough, some leading figures of the Enlightenment were priests or pastors. This animosity led to anticlericalism, which became, starting with the French Revolution, a hallmark of all attempts for social change through intellectual persuasion or armed struggle. This anticlerical attitude later supported injustices since the evidence shows that most clerics lived a miserable existences. In addition, anticlericalism as an ideological and political tool fostered gratuitous violence which in turn produced social imbalances that became difficult to resolve and, in the end, eroded the Enlightenment project itself.

The Enlightenment also contributed to a greater recognition of the freedom of belief and thought—the previous step for the future revindications on free speech. Many ideas that had raised political or religious authorities' suspicions in the past, for being too bold or imprudent, became admissible. The Enlightenment promoted the value of universal equality, which arose again in the 1960s with struggles for racial and gender equality as I discuss in Chapter 17. Jean-Jacques Rousseau was equality's main advocate. Along with Voltaire, he is most popularly associated with the Enlightenment. This Swiss thinker published *The Social Contract* (1762), as well as other very influential works like *Discourse on the Origin and Basis of Inequality Among Men year?*, and *Emilio, or On Education year?*, which Rousseau considered his best work. In his utopian approach, he studied human behavior free from civilization in order to better understand man's original nature. His approach is considered a precedent to the cultural anthropology studies led by academics such as Edward Evans-Pritchard and Claude Lévi-Strauss, who worked during the first two-thirds of the twentieth century and interacted with remote tribes untouched by Western influences in central Australia, Africa, and the Amazon.

Rousseau also popularized the myth of the 'noble savage,' which later influenced popular libertarian movements, for example, the 1968 Revolution or some Marxist varieties. He posited that humans are good by nature and are only corrupted by the competition that arises from demographic development and the need to share natural resources. The development of the notion of property led to inequality, which had devastating consequences in the form of individualism. The only solution, he argued, lies in returning to the origins of humanity, before Christian civilization, and in recovering the natural social contract upon which the first civilization agreed.

The Scottish economist Adam Smith, author of the influential essay *The Wealth of Nations* (1776), proposed his ideas of liberal-style commercial development and necessary diversity and inequality as an alternative to Rousseau's utopian egalitarianism. Smith set out to improve the conditions of human life by reforming economic activity. He argued that improving nations' material conditions depended on constructing an established legal order, together with citizens' moral reform. The inequalities that this regime produces are the necessary, natural consequence of people's diversity but are fair because they reflect that inherent variety. True progress is to be found on this path, and indeed some nations were already on it. Smith thus consolidated an emerging discipline, which has become vital today: political economy. Nowadays, when it seems that politicians only obtain positive results thanks to applying orthodox economic policies, Adam Smith's work is more alive than ever. Starting from the inevitability of economic inequality, and thus confronting Rousseau's utopian theses, he argued for the development of trade free from fiscal and political obstacles, allowing wealth to flow more naturally and levels to even out. Rousseau and Smith are the standard bearers, respectively, of egalitarianism (whose political outlet is communism, socialism, and populism) and economic liberalism (whose political realization is found in liberal parties and moderate social democrats). These oppositions led to a wide-ranging debate with deep ideological implications, which Chapter 15 explores.

Another basic Enlightenment value pertains to fraternal universalism, which also links to the third principle French revolutionaries set forth: the recognition of a universal brotherhood. Enlightenment thinkers were persuaded that education is one of those basic universal rights. Because of its universalistic aspirations, a major moment in the development of Enlightenment ideas came in 1751 with the publication of Jean d'Alembert and Denis Diderot's *Encyclopedia*. Most of the principles Enlightenment thinkers defended are found in its *Preliminary Discourse*, and it is a real forerunner of today's *Wikipedia*, promoting universalism, progress, popular access to knowledge, and rational knowledge. In a rational approach to nature, knowledge must be ordered by mathematics but ultimately derives from experience. In this approach, knowledge of language is essential for communicating, history is the repository of our collective memory, politics orders society, and rational morality is a substitute for religious faith.

Influenced by early modern essayists, such as Pascal or Montaigne, Enlightenment intellectuals used essay-style writing prolifically and intelligently. This genre, far from the highly speculative treatises by the philosophers or papers by the scientists, allowed them to discuss moral issues and considerably increase their audience since they wrote for a general, rather than specialized, readership. This style was more literary than scientific, more discursive than systematic. It also used rhetorical devices such as satire or irony and reinvented classical genres such as the fable—Voltaire and Rousseau turned back to Molière's model—to get the message across more clearly. In this way, writers managed to simplify their ideas, which were also more easily received by those who were reading them for the first time.

Enlightenment intellectuals also benefited from the expansion of the printing press in the eighteenth century. The increase in commercial publishers generated the creation of 'authors,' i.e., writers who became public celebrities and attracted new readers through name recognition. Just as Frank Capra was the first film director to get his name in his film's credits, Enlightenment essay writers managed to get their names on the first page of their texts, next to the title. This made a wide distribution of historical, literary, and thought pieces possible, many of which are considered the first best sellers in history and brought significant profit to their authors for the first time, including *The History of England* by David Hume, *The History of Scotland* by William Robertson, *The Wealth of Nations* by Adam Smith, *Émile* by Jean-Jacques Rousseau, and *Teatro crítico universal* by Benito Jerónimo Feijoo, who represents the Spanish Catholic Enlightenment. These publications were accompanied by the emergence of new discussion forums, namely idea magazines (*Giornalle de'letterati* in Italy, *Critical* in England, or *Edinburgh Review* in Scotland) and book magazines (*Nouvelles de la république des lettres* or *Bibliothèque universelle* in France), which critically evaluated the latest books and contributed to public opinion, and were spread among the academic world and the cultured public. Finally, Royal Academies were founded, starting with the Royal Prussian Academy of Sciences (1700), which inspired others in France, England, Spain, and Italy, and which were consolidated as a viable alternative to universities. A spirit of enlightened elitism among these academies survives to this day—although not free from some anachronistic academicism resulting from its tendency to function as 'the guardians of tradition.'

Concluding this chapter necessarily involves reflecting on the legacy of the Enlightenment. Our first obvious inheritance thereof transpired at the end of the eighteenth century with the outbreak of the American Revolution in 1776 and the French Revolution in 1789. But these revolutions were not a direct consequence of the application of Enlightenment ideals. They were the result of much more complex circumstances than a simple, radical revision of traditional ideas and instead responded to profound political and social disappointments that went back centuries, and to specific circumstances in those countries. The American Revolution was an archetypical emancipation of a colony from its colonizer, a cyclical process that lasted up to the 1990s with the last throes of decolonization. The French Revolution was a consequence of extraordinary social imbalances accumulated during centuries with the maintenance of a political system anchored in the Old Regime, while the country's intellectual and social reality had changed. In addition, these revolutionaries' radical and violent reactions were little in keeping with the Enlightenment's discursive and (at least formally) dialoguing mood.

However, it is also evident that many of the ideas spread in the eighteenth century, especially those that refer to freedom, equality, and universal brotherhood, were essential for the legitimation of those rebellions, and that revolutionaries moderated themselves thanks to the certain Enlightenment intellectuals—Montesquieu, Rousseau and, later, the Enlightened-revolutionary Condorcet, Tocqueville, and Jules Michelet, among others. As a consequence, the French Revolution caused an anti-revolutionary, anti-enlightened, and anti-liberal reaction in many European countries after Napoleon's expansion. These positions were united in a common front, embodied at the Congress of Vienna (1815) with its proposal to restore the pre-revolution world, thus opposing liberalism as it had come to be understood in the post-revolutionary period. Therefore, the nineteenth century became a constant struggle between liberals (those who defended the values associated with the French Revolution) and anti-liberals (traditionalists who did not accept the new liberal regime), as the periodical revolutions in Europe (1830, 1848, 1870) conveyed. World War I saw the definitive disappearance of anti-liberalism, and opened up a new scenario of struggle among the three great ideologies of the time: liberalism, fascism and communism, which the next chapter will address.

Criticism of the Enlightenment intensified during the twentieth century. The Enlightenment was unable to overcome the contradictions of capitalism, and the world became entrenched in irrational processes such as fascism and anti-Semitism. Social philosophers within the Frankfurt School—a group of intellectuals of social theory and critical philosophy founded in Germany in the 1930s—led the way with this critique, particularly Theodor Adorno and Max Horkheimer. After World War II, authors such as Reinhard Koselleck (inspired by previous studies on the Hobbesian sovereign state from the philosopher Carl Schmitt) and Ernst Cassirer criticized the Enlightenment for its inadequate and insufficient response to (when not open collusion with) absolute monarchy, which he considered an immediate precedent of fascism. A few decades later, postmodernism, with authors like Michel Foucault and Richard Rorty at the helm, argued that the Enlightenment edifice, based on an absolute belief in reason and the unity of knowledge, should be demolished and rebuilt. They postulated instead that knowledge and morality lack a natural, objective foundation.

All these criticisms, built by some of the most influential twentieth-century philosophers and thinkers, clearly reveal a reaction to the idea of modernity generally considered. The Enlightenment, with its dramatic outcome in the French Revolution, represents something like the zenith of modernity, the moment at which all its values stand together in a quest for greater theoretical coherence and political and social application. This resulted in the hyperinflation of some ideals, such as rationalism, progressivism, authoritarianism, and egalitarianism, all of which end with an *ism*, which usually expresses the exaggeration of some idea. Enlightenment and post-Enlightenment thinkers' exaltation of these values brought effects that even their advocates did not want, or at least did not expect, but that in fact instigated much of Europe's conflict during the nineteenth and twentieth centuries.

Avoiding post hoc projections—in which intellectual fall into the trap of judging events not for what they were, but for how subsequent generations received and experienced them—Enlightenment thinkers deserve recognition for having provided us with concepts and values such as universalism, freedom, egalitarianism, the autonomy of reason, and the progress of societies, which are still very useful today when placed in an appropriate intellectual and moral context. However, some Enlightened thinkers who aimed to erase religion from society, such as Voltaire, did not foresee the unintended consequences of their desire, and in their slide toward supremacism would bring with it. Powerful ideologies soon occupied the space traditionally occupied by religion. Unable to consider transcendent goals because of their political nature, and functioning in a certain sense the same way of the religions they aimed to replace, these ideologies soon focused all their energy on newly emergent conflicts. From this moment on, the typical revisionism of Western societies was divided into a gradual reformism or a rupturist revolution, in which ideologies rather than ideas came to play a radical role.

PART IV

REVISIONS

CHAPTER 15

IDEOLOGIES

Poets and artists have the gift of prophecy although they often exercise it unknowingly. "The dream of reason produces monsters," Goya wrote in an engraving next to a man in a deep sleep within his *Caprichos* series. It dates from 1799, shortly after the collapse of the French Revolution. Indeed, reason seemed to have fallen asleep in a Europe that became dominated by the ideologies that this chapter takes up. Twentieth-century totalitarian ideologies were fundamentally based on political myths spread in the nineteenth century, making them compatible with the systematic application of reason in politics, which enabled them to dream up world domination. Thus, paradoxically, when reason alone guides politics, without considering elements other than power dynamics, it can lead to utopianism with dramatic consequences for the harmony of societies. These ideologies wreaked havoc among many populations when totalitarian states assumed them.

Ideologies are a set of theories that form a political-social program with specific objectives and that are spread through the propaganda of doctrines. There are not just a group of ideas meant to help us understand the world but a body of ideas that entails strategies to *change* this world. Their effectiveness is based on the following six traits. First, they are dualistic, and therefore base their argument on effective simplifications of reality: good–bad, patriot–foreigner, loyal–traitor, friend–enemy. Second, they are alienating, that is, they try to neutralize one's personality, make people submissive and adhere to the consequences of a given ideology, to the extent of eliding personal responsibility. Third, they are doctrinaire, demanding absolute allegiance from their followers. Fourth, they are totalitarian in that they seek not only to organize the political sphere but also have an influence of all other areas of reality (social, economic, cultural, and religious), control personal behavior, and provide a moral code for citizens. Fifth, they are messianic in that they promise to lead to a utopian, paradisiacal culmination of history, albeit an earthly one.

Sixth, they skillfully exploit people's feelings, endowing them with a transcendent motivation in times of social imbalance, especially serious economic crises or moments of low national esteem, for which they also tend to have strong nationalist leanings.

These six principles are applicable, to a greater or lesser extent, to the three ideologies whose origins and historical developments will be taken up in this chapter: liberalism, communism, and fascism. To them, we should add nationalism, which emerged in Europe with the unification of Germany and Italy in 1870 and found formidable allies in communisms and fascism. In this chapter, we analyze the period between the outbreak of the French Revolution and World War I, that is, an extended view of the nineteenth century.

Before the outbreak of ideologies, the West experienced the emergence of intellectual tendencies characteristic of the nineteenth century. The first was Romanticism. Developed in the first decades of the century in France and Germany, it reacted to intellectualism and enlightened rationalism by proposing a sentimental and emotional reading of the past, literature and art. Concepts such as shared tradition and collective identity were consolidated in this period, which greatly influenced nationalism in the second half of the century.

From the mid-nineteenth century, cultural and intellectual phenomena significantly influenced specific ideologies and a good number of 'isms,' including historicism (Leopold von Ranke), positivism (Auguste Comte), evolutionism (Charles Darwin), Malthusianism (Thomas Malthus), and pragmatism (Charles Peirce). They all share a desire to give secularized alternatives to essential questions whose explanation had previously been dominated by the Jewish and Christian traditions, but they were unable to avoid a fascination with providence, especially in the case of German historicists such as Ranke and Dilthey. Historicism opted for historical experience to the detriment of the stability of traditional natural law, thus privileging the changing nature of the human condition over its permanent condition, the construction of culture over that which nature endows us with. Positivism based its interpretation of knowledge on inductive science instead of on metaphysics or theology. Evolutionism based its explanation of nature on the impersonal selection and progress of species instead of biblical creationist ideas. Pragmatism reduced reality and human action to changing truths according to their applicability and consequences, instead of belief in absolute and immutable truths.

The nineteenth century was tremendously creative—a variety of genres thrived, including the novel, the symphony, and the opera, as well as original intellectual, artistic, and literary styles such as romanticism, realism, naturalism, symbolism, impressionism, and modernism. In addition, much energy was directed toward political debates around social issues and material progress. On the one hand, industrialization generated economic imbalances and social unraveling that created internal tensions. On the other hand, technological advances and material progress in the West launched it toward global expansion through colonization. This generated anxiety among the various European powers that soon exploded in open competition and created external tensions.

In this context, intellectuals devoted themselves to examining and justifying the situation and legitimizing sovereigns' behavior rather than creating new ideas. Ideologies emerged as a blend of ideas destined to legitimize a given political situation, rather than intellectual currents that materialize a shared mentality or search for answers to emerging problems. In general terms, we can say that ideologies impose structured ideas from above, while mentalities are generated spontaneously from below. They became secularized religions that seek to replace old convictions, already clearly discredited and delegitimized by successive waves of modern humanism, rationalism, enlightenment, and positivism.

Liberalism, communism, and fascism emerged from the spoils of the French Revolution. After the revolution, everything seemed reduced to a power dynamic. Rulers intend to transform societies, demolishing past tradition through the creation of a present legitimized by ideologies. In ancient and medieval societies, novelty (whether religious, political, social, economic, cultural, intellectual, or artistic) had to be compared and contrasted with tradition. In the modern era, it became enough to generate discourse, symbols, or rhetoric that set the tone for an ideology. Innovation begun to dominate over tradition as a rule for social life.

In the amazingly short period of a decade, France went from Jacobin republicanism after 1789 to the communitarian socialism of François Babeuf after 1796, and to Napoleonic authoritarianism after 1799. Over time, these three moments represented the three great ideologies dominating in the next two centuries: liberalism, communism, and fascism. Republicanism, transformed into different forms of capitalist democratic liberalism, remains hegemonic among them. Socialism, experienced in the final stages of the revolution, flourished as an ideology starting with the great European revolution of 1848, and diversified into utopian socialism, communism, anarchism, trade unionism, and, during the second half of the twentieth century, into a more moderate social democracy. Authoritarianism, which has a long tradition, was revitalized by the Napoleonic Empire, which endowed it with a revolutionary ideology and later continued with twentieth-century totalitarianisms and fascisms.

We will analyze them in chronological order of expansion, namely liberalism, communism, and finally fascism.

Liberalism, in its most theoretical and foundational sense, defends the freedom of the individual and advocates for only minimal state intervention in social, cultural, and economic life. Since its original formulation, the concept has evolved in a complex manner, such that thinkers like Spinoza, Locke, and Smith, who forged liberalism's foundations in the seventeenth and eighteenth centuries, have little in common with the liberalism developed in the nineteenth century which tries to neutralize the state's anti-liberal weight. In the next paragraphs, I will develop liberalism's four main dimensions and manifestations: intellectual (free-thinking), politics (parliamentary democracy), economic (free trade and equality of opportunity), and social (majority middle-class societies).

Firstly, liberalism is an intellectual movement fostered above all by philosophers like Locke, who privileged private property as an inalienable right because he saw it as synonymous with freedom and life, and by Enlightenment activists such as Voltaire, who prioritized freedom of thought and conscience above any other consideration. Human reason is seen as fully reliable as a source of knowledge, making it necessary to promote its autonomy and not interfere with its functioning. This aroused abundant misgivings on the part of more traditional institutions, such as the Church and the state, focusing debate on religious tolerance and on new ideas. After their initial alarmed reaction, both the Church and the state eventually accepted free thought. The state gradually abandoned its most ostentatious censorship practices, such as the Inquisition, although today they have re-emerged through diverse forms of control, including the banner of preserving security and autonomy. The Catholic Church, for its part, after experiencing anti-religious violence for many centuries, was forced to recognize that confessional plurality or simple religious indifference were not going away. This fostered a more in-depth reflection on the issue of religious freedom, especially as a result of the Second Vatican Council (1962–1965), which steered the Church toward becoming one of the most prominent supporters of religious freedom.

Second, the political version of liberalism materialized in parliamentary democracy. This system emerged from the ashes of the American and French Revolutions. Alexis de Tocqueville was a key thinker in its dissemination; in *Democracy in America*, he revealed a kind of fascination for the political system established in the United States of America after its independence and highlighted, in particular, its distinction between legislative, judicial, and executive powers. The legislature creates laws, which are enforced by the government and monitored by judges. The doctrine of the vesting of the legislative, executive, and judiciary powers of government in separate bodies, based on the ideas of Montesquieu and Tocqueville, among others, is one of the bases of political liberalism. Respect for each branch's autonomy is the only guarantor of political stability, equal rights, and the possibility of harmonious economic development. Parliamentary democracy has assumed a monarchical or republican system, depending on each country's political experience and attachment to tradition, but a balance of powers is equally exalted in both. Based on the conviction of all subjects' equality, democracy guarantees a government representative of its citizens. The universal right to vote was gradually implemented (mainly due to a lack of technical resources and resistance to admitting female voters), but it finally won out in all democratic countries.

The democratic system obviously has its limitations and shortcomings. The most worrisome at present is politicians' tendency toward corruption which, uncontrolled, can pervert the entire system. The alleged separation of power is sometimes hard to achieve. But democracy's enormous advantage over other systems, such as dictatorial or populist ones, is its reversibility. Democratic political offices have established term limits, which generates a sense of transience among politicians, who are often more concerned about the next elections than their day-to-day work. But there are many more advantages than disadvantages to this system, especially because it blocks any possibility of tyranny.

Economic liberalism, in the third place, defends free trade and the development of capitalism free from state or political interference. It asks the state to guarantee a minimal framework of political stability, a system of rules, respect for private property, and the right of association, guarantee of freedom of opinion, as well as the promotion of individual autonomy and personal creativity. Liberal capitalism now dominates the world, even having been adopted by nations such as Russia or China, which, based on their tradition, historical experiences, and idiosyncrasy, did not seem to be likely candidates for adapting it as an economic system. In these countries, pure capitalism does not exist because their authoritarian governments tend to control and plan the economy. But, for now, we have not found realistic alternatives to the capitalist system, in spite of the crises it periodically engenders—which have been particularly problematic in the last hundred years—especially the Wall Street Crash of 1929, the energy crisis of 1973, and the speculative one of 2007. And, what is worse, capitalism has an extraordinary ability to forget the mistakes it made even in its recent past, which prevents the establishment of effective means for preventing them from happening again.

Historical experience also reveals liberalism's ability to create a vast middle class wherever it is implemented, giving large masses purchasing power.

This middle class also has unprecedented access to culture and, therefore, has become more immune to ideological manipulation and less tolerant of tyrannical, authoritarian, demagogic governments and despots. Here we find the feedback loop between free thought, democracy, and capitalism. However, capitalism also clearly generates significant economic inequalities (although they are not typically greater than those generated by communist or populist regimes), especially in countries that resist regulation or where corruption prevail overs legality. Thus, the current gap between the rich and poor has been on the rise, especially in urban pockets of Asia, Africa, and Latin America. But it is precisely in these areas where true capitalism is polluted by anti-liberal political systems.

The introduction of certain market regulations and partial state intervention, particularly after the crash of 1929, has been shown to alleviate some of these imbalances. Based on the ideas of British economist John Maynard Keynes and fostered by post-war Christian Democrats such as Alcide de Gasperi, Maurice Schumann, and Konrad Adenauer, the most advanced European nations— England, Germany, France, Switzerland, Holland, Belgium, and the Scandinavian countries—implemented a social democratic system. This system involved smooth planning of the capitalist economy, an alternative to the savage capitalism underway in the United States and Japan. This resulted in standards of living like the world had never seen, as well as the implementation of the so-called welfare state with three pillars: compulsory and free education, universal healthcare, and a basic retirement pension.

Time has shown that these material levels and public benefits are difficult to maintain, but contemporary Europeans must at least try to pass on this model to the coming generations, imperfect though it may be. In this effort, perhaps Europeans should start talking more about realistic modifications and reforms than about cuts in the public services. The word *cuts* has negative implications that generate a kind of animosity toward the welfare state, and suggest that it is practically impossible to maintain. Politicians categorically proclaim that the rights associated with the welfare state must be preserved at all costs, and they get elected based on their promises to guarantee them. Yet they know that the whole system will be impossible to maintain without applying serious and realistic reforms. But it seems to be that nobody, not even politicians in favor of an unmodified welfare system, is willing to make the sacrifices in the present that are required. We cannot forget that those who worked hard to create this system during the decades after World War II not only paid higher taxes but also work hard for rebuilding Europe. We should keep this spirit alive.

Looking at the world today, it is difficult to find a more balanced model between liberal capitalism and state planning, between private initiative and public services, than that implemented in several European countries from the 1950s to the 1980s. Europe's achievements in this area certainly seem to shape a better reality than the extreme capitalism in the United States and Japan, the controlled planning in Russia and China, the brutal inequalities of developing countries in Asia and Latin America, and the clearly underdeveloped countries of sub-Saharan Africa. Certainly, there are many threats to European stability, including increasing global competition, division, the alarming increase of public debt in southern Europe, and the need to combine the reception of immigrants with retaining national identity. However, taking into account all the challenges that the future poses, the strength of historical experience also opens up a path to follow.

Finally, the fourth dimension of liberalism is social mobility. In traditional societies, social hierarchy was set at birth: when one was the son of a nobleman, that condition was hard to lose, just as when one was born the son of a peasant or an artisan, that trade and social status generally remained unchanged. Social level thus originated with both position at birth and the professional activity of one's family. The famous 'three orders' of the Middle Ages—*oratores*, *bellatores*, and *laboratories*, those who pray, those who fight, and those who work—reflect this socio-professional dimension. The incorporation of merchants into public life entailed growing fortunes, their introduction into the social elite through marriage or investment and their conversion into the contemporary business class, all of which blew a hole in traditional social rigidity. Being part of the elite no longer exclusively meant coming from a family with a storied ancestry but could now be based on one's purchasing power. Social categories went from being socio-professional to socioeconomic. Thus, from the historical point of view, we cannot correctly apply the notion of *class* to traditional societies like the ancient, medieval, or early modern ones. The Marxist class concept responds to a specific socioeconomic reality of Marx's specific historical context (basically, Europe in early industrialization), but it is hardly applicable to previous periods' socio-professional stratification and hardly accounts for today's more complex socioeconomic reality in which Marxism's reading of society as extreme poles does not fit at all.

Indeed, the social mobility characteristic of capitalist societies has allowed for the emergence of very large middle classes. Therefore, the polarizations typical of the ancient world (free and slaves), the medieval world (lords and vassals), the early modern society (bourgeois and craftsmen), and even of late modern industrialization (capitalists and proletarians) are no longer applicable. Today, workers and patrons are linked by a commercial contract rather than by legal requirements, social status, or economic domination. When considering today's social relations, we must bear in mind other factors that influence the social question, such as those related to massive migratory movements, the implementation of globalization, the growth of the service sector, the hegemony of finances over production, the relevance of civil servants, and the spread of urbanization. The current professional contract system is clearly an improvement over the subjection exercised in other systems of domination like slavery and feudalism. Yet, there may come a time when society finds new socioeconomic systems. It may seem hard to believe now, because we always tend to think that current circumstances are the best or the only ones possible, that they are insurmountable, and that, therefore, they represent 'the end of history.' Slavery seemed like the most appropriate system to the Romans until Christianity arrived. Medieval societies thought that feudalism guaranteed security to people who would not otherwise have it, until the commercial revolution and urban development changed society's configuration. The moderns created the capitalist model with contractualism as the foundation of economic stability. Each one of these previous systems was replaced, and, therefore, it only seems logical that the current system may someday be overcome. For now, we should focus on improving the contractual system, based on fair labor and commercial law, to avoid any form of human exploitation that professional relationships may generate.

This brings us to the second of the great ideologies that the contemporary world has experienced. Marxism, the theoretical basis for the communist ideology, responded to the desire for a minimum of stability and justice in social life. In its original formulation, it sought to alleviate the dreadful consequences that industrialization imposed upon the most disadvantaged, as described in the analysis of capitalism. But Marx wanted to go further and intended to move from theory to practice (*praxis*). The first front of battle was property—that crucial issue originally raised by John Locke, not by chance. Since he believed that owners (capitalists) would never voluntarily share their industries, the workers (proletarians) had to take them by force. The first step entailed uniting all workers at the same factory into unions, and, if possible, linking with workers from a whole sector (construction, textile, or the press) and around the world through international Unions (Figure 15.1).

Uniting the proletariat based on class consciousness was meant to supersede other identity categories, such as politics, nationality, race, gender, religion, or culture. For this reason, Marxism is a universalistic ideology like liberalism and unlike fascism, which usually has an extraordinary nationalist dimension. Unions put pressure against capitalists with workers agreeing to increase demand for certain jobs, and capitalists would then have to pay better wages to

FIGURE 15.1 Portrait of Karl Marx, around 1875.
© Everett Collection/Shutterstock.

the few available workers. Or they would agree to stop working on certain days, striking in order to put pressure to improve their working conditions or pay. Workers were meant to rebel against capitalist domination, detonating a class struggle with the aim of appropriating the means of production and finally abolishing all property. Then classes would cease to exist, and the world would be transformed into an earthly paradise.

Marx systematically exposed these ideas in his *The Capital* (1867). But he had already simplified his ideas in his 1847 treatise *Communist Manifesto*, which he co-authored with Engels, just a year before a revolutionary spark spread throughout Europe. The argument seemed logical and impeccable and, of course, was moved by a desire to improve working conditions. But its failure also made sense. In the first place, society was not as simple as Marx had imagined it, polarized exclusively between capitalists and proletarians. It soon became clear that in addition to industrialists and workers, there were many craftsmen with long-standing workshops, merchants who lived on exchanges, sailors, shopkeepers, soldiers, teachers, liberal professionals, small agricultural owners, officials, civil-servants, and beggars. Moreover, a few decades later, the most advanced countries (England, Germany, Austria-Hungary, France, Holland) saw the emergence of what would later be known as the middle class, which began extraordinary expansion in the twentieth century and which also served as an important counterbalance to Marx's diagnosis, nullifying his social strategies.

Marx based his theories in the belief that people—capitalists and proletarians—are moved by hatred and would therefore be willing to wield violence without second thought. He and his followers forgot that people are not continually mired in violent thoughts. They do not go around in the street trying to do violence to other passers-by. For centuries, Christianity had fostered the idea of charity toward one's neighbor, a behavior that directly opposes Marxist strategies. Thus, combining Christianity and Marxism is usually based on well-intentioned voluntarism, but ends up failing because the former believes history is moved by love, while the latter believes it is moved by violence. In fact, Christianity's response to the social problems of the day was very different from, if not completely opposed to, Marxism. During the nineteenth century, religious orders proliferated and their members, usually nuns, devoted themselves tirelessly to caring for and alleviating the needs of the overlooked (in hospitals, asylums, hospices, orphanages), as well as projects to care for and give training to the most disadvantaged. Along with this effort on the part of the Church, the state, which was more and more stabilized, could not remain impassive in the face of such a social situation, and it began to organize compulsory education for children, regulate working conditions, ensure healthcare, and guarantee a retirement pension.

All this culminated in a very intense century of reforms with its fair share of upheaval, basically between the Social Revolution of 1848 and the Cultural Revolution of 1968. The work of a few visionary politicians, the long view that business people began to take, and a lot of suffering on the part of workers make it possible for some European and North American countries to correct the working conditions without resorting to Marxist praxis. They showed Marxism to be a utopia, that is, functioning on paper rather than in practical implementation, as experience began to demonstrate. Marxism prevailed in Stalinist Russia and Mao's China because of the establishment of police states, but at the time, paradoxically, both countries were economically backward, industrialization had barely begun, and social cohesion was precarious. The greatest ideological weakness of Marxism became clear there, engendering tremendous contradiction when applied. Russia in 1917 and China in 1945 were extraordinarily poor; capitalists and owners barely existed because there was hardly any industry. Thus, ironically, Marxism flourished in places for which it was not designed.

In addition to the ideologically legitimized territorial expansion associated with the Soviet and Chinese empires, many Latin American, African, and Asian countries also strategically adopted communism as a political weapon as part of their processes of decolonization. Yet, communist dictators simply replaced authoritarian military leaders and sadly tended to perpetuate the social ills they had promised to resolve, losing their eventual original legitimation or good intention when it existed.

Communism began to break down, as could not be otherwise given its internal contradictions. After the fall of the Berlin Wall in 1989, communist regimes tumbled one after the other and, in the span of about a decade, communism disappeared as a political structure and ideological doctrine in Europe. Since the September 11, 2001 attacks, the great East–West and capitalism–communism geopolitical clashes that were in force since the beginning of the Cold War gave way to the north–south and West–Islam confrontations that still plague us today. The political presence of communism is nowadays limited to a few anachronistic experiments, such as post–Castro Cuba, militarized North Korea, and the unorthodox Chinese regime. However, its shadow certainly remains in ideological terms with the capitalists–proletarians simplification extending almost literally to left-leaning populisms (neo-Marxisms) in bipolar rhetoric between the rich and the poor.

In its various forms, fascism became the third ideology that expanded out of the West. During the interwar period, it materialized with German Nazism, Italian Fascism, and Japanese Imperial totalitarianism. Fascism shrewdly allied itself with another of the great ideologies of the time, nationalism, and gained enormous momentum. It was thus able to mobilize large sectors of the population during the between-war period, collapsing during World War II (1939–1945). In addition to taking advantage of national sentiment, fascist regimes also skillfully employed *propaganda* with the use of new language and images full of symbolic connotations and capable of streamlining complex messages through simple words, gestures, and representations.

Fascist regimes also established new rites, which Christian traditional societies, along with secularized French revolutionaries, had already implemented. A new secular liturgy, as the historian George L. Mosse has explained, took hold. In this context, these rites adapted to the emerging phenomena of the de-personification of the masses—as famously argued by José Ortega y Gasset in 1930 in his book *The Rebellion of the Masses*—like large military parades, colorful settings, eloquent greetings and farewells, and a whole wardrobe meant to dramatize the situation. Scholars have analyzed Hitler's speeches from this perspective—for his discourse to take full effect, it had to be paired with flashy ceremony, paraphernalia, and a variety of gestural and vocal registers, including specific intonation and intentional pauses.

Fascisms organized totalitarian states by creating monopolizing political parties. They subjugated both the public and private spheres, making everything political and ideological. Citizens ceased to have their own criteria and were forced to direct all their energy toward serving the totalitarian-fascist state. This partially explains the large number of middle managers, particularly in Nazi Germany, who followed orders and carried out unspeakably brutal acts, such as humiliating and massacring concentration Holocaust camp prisoners, as well as torture of and medical experimentation on the living—something denounced by Hannah Arendt in her book *Eichmann in Jerusalem: A Report on the Banality of Evil* (1963).

Films such as *Judgment at Nuremberg* (1961) and *Hannah Arendt* (2012) reflect ordinary people's perplexing actions based on obedience, submission, or simply paralyzing fear, which they committed apparently without much awareness of their evil, or at least anesthetized themselves with drugs in the face of it. Ultimately, the mediocrity of people who went with the flow (and madness) of evil played a more decisive role than the powerful few at the top of the system. I have always found the response of an American official at the Nuremberg trials very telling. A Nazi official, shocked and horrified by what he had done, asked the judge, "How did we get here?" The official replied, "We got here the first time you accepted an unjust order that contradicted your own conscience."

Fascism, communism, and populism intersect in the use of prophetic and messianic language. The promise of an immanent, earthly paradise contrasts with traditional religions' promise of a celestial, transcendent one. Prophecy thus became an essential element of political leadership with rulers promising things they cannot give and predicting future events they cannot foresee. Veracity suffered a setback when strategy began to take precedence over reality (what we call nowadays 'post-truth'). It was a chilling reminder of the often-forgotten millenarian and messianic movements that periodically appeared in the Middle Ages. Contemporary politicians, like those apocalyptical prophets, use these rhetorical techniques to a greater or lesser extent, especially populists on both the left and right (Chávez, Castro, Le Pen).

These three great ideological systems soon clashed, intensified by nationalist ambitions. The Great War (1914–1918) and the Russian Revolution (1917) shook Europeans to the core and produced a crisis of conviction, as well as an awareness that one era was coming to an end and another was emerging. This shift was likely as profound as the fall of the Roman Empire, the transition from the Middle Ages to the Renaissance, and the eruption of the French Revolution. Indeed, a severe crisis of modernity awaited the first half of the twentieth century.

CHAPTER 16

CRISIS

Between World Wars I and II—known as the interwar period—Europe entered into a deep emotional, spiritual, and cultural crisis. Exclusionary nationalism, fueled by ideologies that legitimized territorial expansion at the expense of injustices committed in colonized territories, led Europe to collapse. The hegemonic cultural and intellectual movement of this period, the modernism, was, paradoxically, an anti-modern movement. The West witnessed the humans' self-destructive capacity and the consolidation of irrational ideologies. The myth of Enlightenment progress fade provoked a strong feeling of uneasiness. Many scholars define this era as the 'crisis of modernity' because all the values developed in Europe from the Renaissance to the Enlightenment (seen in Chapters 9–14) seemed to have vanished or lost their meaning. This chapter is devoted to approach the manifestations of this deep crisis during this period (1918–1945), which will finally revise all the project of modernity.

Nowadays, after one century, the West is still licking the wounds caused by this crisis of values emerged in that period. So, understanding what happened during that period, and its main manifestations—in philosophy, art, literature, science, religion, economic, society, and politics—is of great relevance to understand what is happening today. I would like to point out that, paradoxically, along with this evident self-consciousness of crisis and the emergence of radical populisms, the West developed at that time one of the most sublime moments in its history. The art and culture that emanated from cities such as Vienna, Paris, Berlin, London, Amsterdam, Brussels, Barcelona, or Budapest are difficult to emulate, both for its beauty and its originality. It remains a mystery why societies tend to give their best, culturally and artistically, during periods of greatest difficulty and economic decline. But it is a fact proven by history.

The rupture of Picasso's figure in art, Nietzsche's iconoclastic philosophy in thought, and Einstein's theory of relativity in science are three icons very expressive of the breakdown of the monolithic security of modernity in this period.

Few things help better understand a certain era's mood than art. Picasso's *Guernica* (1938) exemplifies this cultural anxiety, the profound questioning of the modern tradition, and the existential crisis of the interwar period. The painting's most evident purpose was to express the horror, the wounds, and the misery of war, in this case with the additional weight of the strongly ideological, violent, fratricidal Spanish Civil War (1936–1939) (Figure 16.1). Broken facial expressions and the horrified cries that the viewer can almost hear and the use of animals transmit the depth and mystery of human suffering, which in this case was increased by the confusion that citizens can inflict such pain on one another. The painting also reveals a fundamental cultural aspect during that period, namely the waning confidence in modern values reflected in the figures' distortion, composed of more or less geometric, but also disproportionate, cubes. The human being would no longer be a unified self, describable from the outside, but an unsteady addition of different fractions desperately fighting to survive through an agonistic battle.

From the fifteenth century, art had largely been based on Renaissance perspective studies, which the artist used to help the viewer discern the image's central aspects from marginal or accessory ones and understand the scene

FIGURE 16.1 Effects of a bombing in the city of Guernica (Spain). © Shutterstock.

at first sight. Artistic production in the interwar period lacked a clear center, protagonist, figure, geometry, and perspective. Modern confidence, based on the figure of man as a nerve center, disappeared amid the collapse of his own gaze, the loss of a privileged point of view, the need to share his space with beasts of nature, a break in the ideal of classical beauty, and the appearance of geometric figures taken from the dehumanizing urban environment, contrasting with the harmony in the serene representation of a bucolic landscape or the classic genre of *still life*.

Along with art, philosophy also produced a thinker who embodied the crisis of modernity and also announced the irruption of postmodernity: Friedrich Nietzsche. His philosophy of power appears as the apotheosis of modernity, of the superb power that modern humans have achieved. When it turns to madness, as experienced by Nietzsche himself, it exemplifies the impasse to which modernity had come with its project to substitute God ('the death of God') for the greatness of modern humans. Understandably, Nietzsche was considered throughout the twentieth century as the paradigmatic forerunner to postmodernity. Yet, the question remains as to whether postmodernity is the culmination of modernity, its point of arrival, or an alternative to modernity and the starting point of a new era.

In addition, Einstein and Bohr's development of relativity and quantum theories revised Kepler, Copernicus, Galileo, and Newton's theories. People still had confidence in science, which they considered more reliable than other forms of knowledge, but new discoveries, which aimed at examining the universe at its two extreme dimensions (the infinite with relativity and the infinitesimal with quantum theory), showed that blind trust in material progress and rational knowledge are also shaky foundations. In light of the discovery of the electron, Vasili Kandinsky, a champion of artistic abstraction, reacted with a phrase that is telling of the scientific method's precariousness: "The collapse of the atom model was equivalent, in my soul, to the collapse of the whole world. Suddenly the thickest walls fell. I would not have been amazed if stone appeared before my eye in the air, melted, and became invisible. Science seemed to me destroyed." Scientists began to trust in the Socratic maxim ("I only know that I know nothing") over any of the optimistic hypotheses associated with nineteenth-century positivism.

Modern science also received a severe blow when humanity was horrified to find that its discoveries could be used for self-destructive purposes and inflict unprecedented damage. The dropping of two atomic bombs on Hiroshima and Nagasaki in August 1945 destroyed the idyllic dream of modern science for the few who still had blind faith in it. A feeling that science should be controlled and regulated also increased, just as with the state after Nazism and the capitalist economy after the 1929 crash. This feeling affected science, as well as technology. Knowledge of dramatic events, catastrophes such as the San Francisco earthquake (1906) and sinking of the Titanic (1912), quickly spread thanks to the massive expansion of the press and new photographic and cinematographic technologies. Experience of nature's extraordinary force contributed to the conviction that technological development must respect natural forces more. Thus, the first environmental movements emerged, which have been very influential since then and which have brought back many people's desire for direct contact with nature in reaction to the monotony of cement, concrete, steel, glass, engine noise, pollution and, ultimately, the overcrowding of urban life.

From a political perspective, global war shook the foundations of the peaceful security on which the modern state was built. International stability, precariously underpinned in previous periods by balancing out the great powers, was destroyed and, what was worse, a desire for revenge emerged in the years following the Treaty of Versailles in 1919. While some naïvely believed that all accounts had been settled, the worst was yet to come. England and France were satisfied with victory, but Germany continued to lick its wounds amid the chaos of the Weimar Republic, which was an alternative to radical communism, but proved itself unable to stop Nazism. The disintegration of the enormous, multicultural, and multiethnic Austro-Hungarian and Turkish empires led to enormous instability along their previous territories, from Central Europe to the Middle East.

Instability and political unrest grew with the outbreak of the Russian Revolution in October 1917. Russia abandoned the Great War to face its own devastating civil war from which a totalitarian political regime emerged, underpinned by the radical application of communist ideology. Moreover, the Russian Revolution took the same course as the French Revolution a century and a half earlier—just as Napoleon built an empire to expand the republican values that emerged from the revolution, Russia began empire building to expand communist values all over the world through the Union of Soviet Socialist Republics (USSR). Thus, three enormously powerful ideologies converged with international communism, Russian nationalism, and Soviet imperialism. Russia not only threatened to destabilize the international order again, it also created tremendous anxiety in those convinced of the liberal system's supremacy.

The Wall Street Crash of 1929, the first economic crisis with global effects, further intensified Europe's political fragmentation into irreconcilable ideological and nationalist factions. If the Great War was the first global war, the crisis of

1929 was the first global economic crisis. After the *Roaring Twenties*, the United States and Europe entered a critical period, known as the Great Depression. Some of liberal capitalism's profound contradictions were then dramatically revealed. The left's protests against liberal capitalism in the 1930s, promoted largely by international communism, assumed different labels, such as radicalism in the United States, trade unionism in Britain, and anarchism in continental Europe. They managed, for the first time, to unite heterogeneous groups made up of intellectuals, artists, students, and workers.

These two political and economic global cataclysms powerfully reflect the dimensions of this crisis, revealing the state and capitalism as less than the perfect creatures their founders had foreseen. While the Great War questioned the state model, whose authoritarian tendencies had grown into the monster of totalitarianism, the 1929 crash promoted a review of the capitalist system as it had been designed and practiced since the dawn of modernity.

The financial dimensions of the crisis brought about the need to minimally regulate the capital market. New Keynesian theories, based on greater state intervention in the economy and increased control of investment markets, did not question the capitalist system in its entirety, but they alerted society to the damages of its complete deregulation. Blind faith in market laws, which the Austrian school under Friedrich von Hayek had promoted at the beginning of the century, was obliterated, prompting moderate financial regulation standards, interest rate controls, review of public debt, and greater budget planning. The fruits of this new economic policy were the *New Deal* promoted by Franklin D. Roosevelt in the United States in the 1930s, and the spreading of Keynesian doctrines, social democracy, and the planned economies in Europe after 1945.

Paradoxically, reconsidering modernity on its artistic, philosophical, scientific, political, and economic fronts did not lead to increased spirituality. In an apparently anachronistic phenomenon, in the first decades of the twentieth century, modernism infiltrated the Catholic Church, and some of its priests and theologians postulated that the Church should adapt to the spirit of the times. Curiously, many ecclesiastics were fascinated by the modern values that the West was beginning to reject. This ecclesial modernism promoted a reform from within the Church (not from the outside, like the Protestant Reformation), threatening to demolish the Church's ancient, but effective, structure. Pope Pius X's determination helped overcome this crisis, but modernism forcefully re-emerged during the mid-twentieth century, especially among a part of the hierarchy and clergy that journalists coined as 'progressive' in an ill-advised application of a political-ideological category to a spiritual reality. The crisis of modernity led the Second Vatican Council (1962–1965) to seriously consider the Church's necessary dialogue with contemporary ideas, which was especially reflected in the text *Gaudium et Spes* (1965). But the Church did not ultimately compromise with radical modernist currents that tried to turn it into a simple association of people, de-sacralize the sacraments, reduce the priesthood to merely representative and ceremonial functions, abandon spiritual life, and relegate Church governance to a mere balance of power.

All these currents and events, that emerged in the interwar period, conveyed in the previous pages, also leave no doubt about the reconsideration of modernity's values, if not their open and radical questioning. Irrationalism extraordinarily expressed the unrest of the moment, advocating the exact opposite of modernity. The well-known avant-garde movements, so characteristic of the interwar period, reflected fading confidence in conventional modern values. French Dadaism in the 1920s completely discredited the hegemonic power of the nineteenth century's culture and system. The hippies of the 1960s promoted ironic performances to demonstrate the anachronism of the old culture and to spread new countercultural tendencies and values. Replacing intellectuals and politicians, avant-garde artists and writers became the true representatives of the new culture. From the 1920s onward, the artistic and literary world led the appropriately expressed 'cultural vanguard.'

Salvador Dalí's and Luis Buñuel's Spanish surrealism adopted overtly irrational, or at least nonrational, forms. Their intention was clearly subversive, as interpretation became subject to the art critic and spectator's free reading. Expressionism in painting connected with existentialist philosophical positions, and few pieces better reflect the unease of the moment than Vincent van Gogh's disruptive representations, Edvard Munch's *The Scream*, Odilon Redon's surrealist faces, Fritz Lang's Expressionism films, and Gustav Klimt's symbolic paintings. They also reflect a marked tendency during those years to explore the limits between the conscious and the subconscious, which Sigmund Freud systematized in his theory of psychoanalysis.

Cubism, the pioneering work of Georges Braque and Pablo Picasso, explicitly reflected the reaction against the univocal reading of reality for which modern thinkers, scientists, and artists advocated. By representing the same figure from the front, side, and back, the image reflected the idea of the many existing points of view, which generated greater knowledge of reality but also fostered postmodern skepticism and relativism. The distortion of images, or the abandonment of traditional painting canons, convinced the viewer of the impossibility of representing reality with the objectivity and self-sufficiency that modern scientists such as Newton, artists such as Velázquez, thinkers such as Descartes, and social scientists such as Comte intended. Many artists of the moment followed this abstract or non-figurative movement, giving rise to new genres, like Joan Miró's huge and harmonic geometric shapes. Architecture also captured these irrational tendencies. Architecture easily adopts new trends, because it is a profession that blends art, design, technology, and functionality. Paradoxically, interwar architecture was labeled rationalist because it aligned squarely with new urban forms found in the great American cities, whose gigantic skyscrapers expressively voiced to the world that modernity would not disappear so easily. Projects from Walter Gropius, within the German Bauhaus School, and from other famous architects, such as Le Corbusier and Alvar Aalto, assumed avant-garde tendencies with geometric shapes, but rationally used new materials (cement, wrought iron) for structural purposes, as well as for ornamental embellishments. For this reason, they are also called functionalists.

It did not occur to functionalist architects to hide these materials; they preferred to structurally incorporate them. In this way, pioneers in New York and Chicago, like German immigrants Walter Gropius and Ludwig Mies van der Rohe respectively, left their mark. They followed the example of the Greeks, who succeeded in making beautiful columns, elements whose functional purpose is simply structural, or that of the Gothic architects, who designed flying buttresses to relieve pressure on the walls and thus achieved greater interior luminosity, gifting gothic buildings with a beauty that still stuns today. Another branch of contemporary architecture went in another direction, toward nature, thus earning the name organicist. Its most representative exponent was Frank Lloyd Wright. His *Fallingwater* house, for example, continues to impress with the extraordinary way it mimics the surrounding landscape.

The proliferation of such diverse and complex pictorial and architectural tendencies also led to the appearance of influential art critics. The Warburg Institute, founded in the 1920s in Germany, soon emerged as a leading laboratory of artistic analysis with social implications. Its founder, Aby Warburg, an independent scholar from Hamburg, was fascinated by classical antiquity and the way in which its forms and values were transmitted in latter periods. In addition to a still operational extraordinary library at the Institute's headquarters in London (where the Institute found accommodation after the expansion of Nazism), Warburg left for posterity an interdisciplinary humanistic method based on integrated interpretation of images that draws from disciplines as apparently disparate as theology, philosophy, history, mathematics, and anthropology. Others within this school marked a crucial turning point in their respective disciplines. Erwin Panofsky devised a brilliant system for interpreting non-figurative art, known as the iconological method. Ernst Cassirer developed criticism of the modern state, associating it with the category of myth, whose reading is still illuminating. The medievalist Percy Schramm combined interpretation of events, symbols, and representations in his analyses of medieval Europe's power dynamics. Ernst Gombrich published *The Story of Art*, which has sold millions of copies and that completely transformed art criticism, promoting it to the interpretive and hermeneutic realm rather than just the descriptive or cataloging level. Gombrich's original contribution stems from his study of experimental psychology and collaboration with psychologists such as Richard Gregory. He introduced the ideas of *schema*, which designate reality by force of convention and through which the artist begins her own process of trial and error.

Literature was one of the clearer manifestations of the beginning twentieth-century crisis of modernity. Marcel Proust's *In Search of Lost Time*, James Joyce's *Ulysses*, and Virginia Woolf's *Mrs. Dalloway* replaced structured and lineal modern narration with stream of consciousness and decentralization of modernist accounts. Literature also expanded the nihilism of Samuel Beckett and Eugene Ionesco, and the existentialism of Albert Camus and Frank Kafka's *The Metamorphosis*. Gloomy diagnoses also influenced the way historians approached the past, as evidenced by Oswald Spengler's voluminous work, *The Decline of the West*, which garnered much attention in the 1920s in Germany, as well as in all the English-speaking countries where it was published. Spengler popularized an organicist argument of history, which lingered into the post-war period with other famous historians such as Arnold J. Toynbee and his monumental *A Study of History*. All civilizations behave as living beings, that is, they have an organic cycle from their birth and adolescence to youth, maturity, and decadence, and these historians saw the West as beginning to suffer from the ailments associated with aging. Spengler concluded that only a charismatic leader could save it, clearly contributing to the rise of Nazism. Metaphors of a civilization as a living being is a dangerous one, as Johan Huizinga, who once took it seriously, came to think later.

Existentialism and personalism were more proactive than iconoclastic irrationalisms, nihilisms, and vanguardisms. Concerned with the incessant dehumanization of modern man, they proposed a return to a philosophy centered on the person. Existentialism was previously forged with authors like Søren Kierkegaard, Gabriel Marcel, and Miguel de Unamuno, and then blended with Catholic (Gabriel Marcel and Jean Daniélou) and Protestant theology (Karl Barth) in the interwar period. Existentialism also houses two of the twentieth century's most influential philosophers such as Martin Heidegger, disciple of Edmund Husserl. They are best known for pioneering phenomenology and hermeneutics, respectively, but their rejection of rationalism and exploration of the scope of the will also places them in the existentialist orbit, which Jean-Paul Sartre skillfully latched onto during the post-war period.

Emmanuel Mounier and Romano Guardini developed personalism, among the few intellectual interwar trends that have survived to the present day. Their arguments resurfaced in the twentieth century with intellectuals like Emmanuel Lévinas, Karol Wojtyla, and Martin Buber, who begin with a vision of the person as singular, unique, and unrepeatable, and then reflect on the applications thereof. Personalism is a direct reaction to the immense and dehumanizing brutality of Nazism, and it is no coincidence that the Nazi regime persecuted some of its most representative proponents. Multidisciplinary scholars such as Étienne Gilson, Henri de Lubac, and Hans Urs von Balthasar were the last generation of theologians who built a solid dialogue with the humanities and general intellectual tendencies. Joseph Ratzinger's most recent contributions are the last reverberation of this rich Central European theological tradition.

A reconsideration of modernity also appears in dystopian novels, such as Robert H. Benson's *Lord of the World*, Aldous Huxley's *Brave New World*, or Georges Orwell's *1984*. These fictions come closer to reality than perhaps even their authors could have foreseen, with some predictions literally becoming part of everyday life. In his novel, Orwell created an omnipresent being called Big Brother that controls citizens' every move. What he conceived of as alienating has now become a pastime for millions of viewers across the globe. Orwell probably did not expect that we would develop the technology so quickly and that televised amusement would one day become a real threat to privacy. Set in the future, these texts foretold a world in which modern values (especially absolute confidence in reason, science, progress, mechanization, and technology) are taken to the highest degree; they thus describe a dehumanized world in which pleasure is people's only motivation at the expense of freedom, autonomy, and even conscience.

These dystopias prefigured the future movements of posthumanism or transhumanism. Julian Huxley, brother to Aldous, first explored the concept of transhumanism, meaning the tendency in certain areas of contemporary science toward overcoming human beings' somatic and intellectual limitations through control and technological design of their very biological disposition. Little by little, the discipline of human genetic engineering is emerging, which aims to influence our genetic configuration and design a new, immortal human free from imperfections. This has been depicted in futuristic films such as *Gattaca* (1997).

These futuristic tendencies, already a present reality, also foster the technology that has begun building artificial intelligence, that is, machines that mimic human intelligence. Thus, dystopian interwar authors also predicted a theme relevant to contemporary debate, that is, the relationship between humans and machines, and the eventual rebellion of the machines they create. Stanley Kubrick and Ridley Scott pioneered reflection on the autonomy of machines in masterful science fiction films: *2001: A Space Odyssey* (1968) and *Blade Runner* (1982), with the respective rebellion of the computer *Hall 9000* and the artificial humans called *replicants*. These geniuses showed, once again, that cinema may foster reflection on important human and ethical issues. Along with visionary film directors, poets and artists also have had much to say about a debate that scientists seem to monopolize. As Victor Hugo aptly expressed, "What drives and drags the world are not machines, but ideas."

In scholarship, linguistics had grown traditionally under the umbrella of philology, but became independent from it at this time thanks to the pioneering task of Roman Jakobson and Leonard Bloomfield, among others. The development of a new philosophy of language unleashed 1970s postmodernism, influencing diverse social science and history fields. The Swiss Ferdinand de Saussure's *Course in General Linguistics*, originally published in 1916, was taken up with enthusiasm in the 1960s. His approach was very much nominalist, that is, it started from the reality that the way in which words appear (the *signifier*) does not necessarily reflect a universal meaning—the *signified*. Words do not reflect essential realities that are applicable to universal ideas, but rather are an arbitrary means for understanding one another. Richard Rorty and Hayden White, who introduced the *linguistic turn* in philosophy and history, respectively, later took up this divorce between signifier and signified. In addition, Wittgenstein developed the philosophy of language in England, further driving relativistic tendencies in the humanities and social sciences, starting from the priority of language over reality in everything that concerns the process of knowledge.

Few intellectual phenomena from the interwar period so clearly reflect its uneasiness as psychoanalysis, a new discipline that profoundly impacted later decades, especially the sexual liberation movements of the 1960s. Sigmund Freud's work clearly manifests this period's anxiety. In 1929, he published *Civilization and Its Discontents*, arguing that society evolves based on the need to control individuals' rebellious, aggressive, and sexual instincts. Civilization, repression, and neurosis are thus intimately interconnected because the more the former progresses the more repression is needed, which further increases the latter. Dissatisfaction with said reality is manifested in escapism through sex, alcohol, or drugs. Freud was a rationalist who studied the irrational but hoped that the more rational ego would overcome the less rational.

Freud did not offer a simple compendium for curing these psychological illnesses, but rather intended to highlight the real problem of selfishness. His psychological reductionism recalled Marx's reductionism, for which violence is the engine of historical change, as well as Nietzsche's reductionism, for which the will to power is man's main motivating force. These three authors' influence on posterity is a visible sign that postmodernity or, perhaps better said, the late modernity through which we are still living, has not yet come up with the right recipe. Nietzsche, Marx, and Freud failed to present true alternatives, since their proposals all came to dead ends. They certainly emphasize three realities that are typical of the human condition (attraction to power, the seduction of wealth, and the enjoyment of pleasure), but these alternatives proved insufficient based on their reductionism: not everything can be reduced to a fascination with power, to the cultivation of greed or to the satisfaction of sexual impulses. No one can deny the importance of these authors' legacy, but society now needs ideas to rise above, rather than fatalistic diagnoses that further inter society in its own anguish.

The intellectual, literary, and artistic manifestations that dramatically expressed society's malaise sufficiently illustrate the so-called crisis of modernity. Many authors group these early twentieth-century European cultural manifestations into a single current, namely modernism. Others, especially those from Spanish-speaking countries, tend to recognize this concept in the work of the brilliant Catalan architect Antoni Gaudí, in French *Art Nouveau*, in German *Jugendstil*, and in England's Modern Style. But modernism was actually a global movement in direct rebellion against the Victorian world's enormous degree of self-sufficiency in the second half of the nineteenth century. The philosophical, artistic, and literary manifestations found herein help summarize this cultural period into three predominate values, characterized accordingly as anti-modern, anti-historicist, and anti-Enlightenment.

In the first place, modernism is, paradoxically, an anti-modern movement since it reacts against the previous century's self-sufficient and universalistic tendencies, with its blind faith in progress, reason, and evolution. Modernism conforms to the realism of microsystems and micro-narratives rather than macro-narratives or universal explanations. It had a deep influence in literature, history, art, and science. In the field of literature, early twentieth-century micro-narratives and decentered accounts of the everyday life, such as Joyce's *Ulysses*, Wolff's *Mrs. Dalloway*, and Proust's *In Search of Lost Time*, overtook the great nineteenth-century romantic epics, such as Walter Scott's *Ivanhoe* and Victor Hugo's *Les Misérables*, Russian realistic novels such as Fyodor Dostoyevsky's *Brothers Karamazov*, and British Victorian dramas such as Charles Dickens' *Oliver Twist*. History, for its part, reacted to nineteenth-century French romanticism's linear narrative storiessuch as Jules Michelet's *The History of the French Revolution*, to German scientific historicism found by Leopold von Ranke, and to Charles Seignobos's French Positivist School method, finding an alternative in the impressionist approach. Johan Huizinga's famous work, *The Autumn of the Middle Ages*, perhaps best reflects this trend in line with its contemporary French pictorial impressionist style by using hundreds of impressions and historical details rather than touching on big global ideas. Huizinga also discusses big ideas as 'forms of thought.' In art, the styles prior to the avant-garde, such as Pointillism and Impressionism, had already clearly opted for detailed extremes with little dots and the blur of thick brushstrokes in reaction to the realistic confidence of previous periods characterized by the works of Velázquez and Caravaggio. Francisco de Goya's peculiar style of thick brushstrokes was, in this context, extraordinarily advanced for his time. There are many modernities, many styles coexisting at this time, which is something new, since brushstrokes are characteristic of late Titian, late Rembrandt, and late Turner, among others. But the French Impressionists went certainly further. And, finally, in science, interest in analyzing the smallest unit (the atom) increased in reaction to the more traditional field of analyzing the universe and infinity.

In the second place, modernism is anti-historicist with its violent reaction against nineteenth-century "neo" tendencies, Victorian triumphalism, and nostalgic romanticism. The present is what really matters and, in any case, we must contemplate the future, as dystopian experiments and futuristic artistic movements (both pictorial and architectural) showed—the *Art Decó* Chrysler Building in New York stands as one of its most iconic and durable examples. Modernist anti-historicism also had its counterpart in functionalism, which was manifested above all in rational architecture and in literary formalism: the object exists in itself, in terms of the freely assumed function it performs and it is not bound to received tradition. As a consequence of this anti-historicism, modernism reacted against all tradition and continuity. Artistic and literary styles were no longer valued based on their duration or permanence, and the opposite became the case in the spirit of the avant-garde. Modernists represent a relativist rebellion against the weight of tradition, while previous romantic and Victorian generations derived value from it.

Third, modernism is an anti-enlightenment movement, opting for the fractured, the fragmented, and the discordant in opposition to the Victorian era's harmony, order, and sense of proportion. This is reflected in the lines of artistic styles such as cubism, in its eloquently distorted figures, its attraction for the *ugly*, the grotesque, and the gothic, and its rejection of everything that supposes the imposition of a *canon*—whether theological, literary, or artistic. Opting for fragmentation, for the idea that reality is so complex that it requires a multifaceted point of view, led to the rejection of classic binary notions surrounding good–evil, man–woman, object–subject, high–low, center–margin, or tradition–innovation. This rejection planted the seed for the most influential post-war cultural trends, such as moral relativism, gender theories, the relativity of knowledge, social equality, respect for minorities, and detachment from tradition. New theories of relativity even confirmed this, questioning for the first time the binary notions of time–space and mass–energy.

All these trends show that *modernism*, beyond its elusive name, was a movement that combined hyper-modernity with anti-modernity. It is not surprising that from this point onward the notion of *post-modernism* and *post-modernity* began to spread. The former would be an artistic and cultural reaction to modernism and the latter a supposed new epoch, subsequent to modernity. Yet, all these intense artistic, philosophical, literary, and scientific innovations were abruptly cut short with the outbreak of World War II and would not recover—then with unusual force, with the force of an enormous decompressed spring—until the 1960s and the outbreak of the cultural revolutions and liberations.

CHAPTER 17

LIBERATIONS

The (anti-modern) modernist tendencies and the feeling of deep crisis, combined with the devastating material consequences of the war, grew in the West when World War II finished in 1945. The horrors of the war also increased the desire that they should not be repeated. The Universal Declaration of Human Rights in 1948, promoted by the United Nations, allowed for a global expansion of Western values, this time in the form of the struggle for universal civil rights – this universalist idea has sometimes been criticized in Asia and Africa as an attempt to impose Western values. The Declaration included and promoted the main values spread by Western civilization from its origins. It confirmed that the West still had much to contribute to the whole world, because its strongest convictions such as freedom, equality, universality of rights, and free speech and thought continued to set the agenda for the struggle for civil rights. In this struggle, there was still much to be done. But the foundations were established by that Declaration and, most important, by the incorruptible and courageous struggle of many of those who risked their lives for their defense in the following decades, in their struggles for racial and gender liberations. This chapter examines how these battles, so crucial to the development of a stable society, have developed from that time to the present.

The fight for liberation was compatible with the certainty that for the first time from the Axial Shift of the twelfth century, Europe became aware that it was no longer the center of the world. Former world powers, especially France and England, commenced the decadent empire syndrome, which Spain and Portugal had already been suffering for centuries. The new superpowers, the United States and the Soviet Union, came from outside Europe for the first time since late Antiquity. Historians coined the term *Cold War* to describe the dispute between Americans and Soviets and tension was high since these two new superpowers were driven not only by a struggle for hegemony but also by imperialist aspirations for their opposing ideologies—democratic liberal-capitalist and authoritarian communist, respectively. Nationalism and ideologies came together, once again, to legitimate imperialism's destructive tendencies. If European states buried themselves in religion during the great seventeenth-century conflict and in nationalism during World War I, the Cold War combined nationalism and ideology, with the religious-secular burden these forces bring with them.

The new geopolitics represented a clash of civilizations between the Slave and Western European tradition—a resonance of that other breaking between the Latin-West and Greek-East, as discussed in Chapter 5 regarding the clash of late-Antiquity civilizations. This new confrontation was therefore not as new as it seemed. The tectonic movements of the past often remain hidden, until they resurface. The long-term perspective shown in this book allows us to glimpse some ethnic and religious continuities that explain many things. The old division propitiated by Constantine in the fourth century, between the West and the East of the Empire, between Rome and Constantinople, between the heirs of the Latin and Hellenistic culture, between the Carolingian and Byzantine empires, between Catholicism and Orthodoxy, between Latins and Slavs, was now exploding again in all its rawness.

In military terms, the Cold War globalized armed conflict. Direct confrontation between the two superpowers would have clearly meant an atomic cataclysm and so others, located on the margins, suffered the consequences of that confrontation. The internationalization of the Cold War was a tragic effect of global acceleration. This tension was then projected toward various developing countries in Asia, Latin America, and Africa, where this tension rained and then poured on three major fronts. First, open declarations of war in which the dynamics of the Cold War blended with civil wars, as seen in Korea (1951–1953), Vietnam (1959–1975), and its derivations in Laos and Cambodia. Second, the subversive struggle of guerrillas and terrorist groups of Marxist ideology intensified in many Latin American countries, most of them intending to overthrow the military dictatorships in power and, at least, to destabilize the whole system. Movements such as the FARC in Colombia and Shining Path (*Sendero Luminoso*) in Peru or individuals such as Che Guevara and Fidel Castro in Cuba became icons of liberation in the Western world, yet their admirers often ignored the complex circumstances and consequences these movements had for the civilian population. Third, independence movements in former colonies exploded—more or less violently—throughout the world, affecting both newly independent countries and the former colonizers themselves. India and Algeria's independence, for example, had a huge impact on domestic politics in England and France.

This tense militarized panorama defined the bewilderment of the post-war period and delayed the release of cultural tensions until the 1960s, which, when they finally rose to the surface, did so with great force. All the energy accumulated in the interwar period seemed to reach the surface, as if driven by an enormous spring that released the tension from the two World Wars all at once. It is thus understandable that manifestations of cultural revolution first emerged in the United States, where the war had not been as materially destructive.

In the early 1960s, dissent, agitation, rebellion, and protest gradually shook the West as a whole and, with it, the nascent global world. Unlike at other times, these protests were not just political or social, that is, they did not just aim to demolish the authority of despotic governments or blow up the privileges of established social elites. Rather, they involved a rebellion of much greater scope against all received tradition and established authority, as well as the radicalization of the generational confrontation between parents and children. Indeed, one of the best ways to describe this movement is with the word *contestation* (in its original French). This movement, and the main topic of this chapter, is known as the "cultural liberation" of the 1960s. For the first time in history, revolution became eminently cultural, thus generating far more lasting and global effects than previous political, economic, or ideological previously experienced in Europe.

Yet, more relevant for the West, when things seemed more complicated, this circumstance allowed the West to universally expand many of its specific values—especially those related to freedom and equality—that it had treasured throughout history, and whose attainment had cost it blood, sweat, and tears. The main cultural liberation movements, raised from the 1960s, have had long-lasting effects in society, and included the civil rights movements of racial (notably the African American struggle), intellectual (particularly through student revolts of Berkeley and Paris), national-postcolonial (based mainly in new countries that emerged from decolonization), and gender equality. These four fronts of the battle for civil rights were supported by countercultural movements and communist subversion, and legitimated by new areas of academic fields such as the cultural, postcolonial, and gender studies. In what follows, I will define and examine these civil movements and track their effects to date.

The civil rights movement first and very visibly manifested itself in the United States' process of racial equality. The unsettling history of black slavery began with European ships headed for the Atlantic and eventually the United States. There, in the South, huge cotton plantations with extraordinary productive demand used enslaved Africans as economic property.

A free black population began to increase during the nineteenth century, either based on an owner's decision to free his slaves or on the enslaved buying their own freedom. But they did not have the mentality of natives struggling to emancipate themselves from a colonial power through independence because, after a few generations in the country, they already felt more North American than African. And yet, once liberated, they were not considered by their compatriots as citizens with full rights either. They were more like second-class citizens.

Racism aggravated the situation, for in many cases it was not only the lack of their rights, but also a visceral, irrational, and anti-Christian hatred. To what extent the racists actually believed the theories that considered blacks to be 'subhuman' or 'intellectually inferior' we do not know, although it is certainly hard to believe. Attitudes varied greatly. Many white Americans resisted considering them citizens with full rights and the racism of organizations like the Ku Klux Klan intensified the situation by actually acting on visceral, irrational, and anti-Christian hatred. It was rather a mixture of lack of culture, insensitivity, economic interests, and inherited family and social traditions. Jews were also persecuted to death in many Mediterranean cities during the Middle Ages, but there it was more openly stated that the motive for the attacks on their neighborhoods was purely economic. Moreover, seen from the perspective of the blacks, if they wanted to assimilate into the white culture, they had to detach themselves from their own traditions and heritage: this is why they tended to conglomerate all in the same neighborhoods, where they could develop their own folklore, their devotions and religious practices, and their traditions. The difficulty of assimilation was therefore twofold.

In the mid-nineteenth century, Catholic and Protestant reformers and churchmen began the abolitionist movement. The abolitionists agreed that slavery should disappear on moral grounds. But they could not agree on the role of blacks in the new slave-free society. Only some of them were willing to wholeheartedly support the black leaders who demanded full citizenship with full rights.

The American Civil War, also known as the War of Secession (1861–1865), was spurred on by abolitionism and the North's victory ended slavery. However, problems of black poverty, marginalization, and social exclusion culminated in segregation laws, enforcing conditions for black Americans not all that superior to slavery. The twentieth century brought with it the first ray of hope for improving this situation given renewed interest in egalitarianism on the part of the new American left, who were mostly reformists, progressives, and radicals. Massive immigration to Northeastern urban centers stifled attempts to organize a rational structure for black workers, whose labor skills and cultural preparation were far below that of whites given years of educational and social segregation. Blacks were thus systematically placed in difficult, underpaid positions with no possibility of promotion. For a moment, it seemed that labor integration, promoted by intellectuals such as Booker T. Washington or W.E.B. DuBois, appeared to be a viable path. But the massive black immigration to the large urban centers of the Northeast stifled any attempt to organize a rational structure for the work of blacks, whose labor and cultural preparation did not have the minimum level to compete with whites, and were thus systematically sent to the hardest jobs and without the possibility of promotion. During the interwar period there was rather an enormous tension, which was released from time to time with terrible outbursts of violence in the ghettos between whites and blacks.

By 1940, advances focused on legal battles, where success or failure did not just depend on what the masses thought, but rather on a supposedly external and neutral force, the courts. Though neutrality did not exactly play out, during those years, activists (among them white reformists and clergymen who joined this struggle for moral reasons) did manage to lay the foundations of the civil rights movement that exploded in the following decades. They also managed to overturn the legal doctrine of 'separate, but equal,' winning an important Supreme Court case that allowed black students to study at previously all-white schools and universities. In the 1950s, all these internal experiences were joined by the experiences coming from the processes of emancipation and independence resulting from African decolonization.

The claims seemed to be making moderate progress when a seamstress named Rosa Parks took a dignified and courageous stand. On December 1, 1955, she got on a crowded bus after leaving work in Cleveland and refused to give up her seat to a white person, despite the driver's request (Figure 17.1). Parks was arrested, but her symbolic gesture decisively contributed to the beginning of the civil rights movement that ended legal racial discrimination. Parks did not originate the idea of protesting segregation with a bus sit-in, as it was preceded in the previous decade by Bayard Rustin, Irene Morgan, Lillie Mae Bradford, and Sarah Louise Keys. But his gesture, unlike the previous equally dignified and brave ones, achieved great notoriety.

History shows that sometimes a heroic demonstration by a brave individual is enough to ignite the fuse of a true revolution in favor of human rights. All this is thanks to some heroic gestures, although whoever performs them never knows for sure if they will have any visible effect or not. In this case, it did. Martin Luther King, then a 27-year-old Baptist pastor who had studied theology in Boston, ably orchestrated a campaign for Park's liberation.

FIGURE 17.1 View of the aisle of a restored 1959 city bus. Just like the bus Rosa Parks made it stop with her dignified and courageous gesture. © Shutterstock.

A year later, a Federal District Court ruled that the segregation of municipal buses was illegal, a ruling that the Supreme Court later upheld. Not only had a battle been won, but this victory also confirmed the movement's strategy of fighting from a moderate, nonviolent stance, and of focusing on cases against humiliating discrimination.

The racial liberation movement merged at the March on Washington in August 1963, where the activist Martin Luther King gave his famous "I have a dream" speech in favor of the equality between blacks and whites. Years later, watching that March on YouTube is enough to confirm just how tense that moment was, as well as Martin Luther King's brilliance and knowledge that he was directing a historic moment. He not only articulated African Americans' long-accumulated impatience and indignation, but also knew how to express it in terms that people could understand and how to find the way to make possible the protest. He convinced the audience, and generations to come, that restraint is the best method of protest, incorporating into the civil rights movement the principle of nonviolence that Gandhi had applied in India, as well as the Christian doctrine of love for one's enemy. He was persuaded that a patient and dignified protest would awaken the conscience of the nation, fueled by a context in which the media were acting more feely than in the past. This strategy continued with small acts of defiance against discriminatory practices, like sit-ins at bars that would only serve white people or organizing interstate bus trips with white and black passengers. Since these discriminatory practices no longer had any legal basis after all the court rulings the movement had won, the criminal proceedings that followed their protests were easily won.

However, despite the progress made, the gap between the laws passed against discrimination and the reality of discriminatory social and administrative practices only increased. People became exasperated and Martin Luther King's moderate strategies no longer seemed enough to many. Marcus Garvey's separatist ideology and Black Nationalism, which he had militantly advocated for forty years earlier, were thus revived. New radical militants, led by Malcolm X, were mainly Muslims and they believed that whites were a 'collective demon' who must be removed from the face of the earth, a stark alternative to Martin Luther King's Christian 'love thy enemy' approach. The eclectic theology of these new militants had little to do with true Islam, although they skillfully manipulated its simplistic dualism, a strategy that continues today with the expansion of new Islamic fundamentalisms.

A phase of unrest arose, especially in urban ghettos in large cities. Riots broke out in New York on July 16, 1964, when a white policeman who was not on duty shot and killed a young African American man. History indeed repeats itself. Police brutality instigated almost all of the ensuing riots, whose participants were mainly young, unemployed African American males with nothing to lose. They did receive support from their elders, who encouraged young people and gave them refuge when fleeing the scene. This inter-generational collaboration originated in previous protest movements against colonial oppression, such as the Irish rebellion of 1916. In this phase of the struggle for liberation, racial interests—the black condition—prevailed over class interests, fostering a strong feeling of solidarity among blacks. This rioting phase, which began in 1964, culminated in the assassination of Martin Luther King in April 1968.

The struggle for racial equality of African Americans, as well as other ethnic groups, including Latinos and Asian Americans, continues to this day. Once legal rights were guaranteed, the struggle began to focus on the guarantee of civil rights, that is, recognition in practice of equality between whites and other North-American ethnic groups, especially in terms of education, professional opportunities, civic participation, and economic prospects. This struggle has gone down different paths, including violence (now nearly an everyday reality that usually springs from discriminatory police action) and dialogue. The West benefited from the struggle for racial equality in that it gained greater awareness of the importance of acknowledging all ethnic groups and their rights. Today, more than ever, this question remains relevant and lessons from the American civil rights movement still hold true, especially that a moderate approach based on dialogue usually has greater long-term benefits than violent repression.

Meanwhile, historians continue to struggle with the reality of how, once a people's dignity is attacked, the consequences of that attack go far beyond what even the original perpetrators could have imagined. When the wheel of gratuitous violence or unjust imposition begins to turn, it is very difficult to stop, and these processes can last for centuries. Herein, we have discussed the case of African Americans, but the same principle applies to all kinds of cultural impositions, military invasions, planned deportations, social segregation, and linguistic coercion. When not cut off at the root, these conflicts become endless and their solution seems impossible because the initial injustice provokes the oppressed party's desire for revenge, and so on. The only way to stop this cycle is for the more powerful party (who is always easily recognizable) to take the high road and rethink the conflict in terms of long-term strategy, and not simply of 'an eye for an eye' justice. History insists again and again that violence wielded to exterminate a people, a language, an ethnic minority, or a culture is always unjust. Reality ends up imposing itself in the medium term, and those who originally supported violence realize how unjust they were, whether explicitly or not. This brings us to one of the West's ethical foundations, summarized in the maxim that Plato attributed to Socrates: "It is better to suffer an injustice than to commit one."

The student revolt constitutes the second major liberation front of the 1960s. They basically aimed to gain equality in the rights of education. Although it wasn't necessarily the most central, it was hugely influential because of media coverage and, above all, because of the expressiveness of the icons that the student revolutions shot to fame in Berkeley (1964) and Paris (1968). University campuses were an apt breeding ground for students' discontent over their social struggles. In the mid-1960s, members of the beat generation and many other young people committed to social causes realized that they could not continue protesting on the sidelines, which provoked more amusement than respect from their elders. As a result, their initial claims achieved very little tangible success.

Although their celebratory and symbolic claims did not lose steam, militant and organized activism took shape. Many students at elite American universities and, later, at European ones, convinced themselves of the effectiveness of direct action for the achievement of social claims. The first clash took place at Berkeley under the slogan 'free speech' and the leadership of Mario Savio, who soon became a national celebrity. Students forced the resignation of two rectors in a row. With time, idealism waned, while ideology gained momentum. Protests turned excessively radical, if not openly violent, and went from airing university-related grievances to focusing on political partisanship. As a result, they lost popularity, and their struggle abated when the new governor of California, Ronald Reagan, decided to confront them by reducing the university's budget and increasing state officials' interference on campus.

The pioneering Berkeley movement spread to many American universities, especially the University of Columbia (New York), where students' demands merged with the civil rights movement. The student movement had an extraordinary social impact and continuous media coverage. Police force against unarmed students further generated empathy for student protests throughout society. Some protests ended in long strikes, which politicized university life by revealing who was for and against the movement among both teachers and students. You could not be neutral in that moving train.

The leaders of the May 3, 1968, revolt in Paris copied almost verbatim the student unrest on American campuses between 1964 and 1968. Some 500 students, who represented a variety of ideologies on the communism–anarchism spectrum, initiated protests in the central courtyard of the Sorbonne against the closure of the University of Paris's suburban Nanterre campus, where students had carried out demonstrations and riots. The police intervened forcefully to disperse students, but they reacted much more violently than expected, and the city was in chaos for weeks. Students began to protest based on the government's limited ability to adjust to and address the university's enrollment growth, as well as based on student leaders' ideological radicalization toward communism, anarcho-syndicalism, Marxism–Leninism, Trotskyism, and Maoism, which clashed with established authority. Protestors were largely inspired by intellectuals who gained attention in those years for their subversive discourse and political positioning, such as Jean-Paul Sartre and Herbert Marcuse. United in reaction against 'capitalist imperialism,' they were spurred on by the wars raging in Cuba and Vietnam, as well as in African and Asian countries that were gaining their independence from old European colonial powers.

Daniel Cohn-Bendit—Dani the Red—led this student insurrection. A student of sociology with a charismatic personality and political skill, he, together with other civil leaders, transformed a student protest into open social insurrection. Many students who attended the May 3 protest did so out of solidarity with their classmates, but once the riots began, they also became revolutionaries. Paris's revolutionary tradition became wholly recognizable in those bright young faces, who echoed the values (liberty, equality, fraternity) proclaimed in 1789 and 1848. Urban conflict intensified until May 10, the 'night of the barricades,' when students formed barricades with cobblestones and overturned cars.

A few days later, in a strategic move, workers' unions joined the revolutionary struggle and gave the student movement palpable social import. A national strike was called on May 13, followed by a massive demonstration of some 800,000 people led by revolutionary students, union leaders, and radical left-wing politicians, since at that socialist and communist moment, many parties were considered too contented and bourgeois. Two weeks later, students and workers gathered at the Charlety stadium in Paris, which signified the beginning of the end of the great revolt and revealed French revolutionaries' absolute incapacity to organize around a common project. On May 29, de Gaulle delivered a categorical speech announcing that, if necessary, he would take decisive measures to prevent the 'communist threat' from attacking France. This warning alarmed businessmen, middle class workers, and loyalists in general enough to mobilize a counterrevolution. The situation was normalized and De Gaulle won further political success in the June elections, obtaining a greater majority than ever. Revolutionary incidents continued into June, but the following academic years developed relatively normally. The student revolution appeared deflated, but, in the long run, May 1968 became a true turning point between old and new worlds in the Western outlook. The values associated with the protests, so characteristic of the 1960s, began to gain the upper hand. In fact, de Gaulle himself, despite having emerged victorious from the crisis, never fully recovered from that moment, and finally retired in 1969.

Many professors at Yale, Harvard, Princeton, and La Sorbonne, Arthur Schlesinger and William Langer among them, later wrote about the psychological impact of seemingly insignificant events, most of them related to traditional university formalities, that became signs of the end of the university as they knew it. Some of these signs of the times included increasingly informal dress on campus, less decorum when addressing professors, open hostility, rebellion, and a lack of courtesy and manners. Many of these professors retired early. After the 1960s, the university definitively changed, and not always for the worse. It became more democratic, somehow rediscovering its medieval roots and original definition given by Alfonso X the Wise, King of Castile at the end of the thirteenth century: "gathering among teachers and students." Both groups regained the ability to influence teaching and administrative decisions, and those with fewer resources gained greater access to a university education. This undoubtedly produced widespread growth that watered down some of the rigor of university life, and was also enormously positive for elevating a wide part of the population's cultural level.

The student movement generated a new spirit, which in turn led to a marked increase in generational differences, yet this crisis was undoubtedly necessary. Now that the waters have settled, the university should remember the idealistic spirit of those first revolutionaries, but shake off their political and ideological baggage. In this sense, universities are like religions: when they become politicized and take sides, they automatically lose their universal spirit, their identity, and their mission. De-politicization and de-ideologization are indispensable for both institutions to effectively carry out their functions— religion, the cultivation of the spirit, and the university, the cultivation of wisdom. Power and ideology are never compatible with genuine spirituality and an authentic search for knowledge and science.

The third front of the movement of civil rights had to do with national emancipation in the context of a galloping decolonization. This new process of liberation was inextricably linked to ideological Marxism. Not satisfied with confinement to authoritarian communist regimes around the world (from Russia to Cuba), Marxism also took on subtle intellectual forms, supplying many of the liberation processes in progress with an ideology. They included political processes, such as independence movements, social processes (clash between classes), racial processes (equality between races), student processes, and ecclesial processes (subversion on the part of ecclesiastics and religious members of the Catholic Church). With the efficacy of its confrontational rhetoric, simplistic dualism, and seductive earthly messianism, Marxism provided these movements with an ideology that proved a very effective weapon in the fight to get their demands heard. Revolutionary figures such as Che Guevara and intellectuals such as Antonio Gramsci were considered icons and heroes of a new struggle. Guevara was represented as the new Redeemer, his image deliberately looking like those popular images of Jesus Christ. The Marxist doctrine provided young revolutionaries with simple but effective strategies for confronting all authority (paternal, university, governmental, or ecclesiastical). All kinds of revolutionaries began to truly worship Marxism, applying it to realities that had little to do with conditions in the nascent, mid-nineteenth century, industrial societies on which Marx based his ideas.

However, communism soon revealed its flaws through the contradictions it engendered when put into practice. Many intellectuals in favor of Marxism questioned their own Communist ideals when they heard Nikita Khrushchev, the new President of the USSR, revealing the atrocities of the Stalin era, specially from his speech at the Twentieth Congress of the Communist Party of the Soviet Union in 1956. From then on, communist parties in Western Europe and intellectuals sympathetic to Marxism did not generally renounce their communist creed, but they became increasingly moderate or openly revisionist of its doctrine. Academics gave a cultural turn to their previous research, which had been based on economic determinism. Ideologues sought greater possibility in political, social, and economic reforms, for which socialism seemed more effective than communism. Thus, socialism often blended with post-war social democratic positions in countries that were beginning to regain their international influence, such as France, Germany, and England.

Khrushchev's airs of reform, although ephemeral, provoked dissent within the USSR and its satellite countries in Central Eastern Europe. The most striking acts of dissent included the 1956 Hungarian revolt, ultimately thwarted by Soviet tanks, and the 1968 Prague Spring, a period of political liberalization and popular protest whose dramatic conclusion clearly served as a reference point for Polish Solidarity led by Lech Wałęsa in 1979, which is commonly seen (along with a failed Afghanistan invasion in the same year) as the beginning of the end of the Soviet Empire.

The notion of intellectuals' moral vocation is deeply rooted in Russian society and collapse soon became apparent with the publication of openly critical novels, such as Vladimir Dudintsev's *Not by Bread Alone* (1956) and Alexander Solzhenitsyn's *One Day in the Life of Ivan Denisovich* (1962). During those years, literature became a moral device both in the Soviet Union and in the West, as Solzhenitsyn explained, "Literature that is not the air of its contemporary society, that dares not warn in time against threatening moral and social dangers, such literature does not deserve the name of literature – it is only a facade." Literature thus lost formal embellishment in favor of functional content which served to efficiently channel a certain sense of social vindication.

The struggle for civil rights, the counterculture movement, student protests, and the communist counterrevolution exemplify the upheaval that took place in the West in the 1960s, whose effects are still present in contemporary culture. However, none of them had such a prodigious effect on the alteration of traditional values as the struggle for women's rights and gender theory. This movement started out as a struggle for equal rights between men and women, in a way that paralleled the struggle for civil rights, decolonization processes, and student equality. During the first half of the twentieth century, activists won almost all the legal battles demanding women's rights, including the right to vote, laws favorable to motherhood, and working conditions free from exploitation. But in reality, in the 1960s, the law was not evenly enforced and the status quo continued to thrive, including discrimination against women at work, the incompatibility of childrearing with a professional career, sexist practices, patriarchal domination, and the glaring absence of women at executive levels both in business, university, and politics.

The first post-war American feminists modeled themselves after reformers from the turn of the century, including interwar British suffragettes like Emmeline Pankhurst (portrayed in the 2015 film *Suffragette*) and other leading figures like Virginia Woolf (see also the film *The Hours*, 2002), a standard bearer of British modernist literature and symbol of female emancipation. Post-war feminism, which centered on equality between the sexes, opened with the publication of Simone de Beauvoir's 1949 essay *The Second Sex*. Feminists began to emphasize gendered cultural differences based on the divergent roles—a cultural reality that may change over time—rather that the two biological sexes developed over the centuries over the complementarity between them based on corporeality or nature.

In their struggle, radical feminists assumed two basic theoretical tools, namely Marxism and gender theory. Marxism outfitted them with a dualistic rhetoric. This allowed them to pose the struggle in terms of radical confrontation, using when necessary the weapon of victimhood. Gender theory provided them with universal legitimization of their claims since the cultural and linguistic concept of *gender* emphasizes cultural differences between men and women and replaces the traditional concept of *sex*, which refers to more bodily differences that are immutable and given by nature. Accordingly, women's assigned roles in society (basically, motherhood, caring for children, and domestic chores) are not based on women's natural inclination, but simply on traditional patriarchal and sexist societies arbitrarily assigning them to women to free men from these tasks. Once the dialectical and theoretical foundations were established, the formula and strategy became clear—society simply needed re-education in alternative cultural values to change this reality.

At the same time, gender theories began to reconsider the relationship between men and women, traditionally based in the West on indissoluble marriage restricted to two opposite sexes. Many began to question the legitimacy of this traditional practice as the only alternative. A different interpretation from gender theory served to legitimize homosexual practices and manifestations. Civil authorities, through education, the film industry, literature, and the media, began to present homosexual relationships as equally conventional as heterosexual ones.

In fact, this movement housed very diverse claims. Psychoanalysis, which arose from the expansion of Freudian and Lacanian ideas, scientifically legitimized many of its ideas. Practices associated with free love, fostered by the beat generation, helped justify ideas that aggressively confronted the traditional, heterosexual, and stable family model, as well those surrounding LGBT demands. Expanding ideas related to sexual liberation promoted the popularization of the contraceptive pill. It shaped, once again (as we saw in the case of the spread of Protestantism after the invention of the printing press), the peculiar connection among the development of new ideas, the big corporations' economic interests, and the development of new technology. Contraceptive methods had certainly existed in all civilizations in the past, especially those with certain levels of material comfort. Yet after the 1960s, the contraceptive pill allowed women to deliberately regulate their fertility, leading to an extraordinary change in their collective mentality. They were no longer obliged to take a passive role when relating to men, which had previously originated practices related to courtly love and the implicit rules in chivalry starting from at least the Middle Ages. Roles were reversed.

Women's liberation movements focused on four demands. The emancipation of women, in the first place, required banishing the idea that a woman's natural role is to marry and have a family. As a result, young women began to leave home for the first time to live alone, single motherhood took on new proportions, and the model of a woman usually marrying an older man was challenged. Secondly, women demanded the same opportunities as men to study whatever they wanted and work in a related field, which required admitting women to universities as both teachers and students. Third, women wanted to secure enough economic autonomy so as not to solely depend on the men in their lives. Fourth, as a result of the above points, family and domestic life became the result of a free and deliberate decision, rather than an obligatory role and a conventional way of life.

The battle for civil rights which characterized the 1960s in these four fronts—racial, educational, postcolonial, and gender liberations—was accompanied by the emergence of the so-called counterculture, a phenomenon whose protagonists belonged to the generation born in and around the 1940s. Although many of them, especially in Europe, had suffered post-war hardships in their childhood, they generally did not experience the war themselves, and grew up in the midst of extraordinary material progress, which gave them access to university studies and later employment. All these experiences manifested themselves in a series of values and attitudes toward life, including a certain disregard for the future, which oscillated between naivety and optimism, a strong dose of idealism, which tended toward a rather unrealistic sense of existence, and a remarkable ability to bypass established norms of authority, especially those that referred to social conventions and religious traditions.

These attitudes began to establish codes of conduct that eventually and paradoxically have become nowadays politically correct, but that, in their origin, were based on the philosophy of disconformity, protest, and rebellion. New icons, mostly from film and media, appeared on the scene, such as James Dean, a young, restless, and aloof actor, who isolated himself from previous generations (*Rebel without a Cause*, 1955) to live out the present with all his energy. After his life was cut short in 1955, he became something of an idol and an icon for having enjoyed a passionate, but ephemeral existence—something similar to what would happen to other stars like Marilyn Monroe in 1962, Elvis Presley in 1977, and John Lennon in 1980. James Dean was a late Romantic figure, which brings us to highlight the Romantic movement and its legacy.

This generation especially tended toward a bohemian lifestyle. In the United States, they were called the *beat generation* because they were *beaten* by the inexorability of life and dedicated to seeking out all of life's positive aspects. Beat also referred to jazz, whose rhythm reminded them of their own time and whose improvisation perfectly matched their bohemian creed. Beat finally referenced beatitude, which was their goal in their spiritual search for infinite love inspired in some Oriental values of Nirvana. They seemed to have replaced modernity's aphorism of 'I think, therefore I am' with 'I feel, therefore I am,' seeking to experience sensations in the most radical and intense way possible, including with drugs and sex. The beats took on the label of 'marginalization' as a banner. Many identified themselves with the beatnik concept and took on the postulates of Jack Kerouac's 1957 novel-manifesto *On the Road*, which described a romantic and bohemian way of life inspired by drugs, poetry, and jazz.

The term beat was later used by the Beatles, changing the third letter of beetle. Although they were not exactly part of the beat generation, which expanded more in the United States than in Britain, the Beatles represented (or, perhaps, actively created) the spirit of the times like no other. Their musical production (1962–1970) also coincides with this period. In addition to the quality of their music, which magnetized three generations simultaneously, their songs were full of messages about universal fraternity and authentic love, and their untidy appearance instantly connected with the rebellious spirit of the time. In 1967, they were invited to star in the first globally televised program in history. For the occasion, they chose a song (*All You Need Is Love*) whose theme and lyrics defined the content of the historical moment as the way they dressed, in bright colors and psychedelic shapes, conveyed its aesthetic and form. The Beatles' songs reflected painful social realities that were emerging at that time. Their song *She Is Leaving Home* (1967) tells the story of a girl who unexpectedly leaves their parents who, baffled, mourn their loss, as the chorus sadly sings "we [her parents] gave her everything money could buy." Their vibrant *Lady Madonna* (1968) describes an exhausted woman facing the urgent problems of a single mother raising their children—a sociological fact more and more common at that time.

Many of this generation faced their futures with less worry than their parents, which led to a certain loosening of social conventions, one of this generation's central legacies. Shirt collars softened and social forms relaxed. Suffice it to compare photographs of young people gathered before and after the 1960s to verify that ties completely disappeared and that clothes became much more colorful or tacky, to use an expression typical of that time. This new subculture was based on love over hatred ('make love and not war'), although this outlook often degenerated into a kind of naivety that hindered them from understanding the complexities of the world and of existence. Pacifism often devolved into the abandonment of duties and rights. Rebellion degenerated into detachment, if not a disdain, for those in authority (parents, teachers, politicians), which led to much tension and, occasionally, violence. Yet, no one can deny that this generation had a capacity for idealism that has yet to meet its match. The idealism of the mentioned Beatles' *All You Need Is Love* (1967) contrasted with the realism of John Lennon's *Imagine* (1971), composed shortly after the dissolution of the group, which convey the radical difference between the idealism and optimism of the 1960s and the nostalgy and pessimism of the 1970s. The cold cement of the working-class neighborhoods replaced the housing warm wood that the Beatles had popularized with their *Norwegian Wood* in 1965. The weapons exceeded the flowers that Bernie Boston had captured in his *Flower Power* in 1967. Bob Dylan's and Joan Baez's denouncing songs surpassed the ideals of universal love spread by the Beatles and other pop music groups during the 1960s.

Seen in perspective, the fronts of the liberation that arose in the 1960s confirm that theories from the interwar period found their footing in the post-war period. Although its effects have been long term, the 1960s' idealistic effervescence was quite short lived. The 1970s were entirely different from the 1960s, just as, half a century earlier, the 1930s (with the Great Depression) contrasted starkly with the roaring twenties. The 1973 economic crisis was different from the financial crises of 1929 and 2007 because it revolved around the energy sector, although it was no less devastating. The upsurge of the Cold War, combined with the psychological and material effects of this crisis, gave rise to a panorama so grim that it caught the leaders of the previous decade's protests by surprise, leaving those that remained idealistic paralyzed, while those that jumped on the gentrification bandwagon became openly cynical and accommodating once in power. Political debate predominated over any cultural, intellectual or artistic debate.

The economic, psychological, and cultural depression of the 1970s was exemplified, in a way, in the reactivation of various particularly bloody war fronts like the Vietnam War, which later expanded to other countries in the region. The small, revolutionary groups inspired by Marxist ideology that many Latin American countries had seen develop became bloodthirsty guerrillas capable of paralyzing a whole country with terrorism. They began to break away from their naïve and idealistic beginnings and fell into senseless violence promoted by the Cold War's ideological factions and financed through the drug trade. The end of the 1970s coincided with two events that foretold huge geostrategic change in the form of confrontation between the Western and the Islamic worlds replacing the Cold War between the United States and the USSR. The first was the USSR's invasion of Afghanistan in 1978 and the second, Iran's Islamic Revolution in 1979 with Ayatollah Khomeini's proclamation of the United States as its mortal enemy. All the tension that the end of the Cold War disbanded was transferred to the vast Persian Gulf region, a very different ideological and religious scenario indeed.

The 1980s experienced the rise of a few leaders with greater stature and charisma than their predecessors, namely Mikhail Gorbachev in the USSR, Ronald Reagan in the United States, Helmut Kohl in Germany, and Margaret Thatcher in Britain. They succeeded in ending the Cold War, dismantling the Soviet Empire, and reinforcing a free-market liberal economy. However, the idea that the economy should run on its own without state intervention or special regulation of any kind undoubtedly contributed to the trivialization of financial activities in the West (the yuppies embodied this reality), which underpinned the great crisis of 2007. In Russia, sudden change from a planned to an ultraliberal economy also had disastrous consequences, stimulating enormous economic inequities, as well as the formation of small mafias backed by different people in positions of power, a situation that far from fading seems to be all the more a reality today. Finally, Pope John Paul II also appeared on the public stage, where he garnered enormous popularity and loyalty, enabling the reintegration of the Catholic Church into global intellectual debates and privileging its pastoral task, after the tormented years of the post-Council.

The long post-war period ended in 1989 with the fall of the Berlin Wall, the rupture of the Soviet Union starting in 1991, and the apparent resolution of the war, Cold War. At the gateway to a new millennium, a new period opened up. Here, communism has practically disappeared from the political and ideological map, like fascism after 1945. Yet both ideologies will find new forms of living and spreading, with the emerging of Left-wing and Right-wing Populisms and, crucially, *new* forms of communism have emerged. This new situation is more marked by the prevalence of a model of civilization than by the struggle for political and ideological hegemony in the mercurial confrontation of the since resolved Cold War.

CHAPTER 18

CHALLENGES

Since the 1980s, the West has been challenged on two major fronts, which have come to threaten its very existence and the possibility of its future: the geopolitical and the cultural fronts. This final chapter examines these two major challenges and how the West has responded to them.

At the end of the 1980s, liberalism lingered on a euphoric moment after having rid itself of fascist and communism challenges. Everyone seemed quite satisfied with the triumphs won on battlefields, as well as, and especially, with ideological supremacy and economic hegemony won at the universities and markets. In 1992, Francis Fukuyama, a young American political scientist, published a book with the enigmatic title *The End of History and the Last Man*. He argued that liberal democracy in politics and free-market capitalism in economics had achieved such a global consensus and sense of legitimacy that it would be hard for anything better to come along in the future, so that 'the end of history' might be proclaimed. Having survived a fight to the death against monarchical-autocracy, fascism, and communism, nothing seemed to overshadow these new Western systems and way of life. While previous forms of government and economic practice had serious irregularities that led to their ruin, liberal democracy and free-market capitalism were seen as free of internal contradictions. Thus, problems, tensions, imbalances, and destabilization could not be blamed on a defect in the system, but rather on incomplete or erroneous application of modern democracy's fundamental principles of freedom and equality. While its principles are infallible, its application may fail. Accordingly, historical experience seemed to show that improving upon the ideal of liberal democracy is impossible, and the ideological evolution of humanity was complete. It was assumed that an age of *Pax Romana* was beginning, and the *end of history* was declared, since things could not improve in the future once the perfect civilization was established.

Four years later, in 1996, another American political scientist, Samuel P. Huntington, published a book that also garnered much attention entitled *The Clash of Civilizations and the Remaking of World Order.* Huntington postulated that the world was not nearly as convinced of liberalism's hegemony and the earthly paradise as Fukuyama imagined. Global politics produces its own ghosts, and the clash between the four great civilizations that had emerged in the previous centuries, namely the West, Russia, a multifaceted cluster of Islamic countries, and China, seemed to be on the horizon. The readers of this book will understand that Huntington resurrected the three-pronged focus analyzed in Chapter 5—Justinian, Muhammad, and Charlemagne—with the additional inclusion of the Chinese civilization. But his reading is too homogenizing and hostile against the Islamic world. From a global point of view, the problem is surely the rise of extremists or fundamentalists (Muslim, Christian, Hindu) at the expense of moderates.

The concept of civilization is understood as the shape a people's overall lifestyle takes, which is materialized in a culture, a worldview, the development of customs and traditions, shared spiritual values, moral assumptions, and religious forms. This concept is thus more all-encompassing than those of religion, ideology, race, nation, gender, or language, and therefore is better suited to the contemporary process of globalization. The notion of a clash of civilizations seems to have replaced that of imperial expansion (typical of Antiquity and the Middle Ages), wars of religion (those the early modernity), national wars (from the nineteenth century to the First World War), and ideological wars (the interwar period up to the Cold War).

The last few decades have revealed that neither Fukuyama's *Pax Romana* scenario nor Huntington's clash of civilizations have fully materialized, but both were accurate in their diagnosis of two key elements in the contemporary world. On the one hand, Fukuyama guessed correctly that the values proper to modern Western civilization would continue to remain in our lives, at least in their original formulation. Thus, it does not seem that we can definitively identify the end of modernity, as some insist, since its essential values (the state in politics, capitalism in economics, trust in science and technology in culture, secularization in religion) are still fully in force. I tend rather to affirm that we are in the late-Modern age, analogous to the late-Antiquity period that lasted several centuries. Such a state is characterized by a radical questioning of centuries-long values, as well as by not having yet found viable alternatives to this questioning. Yet, on the other hand, nobody can deny the prophetic character of Huntington's diagnosis as the second millennium opened with the September 11 attacks and an ensuing confrontation between the West and

Islamic civilizations, whose ultimate scope remains indefinite, as well as those caused by the war in Ukraine. Huntington's prediction could actually be seen as the classic phenomenon of the self-fulfilling prophecy, as was described by Robert K. Merton, who started his essay quoting one of the fathers of American sociology, William I. Thomas: "if men describe situations as real, they are real in their consequences."

Historians agree that the fall of the Berlin Wall in 1989 was a fundamental turning point, a doorway to a new world, with the collapse of (the classic) communism and the end of the Cold War (Figure 18.1). Yet, our contemporary world still contains four imprints of communism and forms of Marxism: the anachronistic regimes in Cuba and North Korea; the Chinese communist regime, which is really just an external armor that hides its true commitment to robust (state-sanctioned) capitalism; different forms of Left-wings Populisms; and various forms of Marxist subversion that have taken shape in small groups that continue to use terrorism as a form of political action.

Because of its foreseeable effects into the future, the emergence of leftist populism is a post-communist reincarnation that deserves a more detailed analysis. At this point, it appears as a countercultural movement that has not yet passed the test of the realm of possibility, but that has already spread to some Latin American countries such as Venezuela, and even some Europeans ones, such as Greece, Italy, Spain, Holland, Denmark, and Poland. These populisms have not managed to innovate on Marxist rhetoric, since their argument is based on a struggle between the poor and the elite, just as communism was a struggle between the proletariat and capitalists. Nor is it really clear what the 'poor' really means in populist rhetoric and who decides who belongs to the poor and who is part of the ruling, rich elite? Today's society is too socially complex and the variety of jobs and classes too plural to classify all its components into just two categories.

FIGURE 18.1 Berlín Wall. © Shutterstock.

Populist movements remind and warn us that everything that glitters
in modern Western values is not gold—indeed, capitalism can become a savage,
dehumanized machine, and the state may turn into a formidable means for
domination and the promotion of destructive wars. Our great challenge in
the new millennium is not so much to diagnose and challenge these misfortunes,
which we have suffered for centuries, but rather to find viable alternatives.
Leftist populisms are relics of and grew out of modern Marxism, just as right-
wing populisms grew out of modern fascism. Neither can present itself as an
alternative to modernity since their ideological foundations and friend–enemy
rhetoric are unmistakably modern.

From the 1990s, the traditional East–West tensions, based on the ideological
confrontation between the liberal West and communism, slid into a North–
South confrontation based on a clash of civilizations between the West and
Islam. The first great division of the Mediterranean among the Greek-
Slavic-Byzantium, the Islam, and the Latin-West is still present nowadays.
This new tension West-Islam can clearly be traced back to imbalances
produced by decolonization, such as the artificial construction of various
borders in the Middle East, which mainly affected Iraq and Syria, as well
as the abrupt withdrawal of France and England from Saudi Arabia and
Egypt, leaving the future of such a historically complex area in the hands of
a young nation like the United States. Afghanistan was waging a new war of
independence against the Soviets. Iraq and Iran embarked on a war during
the 1980s that badly impoverished both. The presence of refugees coming
from different nations of the area destabilized Syria, Lebanon, and Jordan.
All the while, the United States, Russia, and other external forces regularly
interfered in these complex internal affairs.

This continuous state of war, further intensified by dependence on oil for
economic development, precluded even minimal economic stability in the
area and heightened the gap between a small, wealthy elite and a large mass
with few resources. The lack of educational opportunities, unemployment and
idleness, Western powers' meddling, and visceral hatred of the Jews became
a breeding ground for the emergence of Islamic fundamentalism. In addition,
this situation was exacerbated by Islam's lack of a unified religious authority,
the internal struggles between its different sects and, finally, the survival of the
idea of Holy War, which the West had abandoned many centuries earlier.
With a bit of perspective, it is easier to see how the events of September 2001
and a string of attacks in other European cities, such as Madrid, London, and
Paris, are not isolated events, but rather link in the same chain. The continuity
and intensity of this confrontation will depend on the ability of Islamic

fundamentalism to organize around pan-Islamic and multinational associations such as Al-Qaeda or Daesh. Yet, doubts remain as to whether Islamic union is possible, especially after the falling of the Daesh and the increasing division between the Arabs and the Persians, between the Sunni and the Shiite.

Islam emerged as the only entity capable of bringing together such diverse peoples in the form of a simple creed. The nomadic Arab tribes among which Islam first expanded had never been able to unite in a common project, among other things because of their nomadism. Other groups latched on in waves, like North Africans, Persians from Iran, and Turks from Asia Minor. The many missteps that Western powers have made in their attempts to intervene in the Middle East are due to a repeated inability to recognize that religion is at the base of the current clash of civilizations; however, much irrational violence camouflages it. In the end, international tension has not waned after the end of the Cold War, and the West is apparently losing strength in the face of the unstoppable growth of other civilizations such as China, the tension generated with Islam, and the reactivation of the Slavic front with the Russian invasion of Ukraine in 2022.

If the political and military tensions are even increasing, the economic situation has not much improved. The global economic and financial crisis of 2007 turned out to be as destructive as that of 1929, with the only difference being that the last eighty years of experience prodded economic authorities to initiate from the beginning regulatory mechanisms that mitigated its most devastating effects. But, unfortunately, neither of the two crises incited enough social vigilance to finally introduce forceful and effective reforms. In Europe, policies of cuts in public investments that aim at limiting public debt may be effective in the medium term, but they are not the solution to the problem and rather just mitigate the symptoms. Credit will continue to grow, and with it so will public debt, because large corporations conceive of debt as a business in itself, rather than as a temporary input designed to alleviate the effects of momentary imbalance or to encourage investment. The United States followed a different path during Obama's two terms and Trump's term. During those years, the federal government's debt levels spiraled out of control, further aided by a significant tax cut for high-income groups. This was made possible by the privileged position of the US economy (the dollar as the international currency) and investors' confidence that bond and treasury purchases would be backed by the Federal Reserve Board.

The real long-term problem at hand is that no viable alternative to the liberal capitalist system has been found. On the one hand, earlier possibilities have all ended in practice because they do not work. Slavery in Antiquity was untenable because, despite its productivity, it constituted an attack on human dignity and could not resist the consolidation of Christianity as the predominant religion in the West. The feudal system of the Middle Ages worked for some centuries, but the entangled personal dependence on which feudal-vassalage pacts were based ended up denigrating people and seriously compromising their liberty, when not suppressing it altogether. The capitalist system, which began to develop in the sixteenth century, introduced a contractual system, clearly superior to slavery or feudal dependence. However, its shortcomings have become clear over time, especially in terms of the progressive separation between the person, her work, and the capital that results from that work.

The modern state, unlike capitalism, has found a possible alternative in supranational organizations that emerged with globalization. However, the idealism and enthusiasm with which some of them were founded—the United Nations (UN) and the European Union (EU)—has waned over time. As the first step backward in its existence, Great Britain's attempted exit from the European Union shocked the EU system and its supranational aspirations. The UN largely remains caged in the balance of powers with which it was originally designed, and the tension between nations has generated irreconcilable factions, which in turn have paralyzed the institution or, at least have delayed its decisions to the extent of making them inefficient. Yet globalization has made possible a preliminary establishment of organizations that pursue universal justice and attempt to settle cases that involve crimes against humanity. Globalization's economic forces have encouraged international trade associations. International financial regulatory bodies, such as the World Bank or the International Monetary Fund, have emerged, although these institutions are merely advisory and have no coercive power over sovereign states. Finally, a few international defense alliances, such as NATO, have been established, but they are not especially new since international defense coalitions against a common adversary are almost as old as humanity itself.

Despite the upsurge in global institutions, studying a world map shows that sovereign states, which arose from a model created at the dawn of Modernity, continue on as the basic unit of territorial structuring. Although global institutions certainly influence and pressure them, states carefully protect the sovereignty of their legislative, executive, and judicial branches. Outlier cases, like Venezuela's populism and North Korea's isolationist communism, confirm that states largely remain impenetrable spaces in which, once established in power, rulers can develop diverse policies, even those that harm their own population. The political achievement of a global village would mitigate a good part of these aberrations. Some medieval thinkers, with Dante Alighieri at the head, postulated the establishment of a universal empire in which the sovereign has so much power that he is able to judge all causes with the equanimity of those who know their position is safe. Clearly a utopia when spelled out in those terms, the argument could be taken up again today and transformed to alleviate the perverse effects of states' absolute sovereignty. Yet, on the other hand, state sovereignty also guarantees that smaller countries do not become puppets in the hands of other, more powerful nations—as long as, of course, those countries avoid the economic dependence that credit obligations generate.

If the state and capitalism do not have real alternatives now, the same can be said of the third great modern value, namely dependence on science and technology and the material progress it generates. A rational, scientific, and technological mentality has become so entrenched that we are often unable to consider other types of language or argument. The contemporary world hardly appreciates and understands the richness of mythological and symbolic language found in texts and images from ancient and medieval civilizations. Yet, this kind of language represents realities that cannot be expressed with rational language and that are not easily classifiable with history's traditional categories and chronology. Our prevailing rationalistic mentality is no match for mystical or religious language, which can express supernatural or spiritual realities that rational language cannot even begin to approximate. This deficit can in part be alleviated by a close reading of the Bible, of Greek classics like Homer, of medieval epics from authors like Dante, of novels like that of Cervantes or plays from Shakespeare's theater, and even of contemporary classics like Saint-Exupéry's *The Little Prince*. This book famously alert us that, "What is essential is invisible to the eye." Even with this rich array of texts in hand, we are clearly still far from appreciating languages and argumentations that are outside of the hard sciences—let alone ritual language—and this distance seems insurmountable at present. This point is one of the essentials in the intellectual revolution that has constituted postmodern thought in the last half century.

In 1979, the French intellectual Jean-François Lyotard published an essay entitled *The Postmodern Condition*, whose impact was far-reaching because it described and prescribed, with the exactness of a surgeon, the main trends in scholarship and in his fin-de-siècle society. Lyotard concluded that the West was in a new era that he defined as postmodern and characterized by its questioning of the values inherited from modernity, namely reason as the director of knowledge and action, emancipation of the citizenry, the fulfillment of the state as the new spirit of the times, faith in material progress, science and technology, and classless societies. In the new postmodern society, however, this grandiose version seems to have lost credibility. Postmodernism attacks speculative stories such as Marxism or capitalism because while they dazzle us with their theories' internal and formal coherence, they spin out of control when they are put into practice.

The *great narratives* of modernity no longer work because they define and impose rules that oblige actors to accept a speculative game. Because of this, postmodern theory puts so much emphasis on rhetoric rather than on the content. Marshall McLuhan expressed this idea when he noted that "the medium is the message," an idea that informs current society, so dependent on the media for its information. He argues that the content of any message is only a small part of the story because the means we use to transmit it (a scholarly article, an opinion piece in a newspaper, a popular song, radio, television, a speech, or a family gathering) also involve a series of attitudes, suppositions, and emotions that influence the message itself. Richard Rorty coined the term *linguistic turn*, a phenomenon that has greatly shaped history, philosophy, and the social sciences in general. Rorty emphasized the importance of language as an intermediary in all knowledge processes, which automatically implies a trend toward the relativism of scientific knowledge and revision of many modern ideas that society intuitively accepts.

These theories were formulated in the 1960s and 1970s, serving as a kind of doorway to postmodernity. The most influential thinkers of that period include Michel Foucault and Jacques Derrida, and their ideas are still relevant in their fields and society as a whole. Both were influenced by Nietzsche, considering him a prophet of postmodernity with his passionate and visceral criticism of established ideas. They also admired his writing style, communicating through narrative essays rather than with a systematic style.

Michel Foucault was an extraordinarily prolific writer. His works blend philosophy, psychology, psychiatry, anthropology, and history. He focused on topics such as the analysis of insanity and asylums, sexual practices, public policies regarding punishment and prisons, and the relationship between power and knowledge. His remarkable multidisciplinary capacity made him a herald of a new academic field called *cultural studies*. Although it was founded in Great Britain during the 1960s, this field grew fast on campuses in the United States from the 1980s. It mainly aims historical, literary, and philosophical analyses of the most recent topics on the public agenda, such as gender issues, social organization, the control of knowledge, the imposition of ideas, the preservation of intimacy, and forms of spirituality. Cultural studies have brought humanities discourse to society, but also run the serious risk of a limited perspective that may damage the pastness of the past and force its interpretations in order to achieve a particular cultural and political agenda. This is especially true for cultural studies that exclusively aim to support (albeit completely legitimate) struggles, such as racial equality and linguistic, national, or sexual liberation.

Because of his ability to analyze socially sensitive issues such as marginality, madness, and homosexuality, Foucault also influenced the notion of the *politically correct*, now so embedded in our societies, especially regarding respect for diverse minorities. His studies on insanity and sexuality questioned whether what societies have traditionally considered as normal or conventional is nothing more than a social agreement, conditioned by those in power, rather than a response to the real nature of things. Thus, the notions of normality, normativity, and conventionality were reassessed, and objective moral norms abolished, since what until then was considered unnatural or a moral aberration came to be considered natural and normal. Foucault wondered if the madness was the result of a disease or because the person acted in a way that society considers proper of a madman. Therefore, the condition of madness is a mutable notion according to historical circumstances rather than a condition that derives from an illness.

Mental illness is thus seen as a social concept, rather than an entity, since it is defined and dictated by psychiatrists and psychologists. Foucault used the same epistemic operation he did for the subject of madness to approach other crucial social issues such as sexuality or power. Between essentialism and historicism, Foucault clearly opted for the latter, emphasizing a concept of his that has become more common, genealogy. He writes a discontinuous history, which he defines as the 'archeology of knowledge.' As an archaeologist does while excavating, Foucault digs into a particular culture to find its predominant epistemology or knowledge structure. He dissected society's deepest and long-term immobile structures rather than its short-term historical development. This idea had very much in keeping with Fernand Braudel's historical structuralism and Claude Lévi-Strauss's anthropological structuralism developed at the same time.

Foucault's moral relativism and historicism had many social implications. For example, it encouraged minorities and the marginalized to seek legitimization in public debate, even when proposing a transgressive idea or questioning a secular tradition. In effect, this struggle only needs a coherent discourse that justifies it, while access to and consolidation of power comes through language as an autonomous tool more than through its actual reference to reality. With their artificial nominalism, in which the promises they make do not necessarily correspond with reality, contemporary politicians have learned this lesson very well. In addition, the fact that Foucault was open about his homosexuality, and that he was one of the first well-known victims of AIDS, made him a founder hero among gender theorists.

Derrida's deconstructionism, on his part, emphasizes the audience, that is, the reader or the viewer. In this way, a text or artwork can have as many interpretations as there are audiences. Cubism's interwar artists, like Picasso, applied this idea to the deconstruction of figures, which could then be seen from a variety of perspectives. Here, postmodern deconstruction also connects with analysis of the subconscious, which Jacques Lacan promoted through new ideas in psychoanalysis applied to the social sciences. If Foucault is the author of *otherness*, with his ability to put a spotlight on realities that had traditionally been considered marginal, Derrida is the author of *différance*, making the displacement of language, and its lack of reference to external reality, central. Derrida championed linguistic and literary deconstruction, while Foucault advocated for social and moral deconstruction.

With their relativist and deconstructionist theories, both Foucault and Derrida heralded the demise of modern rational humanism. Both embody the spirit of late modernity, with their willingness to demolish all confidence in the objectivity of reason and knowledge, as well as traditional humanistic and liberal values, through seductive diagnoses. Although Foucault's influence has lasted longer, both constitute two reference points in the West's postmodern rupture, which was especially virulent during the 1970s and 1980s. In those years, marginal and radical thinkers were considered difficult to understand, but, as Foucault himself predicted regarding his own texts, today they are considered prophets of postmodern criticism, models for social behavior, and archetypes for cultural analysis. But they were more denunciatory than proactive.

In the end, postmodernity corresponds to any critical assessment of enlightened rationalism's legacy, which is considered the zenith of modernity. Some postmodern authors consider the modern project completed, while others argue that it is simply unfinished and must be finalized, updated, and readjusted where needed. Most of the intellectuals analyzed in this chapter—McLuhan, Rorty, Lyotard, Foucault, and Derrida—belong to the former group. Those in the latter group are often considered reactionary, for example, Jürgen Habermas. Being modern nowadays implies, according to Habermas, seeing oneself as an active collaborator in unfinished business that Enlightenment authors initiated, aiming to emancipate humanity with rationalist values, and to definitively liberate us from the weight of traditions inherited from the past. And this debate rages on, between those who still advocate for the values of modernity and those who actively seek alternatives, without much success to date. Thus, it seems that we are more properly in the Late-Modern or hyper-Modern era rather than in an anti-Modern or post-Modern one since the essential values of modernity have not yet been replaced by other viable alternatives.

While intellectuals continue to debate these important issues, the world continues to spill blood in cruel and endless conflicts. Some places in Africa and the Middle East are literally in a state of permanent war, while other Latin American and Asian countries endure conditions of alarming insecurity, inequality, populist dictatorships, and discrimination. Immigration from these regions continues to challenge more stable Western countries, which are all together uncertain of the most effective ways to alleviate the problem. These solutions are not to be found in Europe's politically correct *meaculpism*, which is founded on a sterile attitude that usually engenders passivity while employing wrongheaded strategies that divert attention from the conditions of the countries that are suffering the problems. We too often forget that historical experience has shown us that immigration does not signify a problem of cohabitation among different peoples and races, but rather of cultural assimilation. The West puts itself at risk by stubbornly defending the preservation of its own cultural identity, and does not gain anything by insisting on impermeable borders, a utopian delusion that is impossible in our global village, and that is, moreover, likely illegitimate and unjust. My point is that the West has many moral resources at its disposal to avoid falling into either hermetic intolerance or sterile self-punishment. All things considered, though, we rest in the hope that civilization will continue to prevail and that globalization will contribute to greater understanding and respect among the world's different peoples, nations, cultures, and religions.

EPILOGUE

One essential question remains: Does the West still have a key role to play in the future of the world? Challenged by trends such as transcultural, identitarian, post-Christian, anti-universalist, and postcolonial tendencies, and urged by its permanent self-questioning, it finds itself at a crossroads decisive for its existence. This age has some parallels with other critical moments that we have seen in this book, such as the fall of the Roman Empire in the fifth century, the first expansion of Islam in the seventh century, the division between Western and Eastern Christianity in the tenth century, and the emergence of Protestantism in the sixteenth century.

I

A large part of the complexity of the current situation for the West is the proliferation of cultural transfers and assimilations stimulated by rampant globalization. Transculturation has been raised throughout history at a regional or, at most, transoceanic level from the sixteenth century, but in recent decades has become entirely global. Theoretically, this should not pose a problem for the West, since it has never been a 'pure' civilization—and when it has pretended to be, it has run the risk of disappearing altogether. In fact, the West's sensitivity to transculturation has been part of its tradition, whose very history and survival—as I have tried to convey throughout this book—is due precisely to its capacity to absorb and assimilate other cultures. But the challenge of transculturation is now a major one, since it is not about a simple transference or absorption from one culture into another, but a blending of diverse cultures understood as producing something new.

It would be a painful paradox if, in the end, other civilizations came to occupy the space formerly occupied by Western civilization—without whose sphere of freedom the emergence of transculturation itself would not have been possible. The West has historically forged its own identity thanks to its large capacity to absorb a great diversity of ethnicities and cultures within itself, as the chapters of this book *Foundations* and *Maturations* have shown. It has gone through an expansionist phase, as all civilizations do to a greater or lesser extent, coinciding with their colonizing and hegemonistic phase. But it has learned to recognize its errors and limitations and to engage in self-criticism manifested in its successive claims of people, class, race, nation, and gender.

Civilizations breed specific institutions and prescribe models of conduct. But in the West, the moral load has been lightening, with increasing tolerance in matters that do not affect the essential civilizational values. Nevertheless, civilizations need a minimum coherence and continuity in tradition, identity, and culture to survive. Revisionist policies toward one's own past based on denialist stances toward one's own civilization, are not effective, especially when they radicalize or come to form hegemonic policies of memory. Samuel Huntington has coined the concept of 'torn countries' to refer to nations that had oscillated between two civilizations without ever managing to establish their own identity. This had been particularly dramatic in the twentieth century in countries like Russia, which moved between Western modernization and its own Orthodox/Slavic tradition and Turkey, which oscillated between Islamism and Westernization.

This is compatible with respect for minorities, as late Roman and Austro-Hungarian empires allowed minorities to live under their own laws. Yet, if civilizations do not preserve and appreciate that core of their own idiosyncrasy, they disappear—just as the Mesopotamian, Egyptian, Hellenistic, Inca, and Ottoman civilizations did—and end up subsumed in another one. In an age when global politics is shaped by cultural, religious, and civilizational markers rather than economic, political, and ideological values, the West should be more sensitive to the promotion of its own tradition and heritage—and this should have practical applications in terms of politics of memory.

Together with transculturation, identitarianism is another hegemonic cultural movement which is challenging the traditional values of the West. Identity had traditionally been applied to the individual, but in the nineteenth century, it was collectively projected onto nations. Now, in the twenty-first century, it is also being extended to other collectives—ethnic, religious, class, or gender—and particularly to those who have had a marginal position in traditional societies. Foucault's maxim—make the marginal central through the transformation of the discourses—has literally been put into practice again.

Marginal, minority, or peripheric groups have always existed in the West. What is new is that now these minority groups are capable of imposing their criteria on the majority, or at least blocking the majority consensus. Notions of tolerance, promoted on the basis of John Locke's ideas, have been made absolute, becoming—paradoxically—a potential force for intolerance under the form of political correctness. Identity politics has associated elements of postmodern philosophy (social constructivism or hierarchies of power) with the central element of Marxist theory (the dialectic between oppressors and oppressed), resulting in various forms of populisms. In a typically Western movement, two ideologies that arose from within it—Marxism and postmodernism—have turned against its own tradition.

The debates over economic politics, hegemonic in the twentieth century, have turned into identity politics in the twenty-first century. For most of the last century, right-wing politics concentrated on reducing the size of the state and boosting the private sector. The left, for its part, devoted its efforts to promoting redistributive policies centered on the working class. Today, both have adopted identity politics: the right has made its main mission one of protecting traditional national identities, especially against immigration, while the left made central to its activities the gaining of civil rights for the various groups considered marginal collectives coalescing around identities that are mainly ethnic or gender based. This oscillation is heir to the assimilation originating in the Frankfurt School (principally, in the thought of Herbert Marcuse) and in the countercultural movements of the nineteen-sixties and seventies. The problem is that both policies—the right-wing purist and the left-wing marginalist—lead to an exclusivism that generates tensions on both sides that have not yet been resolved through a balanced equilibrium. As a result, political and ideological polarization has grown to unsustainable limits.

The spread of identity politics and the establishment of behavioral and linguistic norms of conduct in defense of the most disadvantaged groups in society have led to the emergence of figures who, from the fields of thought or in the new forms of communication (from YouTube to podcasting), have risen up in protest against the restrictions on freedom of expression, political correctness, and one-track thinking. This phenomenon has created the biggest stir in the United States, Canada, and Great Britain, where celebrities such as Jordan Peterson, Milo Yiannopoulos, Ben Shapiro, and Joe Rogan are promoting a discourse—now they are in the anti-cultural camp—in favor of individuality and against identitarianism.

Contemplating the spread of various brands of transculturation and identitarianism, one wonders to what extent Christianity has ceased to be relevant in the West. This debate was particularly intense in post-Victorian England. Secularist, scientistic, rationalist, and pragmatic intellectuals like Bernard Shaw predicted the disappearance of religious myth in favor of a rational world. More traditionally minded writers such as G. K. Chesterton and C. S. Lewis warned of the pernicious consequences of the disappearance of religion and their moral guidance for individuals and society. In reality, none of them—and of course, not Nietzsche either, with his solemn issuing of God's death certificate—were wholly right, given that modernization has ultimately proved compatible with religiosity. In fact, the second half of the twentieth century witnessed a 'revenge of God,' as defined by Gilles Kepel.

This revival of religion and spirituality has taken many forms, such as the re-Catholicization of North America, the evangelical Protestantization of Latin America, the return to Orthodoxy as the only secular connection to the past in Russia, the revitalization of Islamic fundamentalism, the Christianization of some Asian countries, and the resurgence of a new Hinduism. This revitalization has certainly debunked the 'secularization process' and the 'death of God' forecast by some nineteenth- and early twentieth-century intellectuals. Re-religiosity has won out over paganization wherever they come into conflict, especially where the traumas of rampant modernization or industrialization have caused psychological, emotional, and social dislocations that traditional or modern beliefs have not been able to counteract. The ideological vacuum left by the collapse of Communism and materialism has brought about the resurgence of monotheistic religions, or replacement by ancestral beliefs, in many parts of Asia and Africa. Religion has taken over from ideology, and religious nationalism has replaced secular nationalism. Religion has ceased to be the "opium of the people" (Karl Marx) to become the "vitamin of the weak" (Régis Debray).

All this has led Hans Joas to question whether Christianity is merely a legacy or also a source of contemporary guidance. In fact, the lead-in question ought to be whether Christianity is an essential part of the West and whether the West can survive without its original religion. Christianity, in its diverse forms and confessions, has been an essential part of the West, since it has proved to be more immune to the political instrumentalization to which it has been subjected in other civilizations. In the Orthodox tradition, the Patriarch of Constantinople was soon subjected to the authority of the Emperor of Byzantium, as the Patriarch of Moscow to the Tsar and the Orthodox Church to the political authorities. In Persia, the emperor was in fact the political and religious leader at the same time, as is now the Ayatollah in Iran. In China, the political authorities have completely subjugated the religious hierarchy. In the West, on the other hand, Christianity, both as personal belief and as ecclesiastical hierarchy, has survived despite the clerical and secularizing onslaughts. This autonomy between the temporal and the spiritual, so characteristic of the Western world, confirms the prominent place that Christianity has in the West as an essential value of its specific essence, beyond the personal beliefs of each individual.

II

With regard to external challenges the West is facing, the most perceptible is the criticism of the Western universalism, manifested in the highly visible phenomenon of the debunking and demolition of what had been considered, until very recently, its founding heroes: saints and martyrs of the early Christianity such as Benedict of Nursia, discoverers of the new colonized worlds in the early modernity such as Colón and Magallanes, conquerors such as Francisco Pizarro and Hernán Cortés, evangelizers Franciscan Juníper Serra and Bartolomé de las Casas, and Founding Fathers of the modern West such as George Washington and Benjamin Franklin for the United States or Konrad Adenauer, Winston Churchill, Alcide de Gasperi, and Robert Schuman for Europe.

This historical revisionism has its contradictions. Some of these demystified heroes are today accused of being supremacists, slave owners, or abusers of conscience. Some of these people, admittedly, committed atrocities. History helps us to become aware of them precisely not to repeat them. However, it is questionable to what extent we can project our convictions onto people from the past, just as a judge cannot judge a defendant by applying a penal code that did not exist when he or she did the act for which he or she is accused. It is necessary to contextualize them properly in order to approach the past not with the intention of judging its actors but with the intention of learning, following the maxim that history is the 'teacher of life' (*magistra vitae*), as the classics advised us. It is as simple as it is unfair to judge historical figures from a computer or from the barricades. My point is that we should approach these foundational historical figures not by looking for what they did according to the context of our time, but what they contributed to improve their world in contravention of the moral rules of their time. If we give too much credit to these decontextualized criticisms, we may condemn actions that were a step forward at the time, even if they could not fully complete the reforms they claimed.

Here comes a perhaps more difficult problem to solve: Western supremacism. The three great waves of Western expansion—the twelfth-century crusades, the first American colonization of the sixteenth century, and the great global colonization of the nineteenth century—were concomitant to the conviction on the part of their agents that it was desirable to spread universal values of a religious, ideological, and political nature, without considering the enormous price, in terms of human rights, that would have to be paid for it. Unfortunately, this is a tragedy shared, in one way or another, by almost all civilizations. All major expansionary processes have been accompanied by the commission of major atrocities as experienced in the Persian conquests, the process of romanization, the spread of Islam, the American Aztecs in Pre-Columbine America, the Napoleon's empire, the Chinese and Japanese expansion, the communist Union of Soviet Socialist Republics (USSR) expansion to the world, and so on. So, it is natural that the de-colonization processes of the twentieth century were marked by anti-Western movements that legitimately sought emancipation from colonial powers. The postcolonial movements are the result, in its more scholar and systematized form, of this indigenist reaction, analyzed and legitimized by postcolonial studies as their intellectual reflection.

Postcolonial theories and practices have focused their critique on the hegemonism and supremacism of the West, which automatically refers to the self-consciousness of Western universalism and supremacism. This tendency, whose existence can already be glimpsed in the expansion of ancient Rome, began to show clearly in the rationalization processes that typified the intellectual world of the twelfth century, its Axial Shift. From that moment, Europe promoted this universalizing trend from then until the early twentieth century, with sixteenth-century Iberian and nineteenth-century British colonization its most visible manifestations. On the contrary, Russian Communism, German Nazism, and Italian Fascism of interwar Europe (Chapter 15) were anti-universalist ideologies, in their emphasis on the rule of *one* social class (the proletariat), the purity of *one* race (the Arian), or the hegemony of *one* specific nation (Italy, Germany, and Japan). They were Western movements that ceased to be universalizing, and this entailed numerous problems, for the West and for the whole world. Accordingly, postcolonial theories also face a challenge, since they might fail in anti-universalism in their support for the "universalization of minorities"—a paradox that is not easily to solve.

Another postcolonial claim involves the deepening of indigenization, the search for what is authentic and original in every society. These movements are particularly active in Latin America, trying to abjure its entire Hispanic tradition in order to recover its pre-Columbian ethnic and cultural base in all its purity. Nevertheless, a rigorous historical analysis demonstrates that all societies are forged through a remarkable religious, ideological, and cultural hybridization. It is over-presumptuous to aspire to find a pure society, or to fix the origin of a civilization after which everything is corrupted by the invaders, making it none too convincing to advocate for a civilizational authenticity that ends at the precipice of exclusion. When opting for an indigenist society, applying the rule of authenticity in the oldest, one wonders what exactly the criterion is for setting the chronological limit, and what happens with the cultures, ethnicities, and societies that have been superimposed on that supposedly original one—whether by way of conquest, miscegenation, or cultural colonization. For example, is the *authentic* Spain the Celtiberian, the Roman, the Arab-Islamic, the Roman, the Germanic-Visigothic, or the Western Christianized one? What about the Swabian, Vandal, Byzantine, Frankish, Sephardic, Basque, or Berber-Islamic ethnic remnants in Iberia? Who marks the ethnic and civilizational boundaries? The conclusion is that these ethnic and cultural distinctions cannot be governed by the criterion of purity—unless one wants to fall into precisely the problem one wants to solve: racism, exclusivism, or supremacism. But this is compatible with the acknowledgement of the uniqueness of the different civilizations—in the case of the West, the formulas of state in politics, capitalist in economics, rational in science, legal in organizing society, university-led in research, Christian in religion. These six values have spread all over the world, coexisting with the native forms of other civilizations and, on occasion, replacing them completely. The postcolonial processes have allowed the West to question which of these values and institutions have replaced the preexisting ones (Westernization, as in the case of the British colonization in sparsely populated territories of North America), and which have been shared (Westernization plus indigenization, as in the case of the Hispanic colonization in the rest of America). This is a historical reality that must be considered to face the challenges posed by the new international scenario.

Universalism has been historically the predominant ideology of the West in its confrontations with non-Western cultures. The rule of law is an unequivocal manifestation of this universalism. For the Romans, the law was fundamental to a civilized existence. Medieval thinkers, consolidated in the early modern Salamanca school, developed the idea of natural law by which all—even kings—had to abide. In England, a common law tradition was developed, rooted in common sense, tradition, and jurisprudence. As early as the nineteenth century, the rule-of-law tradition laid the foundations of a constitutionalism and the protection of human rights (e.g., property rights, freedom of religion, and expression), offering protection against the exercise of arbitrary and tyrannical power. In the twentieth century, the West promoted the Universal Declaration of Human Rights, as we have seen in Chapter 17.

It is obvious that the idea of a universal Western civilization that all other civilizations must imitate, or at least take as a point of reference, cannot be sustained. Western supremacism and universalism, which imposed themselves over the whole globe during the nineteenth century, have lost their legitimation. But this should not make us lose sight of the fact that the West differs objectively from other civilizations for having contributed to the consolidation of liberalism, pluralism, individualism, and the rule of law, which made possible modernization, industrialization, liberalism, democracy, and the state order.

III

Finally, one of the most problematic concepts of the West is 'modernization.' Originated in the sixteenth century in Western Mediterranean and northwest Europe, it spread all over the world, influencing political, economic, and ideological aspects of society associated with its inherent processes of rationalization, urbanization, massification, colonization, and industrialization. Part of the effect of the desire to modernize is the consciousness of being backward. One of its immediate consequences is the feeling of the need to imitate other countries. Some remarkable examples are the tsar Peter the Great's determination to follow western models, followed in the nineteenth century by the Russian debate between westernizers and Slavophils, which was the prelude of many later debates and transformations, such as mid nineteenth-century Meiji Japan or late twentieth-century South Korea. Besides regarding modernization as a final stage in the fulfillment of the evolutionary potential of the West, we should also analyze it as a specific manifestation of every civilization, as in one way or another they all experience their modernization processes.

The *modern* belief that modernization—political, economic, ideological, or religious—is an inevitable and beneficial process is currently being questioned by the postmodern, anti-system, and populist movements. Although no one can deny some of its most beneficial effects, especially those related to scientific and technological advances, populisms question some of its more undesirable effects, especially that of depersonalization. Paradoxically, the patent economic globalization has come up against a very marked tendency to localism and attachment to what is uniquely one's own (think globally, act locally). The internal dynamics of the different civilizations and their attachment to their own traditions have in the end counted for more than the apparently fatalistic progress lauded by the nineteenth-century positivists. The variability of the symbolic, institutional, and ideological responses of each civilization has been so great that it is not possible today to speak of cultural standardization.

Modernization challenges and questions the institutional and symbolic premises of all societies—what we generically call 'tradition'—and is thus always met with ambivalence by those societies: some idealize and others demonize it. It raises the debate between conservatism/progressivism and tradition/innovation. Benjamin Nelson questions what are the possibilities for innovation if histories are erased, presents are homogenized, and futures are aborted, by the schematization of histories. Innovation cannot be verified without a confronted tradition. Tradition had been the most important regulator of political and social change in traditional societies. By contrast, the central premise of modernization is the conviction that permanent reflection, revision, and questioning of one's own tradition through philosophical speculation, scientific inquiry, political consensus, and social protest can change a status quo inherited in the past and improve it for the future.

However, the non-Western countries that suffered Western colonization have usually suffer an ambivalent reaction to modernization. On the one hand, they perceive it as an imposition by the colonizer. On the other hand, they appreciate some of its obvious benefits. The global expansion of the West in the nineteenth century opened up new opportunities to the colonized countries in terms of technological and scientific advances. But it also demanded a type of operational response and interaction which many civilizations were not ready for or simply did not wish to accept, especially those who had suffered oppression and economic devastation by the Western powers. This helps to understand the emergence of anti-Western movements, usually in the form of anti-Americanism, promoted by other non-Western but equally colonial powers such as Russia and China. The paradox is that these non-Western powers have assimilated an ideology generated in the West, Marxism, which constitutes the paroxysm of modernity and is being used as an anti-Western tool by other civilizations.

Historical evidence shows that the West has opted for a 'progressive society' as opposed to a 'stationary civilization,' as expounded by Henry Sumner Maine. The West has always been inclined to improve through its commitment to doctrinal and technical innovation, in contrast to societies fearful of change or of going beyond the social habits and customs established by repetition and prescriptive rule. But it was not always so. In the medieval era, a traditionalist conception of life prevailed over the progressive one. As Joseph R. Strayer has argued, in such traditional societies, "every deliberate modification of an existing type of activity must be based on a study of individual precedents. Every plan for the future is dependent on a pattern which has been found in the past." Max Weber ascribed to Chinese, Hindu, and Jewish civilizations a sacro-magical type of consciousness dominated, as Benjamin Nelson has explained, "by prescriptive etiquettes and rituals oriented to the total fulfillment of laws believed to be ontological in character and to have their sanction in the cosmic orders, the commands of the ancestors and the primordial traditions that require that they be preserved through literal performances of fixed obligations." When the prescriptive structures prevail the religious leader is uncritically followed and their absolute authority is never questioned.

The emergence of modernity in the West from the sixteenth century onward altered this course. The commitment to rationalization in philosophy, the inductive development of experimental science, the systematic expansion of capitalism as an economic system, and the structuring of the state as an omnipresent political agent drove the West toward material and mental progress that would not be questioned again until the interwar period in the twentieth century. Territorial expansion, by means of colonizing processes, exported this model to other civilizations that accepted it more as an imposition than something assimilated internally. The sole exception was the reception of Christianity in both Latin and North America, which assimilated this religion wholeheartedly, thereby massively facilitating their Westernizing process.

However, in many parts of Asia and Africa, above all those that had previously been Islamized, Hindu or Confucian, there was wariness not just about assimilating the Christian religion but also the processes of urbanization and modernization. This makes it easier to understand that the rise of a global anti-Westernism as anti-Americanism is in fact a reaction against the least desirable effects of Western modernization, such as relativism, materialism, skepticism, rational fundamentalism, secularism, anti-ecologism, and consumerism. The experience of anti-Westernism should encourage the West to inquire into its roots, question its historical trajectory, self-censor its most perverse traces, filter out those values that have lost their universalism, avoid supremacist or arrogant attitudes, and try to incorporate the best of other civilizations.

This historical revisionism contributes to identifying the positive and negative aspects of the spread of some Western values across the globe. On the credit side of the ledger are undoubtedly the spread of human rights, from *The French Declaration of the Rights of Man and Citizens* (1789) and the American *Bill of Rights* (1791) to the *United Nations Universal Declaration of Human Rights* (1948). Although the latter was clearly an initiative of Western countries, and is seen by some societies as yet another manifestation of Western expansionism, representatives of fifty UN nations took part in the writing of the first drafts. The document was eventually signed by most of the countries in the world, China and the Muslim nations among them. The declaration recognized freedom of conscience, religion, expression, movement, and association. Its application has been patchy, but it is undeniable that it has enabled progress in the development of some civil rights, starting with the practical impetus provided by the movements associated with the cultural and social revolution of the 1960s.

Westernization is different from modernization. The former refers to an entire civilization, while the latter expresses a particular unfolding and a specific phase of that civilization between the sixteenth and twentieth centuries. When distinguishing Westernization from modernization, another question arises: can we conceive of modernization outside of the West, or modernization without Westernization? In Islam, for example, colonization was a determining factor in the formation of a modern elite—often in countries with a long non-Western tradition. But it was not always influential at street level, and was questioned by the fundamentalist movements, as happened in the Iran of the Ayatollah Khomeini as a reaction of the previous regime of the Shah of Persia. The modernization of the Islamic countries entailed a secularization that collided head-on with the popular religious base there. Consequently, the dislocations arising from the collision between secularization and Islamization ultimately revealed a profound continuity in the institutional, religious, and ideological traditions in Islamic societies—and the same may be said of the Hindu, Chinese, and Russian.

Moreover, nationalism and communism have joined forces as anti-Western movements. In many other countries, the nationalist movements associated with decolonization were spurred on, paradoxically, by so typically Western a product as Marxism, as was the case in Asian countries like Korea and Vietnam, Latin American countries like Fidel Castro's Cuba or Sandinista Nicaragua, and African countries like Kwame Nkrumah's Ghana or the Marxism-Leninism implanted in the independence processes of Angola, Ethiopia, Mozambique, and the Congo. In addition, anti-Christian communism has penetrated as an agent of modernization in the Slav, Chinese, and Islamic civilizations, though, in the end, the weight of the previous religious tradition have weighed more than Communist novelty. The Communist Party is rehabilitating aspects of Confucianism such as its heavy emphasis on hierarchical subordination as well as probity, industriousness, and thrift among the people. The Russian authorities always seek the blessing of the Orthodox hierarchy, although in practice they count on its submission. Finally, in other large regions such as Indonesia, the shared traditions of Islam and Christianity are joined by Marxism, which functions for these purposes as a third religious tradition. It is easy to understand the complexity and tensions generated by such a mix of traditions and values. When religions and ideologies join forces, the latter always prevails over the former.

In the West, anti-modern, anti-capitalist, and anti-state postmodernism has proved ephemeral, largely due to their lack of viable alternatives. Ultimately, postmodernism has come up against the great difficulty of setting limits to tolerance, as the debate around freedom of expression in France in the face of Islamism has made manifest after the Charlie Hebdo attack. How does a supposedly tolerant society deal with the declared enemies of pluralism, such as Islamic fundamentalists or radical populists? No matter how deeply skeptical postmodernism has made us about grand narratives and metahistorical constructs, there is now a renewed interest in the founding narratives of tolerance and religious liberty, as set out by their originators John Locke and Alexis de Tocqueville.

The criticism of the West is concentrated nowadays above all on its historical realization of massive urbanization, migration processes, rationalization as an absolute value, the anticlericalism of the Enlightenment, dehumanizing industrialization, blind faith in material progress, and the processes of secularization. Nevertheless, not all of these reproaches count on the fact that these concepts are related to historical processes specifically connected with modernization rather than with the founding values of the West, with their roots in Jerusalem, Athens, Rome, and Christianity, as they have been deployed throughout this book. As a consequence, it is therefore essential to distinguish Westernization from modernization. The former assumes some values (assimilation of the classical legacy, Christianity, separation between spiritual and temporal authority, the rule of law, social pluralism, corporatization, representative political bodies, individualism, and mercantile societies) that are different from what is contained in modernization (full rationalization, dominant state, savage capitalism, omnipresent science, secularization, urbanization, and industrialization). For instance, modernization implies secularization—which is unacceptable for Islamic theocracy or Slav-Orthodox Caesaropapism—while the West, as a civilization, is not necessarily constrained by secularization.

Nonetheless, the great paradox is that the processes of modernization have been assumed by other civilizations, especially urbanization, capitalism, and industrialization, imposed by a runaway globalization that has yet to convince us of its benefits. We are sure that modernization and globalization have raised people's material level and medical care, but not so sure that it has contributed to elevating their moral and cultural levels. As a result, they have had to adopt the Western values that are most alien to them, while others with which they might have more affinity—such as the values of classical culture, universal charity sustained by Christianity, and the spirit of medieval communitarianism—have not spread concomitantly.

In the end, the world is becoming more modern and less Western. The West, by contrast, is becoming less modern—because it declares itself to be in 'postmodernity'—and more Western, because the differences from other civilizations, far from reducing, are increasing. But at the same time, the crisis of Western consciousness has grown, and nobody knows for sure if the West will continue to exist as a civilization. It is possible that Western civilization is in decline, as happens with all civilizations. But history, which in some way always repeats itself, can also take unexpected turns: the future is an open book, yet to be written.

SUGGESTED BIBLIOGRAPHY

Introduction—On the concept of civilization

The spirit of the book is largely inspired by some books that, over the last decades, have reflected on the concept of civilization and its historical development. These are, in order of appearance, as follows: Oswald Spengler, *Decline of the West* (New York: A. A. Knopf, 1926–28), Arnold Toynbee, *A Study of History* (Londres: Oxford University Press, 1934–1961), Pitirim Sorokin, *Social and Cultural Dynamics* (New York: American Book, 1937–1985), Philip Bagby, *Culture and History: Prolegomena to the Comparative Study of Civilizations* (London: Longmans, 1958), Rushton Coulborn, *The Origin of Civilized Societies* (Princeton: Princeton University Press, 1959), Carroll Quigley, *The Evolution of Civilizations: An Introduction to Historical Analysis* (New York: Macmillan, 1961), Fernand Braudel, *History of Civilizations* (New York: Allen Lane, 1963), William McNeill, *The Rise of the West: A History of the Human Community* (Chicago: Chicago University Press, 1963), Matthew Melko, *The Nature of Civilizations* (Boston: Porter Sargen, 1969), Alfred Weber, A. L. Kroeber, *Style and Civilizations* (Westport, CT: Greenwood Press, 1973), Christopher Dawson, *Dynamics of World History* (La Salle, IL: Sherwood Sudgen, 1978), Benjamin Nelson, *On the Roads to Modernity: Conscience, Science, and Civilizations* (London: Rowman & Littlefield, 1981), S. N. Eisenstadt, *European Civilization in a Comparative Perspective* (Oslo: Aschehoug AS, 1987), Adda Bozeman and Immanuel Wallerstein, *Geopolitics and Geoculture: Essays on the Changing World-system* (Cambridge: Cambridge University Press, 1992), Felipe Fernández Armesto, *Millennium: A History of the Last Thousand Years* (New York: Scribners, 1995), and David Graber and David Wengrow, *The Dawn of Everything: A New History of Humanity* (New York: Farrar, Straus and Giroux, 2021).

On the concept and development of modernity: S. N. Eisenstadt, *Patterns of Modernity* (London: Frances Pinter, 1987), Hans Joas and Klaus Wiegandt, *Secularization and the World Religions* (Liverpool: Liverpool University Press, 2009), Cyril E. Black, *The Dynamics of Modernization: A Study in Comparative History* (New York: Harper & Row, 1966).

Introduction—General Histories of the West

Several general introductions to the history of the Western world served to frame my discussion. Ernst H. Gombrich's *A Little History of the World* (New Haven: Yale University Press, 1985) has become a classic in the genre. Philippe Nemo's *What Is the West?* (Pittsburgh: Duquesne University Press, 2009) signals the historical aspects of the West that survive today and that have most influenced other civilizations. Tony Judt's studies (see, for instance, his *A Grand Illusion? An Essay on Europe* (London: Penguin, 1997)) are a continual source of inspiration for those who assess their own cultural heritage, want to reflect on it, and, accordingly, try to develop it. Christopher Dawson's classic, *The Making of Europe* (London: Forgotten Books, 2017) reflects on the historical foundations of Western civilization, offering a philosophical perspective.

Other interesting texts that offer synthesis and a general visions include William H. McNeil, *History of Western Civilization* (Chicago: University of Chicago Press, 1986); John Morris Roberts, *A History of Europe* (Oxford: Helicon, 1996); Norman Davies's *Europe: A History* (New York: HarperCollins, 1996); Judith G. Coffin and Robert C. Stafey, *Western Civilizations: Their History & Their Culture* (New York: W. W. Norton, 2011); Ian Morris, *Why the West Rules—For Now* (London: Profile, 2011); Niall Ferguson, *Civilization: The West and the Rest* (London: Penguin, 2012); Jackson J. Spielvogel, *Western Civilization* (Belmont: Wadsworth Publishing, 2014); the collective volume edited by John Sevenson, *The History of Europe* (New York: Facts on File, 2002); Anthony Grafton and David A. Bell, *The West: A New History* (New York: W. W. Norton, 2014); and Joshua Cole and Carol Symes, *Western Civilizations: Their History & Their Culture* (New York: W. W. Norton, 2016).

Literature, art, and music are three essential manifestations of culture. I would recommend, as historical-critical introductions, for each of these fields the following: Erich Auerbach, *Mimesis: The Representation of Reality in Western Literature* (Princeton: Princeton University Press, 2003); Ernst Gombrich, *The Story of Art* (New York: Phaidon, 2020), and Carter Harman, *A Popular History of Music* (New York: Dell, 1956).

Chapter 1—Jerusalem

There are two excellent summaries of the history of Israel that, despite having been written decades ago, still offer excellent panoramic visions: John Bright, *A History of Israel* (Louisville: Westminster John Knox, 2000) and Martin Noth, *The History of Israel* (New York: Harper, 1960).

For the multiple Judaisms that existed around the time of Jesus and Judaism's relationship to early Christianity, Alan Segal, *The Other Judaisms of Late Antiquity* (Waco, TX: Baylor University Press, 2017). On the Christian-Jew, Paul and his position within the Jewish currents at the time of Jesus, *Paul the Convert: The Apostasy and Apostolate of Saul of Tarsus* (New Haven: Yale University Press, 1990).

Among the vast amount of work devoted to the history of Israel, the nature of the Judaism, and the character of the Jewish people, I recommend Paul Johnson, *A History of the Jews* (New York: Harper & Row, 1987) and Simon Schama, *The Story of the Jews* (London: Bodley Head, 2013 and 2017), which focus on actors rather than on structures or institutions. Anti-Semitism is lucidly examined in David Nirenberg's *Anti-Judaism: The Western Tradition* (New York, W. W. Norton, 2013).

Regarding the foundation of the State of Israel in 1948 and its first steps, Dominique Lapierre and Larry Collins's volume *O Jerusalem!* (New York: Simon and Schuster, 1972) is a fascinating narration.

The reading of the *Bible*, both as primary source and as spiritual inspiration, is the best way to understand the history and identity of Ancient Israel and its legacy.

Chapter 2—Athens

I recommend the following introductions to ancient Greek history: Hermann Bengtson, *History of Greece from the Beginnings to the Byzantine Era* (Ottawa: University of Ottawa Press, 1988); Sarah Pomeroy, Stanley M. Burstein, Walter Donlan, and Jennifer Tolbert Roberts, *Ancient Greece: A Political, Social, and Cultural History* (New York: Oxford University Press, 2008); and Peter J. Rhodes, *A History of the Classical Greek World* (Cambridge: Blackwell, 2006).

For the city and the cultural project of Athens, Christian Meier's *Athens: A Portrait of the City in Its Golden Age* (New York: Metropolitan Books, 1998) is splendid. The book begins with the maxim "Before Understanding, It Is Necessary to Love," which in the case of Greek civilization is not hard to do, and Meier shows how literally he takes the adage, completing a magnificent and illuminating portrait of the golden age of ancient Athens.

Of course, direct reading of the Greek classics in good translation is a more valuable introduction than reading guides and surveys. As introductory readings, I would highlight the works of Homer—*The Iliad* and *The Odyssey*—and Herodotus and Thucydides' histories, as well as Euripides and Sophocles' tragedies. An introduction to some of these primary sources is found in Arnaldo Momigliano, *The Classical Foundations of Modern Historiography* (Berkeley: University of California Press, 1990).

Chapter 3—Rome

For the origins of Rome, see Tim J. Cornell's *The Beginnings of Rome* (London: Routledge, 2015). Summaries of the history of ancient Rome include Paul Veyne, *The Roman Empire* (Cambridge: The Belknap Press, 1997); Brian Campbell, *The Romans and Their World* (New Haven: Yale University Press, 2015); and Mary Beard, *SPQR: A History of Ancient Rome* (London: Liveright, 2015), which have the appeal of excellent writing and undisputable interpretative acumen. Ronald Syme's *The Roman Revolution* (New York: Oxford University Press, 2002), originally published in 1939, to prevent fascism in Europe before the breakout of World War II, is a detailed reflection on the transition from republican to imperial Rome. On Roman institutions, it is always useful to turn back to Leon Homo's classic, *Roman Political Institutions* (New York: Barnes & Noble, 1962). To understand the function of religion in Rome, see Arnaldo Momigliano, *On Pagans, Jews, and Christians* (Middletown: Wesleyan University Press, 1987).

Edward Gibbon's *The Decline and Fall of the Roman Empire* (Frankfurt: Sheba Blake, 2017), clearly influenced by the Enlightenment passion for the *progress* of history and a certain reductionism of the mechanical 'growth-boom-decay' dialectic, retains the strength and freshness of a classic.

Just like with ancient Greece, there is no better introduction to Rome than classic Latin authors, such as Virgil, Cicero, and Seneca, or to Julius Caesar's *Commentaries on the Gallic War* and Plutarch's celebrated *Parallel Lives*.

Chapter 4—Christianity and the Late Antiquity

For the period of late Antiquity and the context of Christianity's first expansion, I recommend the works of Peter Brown, specifically, *The Rise of Western Christendom* (London: Blackwell, 2013), *The Making of Late Antiquity* (Cambridge: Harvard University Press, 1978), and *The World of the Late Antiquity, AD 150–750* (New York: W. W. Norton, 1989). Brown's books were inspired by three historians who created the historiographical label 'late Antiquity' and whose works are always instructive: Henri-Irénée Marrou, *Décadence romaine ou antiquité tardive?* (Paris: Le Seuil, 1977), André Piganiol's *L'Empire chrétien, 325–395* (Paris: Presses Univiersitaires de France, 1947), and Arnaldo Momigliano, *The Conflict between Paganism and Christianity in the Fourth Century* (Oxford: Clarendon Press, 1963).

Three comprehensive introductions to the history of Christianity include Paul Johnson, *A History of Christianity* (London: Weidenfeld & Nicolson, 1976),

William Owen Chadwick, *A History of Christianity* (London: Weidenfeld & Nicolson, 1995) and Tom Holland, *Dominion: How the Christian Revolution Remade the World* (New York: Basic Books, 2019). For basic histories of Catholicism and Protestantism, see José Orlandis, *A Short History of the Catholic Church* (Blackrock: Four Courts Press, 1985) and Mark A. Noll, *Protestantism: A Very Short Introduction* (Oxford: Oxford University Press, 2011).

On the proliferation of Gnostic movements in early Christianity, an area full of controversy and lacking in clarity, see Elaine Pagels, *The Gnostic Gospels* (New York: Vintage Books, 1979) and Karen L. King, *What Is Gnosticism?* (Cambridge: Belknap Press of Harvard University Press, 2003).

Of course, direct access to primary sources is the best way to understand this period. Reading of the *Gospels* represents the best introduction to Christianity. They succinctly tell of Jesus's life and teachings. *The Acts of the Apostles*, written by the disciple Luke, who functions as both witness and insightful observer, is a historical narrative of Christianity's first three decades after the death of Jesus (around AD 30–60) and offers a good synthesis of Christianity's first expansion through the lands of Palestine, Syria, modern-day Turkey, Greece, and Rome. The *Epistles* of Saint Paul, especially those to the *Romans* and to the *Hebrews*, are more doctrinal than narrative, but display remarkable clairvoyance. Finally, Saint Augustine's *Confessions* is a classic not just for understanding Christianity's first expansion and clashes with foreign invasions that threatened to destroy the Roman Empire (around the fourth century), but also as an introduction to how Christianity began to influence the intellectual elite of the time.

There is an infinity of books on the life of Jesus, but the ones that I had most present at the time of writing this chapter were Joseph Ratzinger's three-volume *Jesus of Nazareth* (Washington: Ignatius Press, 2012); Louis C. Fillion's well-documented *The Life of Christ: A Historical, Critical, and Apologetic Exposition* (London: Herder, 1948); and Romano Guardini's *The Lord* (London: Longmans, 1956), which provides a phenomenological perspective.

There is a good biography of Saint Paul that combines deep historical insight, theological seriousness, and a remarkable capacity for contextualizing the Pauline epistles, a task quite crucial to their understanding: Josef Holzner, *Paul of Tarsus* (Strongsville: Scepter, 2002).

Finally, I used an interpretive synthesis regarding specific Christian doctrine, which presents Christian doctrine in conversation and debate with other contemporary ideas: Joseph Ratzinger, *Introduction to Christianity* (Washington: Ignatius Press, 2004). For the access to primary sources on Catholic doctrine, it is very useful to examine the *Catechism of the Catholic Church*, originally published in 1997.

Chapter 5—Clash of Civilizations

This chapter is based above all on the intuition that Henri Pirenne developed in his classic essay *Muhammad and Charlemagne* (London: Routledge, 2008), originally published in 1937.

Histories of the Mediterranean are useful for understanding the drama involved in dividing it into the three big blocks I refer to in the title of this chapter. Various texts serve to explain this: David Abulafia, *The Great Sea: A Human History of the Mediterranean* (London: Penguin, 2014); Peregrine Horden and Nicholas Purcell, *The Corrupting Sea: A Study of Mediterranean History* (Malden, MA: Blackwell, 2000); Teófilo F. Ruiz, *The Western Mediterranean and the World: 400 CE to the Present* (Hoboken: Wiley-Blackwell, 2018); and José Enrique Ruiz-Domènec, *El Mediterráneo. Historia y cultura* (Barcelona: Peninsula, 2004). Although focused on the early Modern period, it is always useful to come back to Fernand Braudel's classic monograph *Mediterranean and the Mediterranean World in the Age of Philip II* (Berkeley: California University Press, 2008), with his three levels of understanding (the geological-geographical, the socio-economical, and the politic) and their corresponding three scales of time, namely long, medium, and short terms.

To write this chapter, I referenced two introductions to Byzantine history: John Julius Norwich, *A Short History of Byzantium* (London: Penguin, 2013) and Warren Treadgold, *A Concise History Byzantium* (London: Macmillan, 2017).

I also found a few texts on classical Islam very useful, among which I highlight John J. Sanders, *A History of Medieval Islam* (London: Routledge, 2015), and P. M. Holt, Ann K. S. Lambton, and Bernard Lewis, *The Cambridge History of Islam, vol. 2b: Islamic Society and Civilization* (Cambridge: Cambridge University Press, 2008). On the difficult subject of the context of origins of Islam in Arabia, G. W. Bowersock, *Throne of Adulis: Red Sea Wars on the Eve of Islam* (Oxford: Oxford University Press, 2013) and G. W. Bowersock, *The Crucible of Islam* (Cambridge: Harvard University Press, 2017).

Chapters 6–8—Maturations (The Middle Ages)

My vocation as a medievalist permeates my approach to this section, which is likely evident in my enthusiasm for it. For a synthesis of this whole period, see Richard W. Southern, *The Making of the Middle Ages* (London: Yale University Press, 1953); Jacques Le Goff, *Medieval Civilization 400–1500* (New York: Blackwell, 1991); Clifford R. Backman, *The Worlds of Medieval Europe* (Oxford: Oxford University Press, 2003); Roger Collins, *Early Medieval Europe, 300–1000* (London:

Macmillan, 1991); William C. Jordan, *Europe in the High Middle Ages* (New York: Penguin, 2002); Maurice Keen, *The Pelican History of Medieval Europe* (London: Penguin Books, 1968); Daniel Power, *The Central Middle Ages: Europe 950–1320* (Oxford: Oxford University Press, 2006); Chris Wickham, *Medieval Europe* (New Haven: Yale University Press, 2016), among many others.

In writing this chapter, I focused mainly on cultural and intellectual issues. I indicate below some of the most representative and comprehensive texts I worked with, some of which are also historiographical references for all studies based on their ability to combine the best of the academic tradition with a remarkable ability to inform. Etienne Gilson, in *The Spirit of Medieval Philosophy* (London: Sheed and Ward, 1936) and *Dante the Philosopher* (London: Sheed and Ward, 1952), makes a convincing synthesis of the main landmarks found in the original and pervasive medieval thought. Charles H. Haskins, in *The Renaissance of the Twelfth Century* (Cambridge: Harvard University Press, 1927), reviews the culturally innovative fronts in the Middle Ages, from the recovery of the classics to the expansion of prose-style historical writing. Johan Huizinga, in *The Autumn of the Middle Ages* (Chicago: University of Chicago Press, 1997), describes the cultural tone and mentality of Europe in the late Middle Ages. Christopher Dawson offers a deep analysis of the religious aspects in his *Medieval Essays* (Washington, DC: Catholic University of America Press, 2002); Jacques Le Goff, in *Intellectuals in the Middle Ages* (Cambridge: Blackwell, 1993), reviews the intellectual history of the period, focusing on the figure of intellectuals and nascent universities. Marc Bloch, in *Feudal Society* (Chicago: University of Chicago Press, 1964), synthesizes the history of feudalism from an all-encompassing socioeconomic approach. Gabrielle M. Spiegel, in *The Past as Text: The Theory and Practice of Medieval Historiography* (Baltimore: Johns Hopkins University Press, 1997), and Jaume Aurell, *Authoring the Past: History, Autobiography, and Politics in Medieval Catalonia* (Chicago: University of Chicago Press, 2012), offer a survey of the medieval historical thought and practice, and of the different politics of memory in Medieval Europe. José Enrique Ruiz-Domènec, *La memoria de los feudales* (Barcelona: Pensódromo 21, 2017), presents an introduction to feudal actors' culture and organization. Finally, for an analysis of the rituals in medieval societies, see Janet A. Nelson, *Politics and Ritual in Early Medieval Europe* (London: Hambledon, 1986).

Art and literature help us understand (and enjoy) the Middle Ages. Dante Alighieri's sublime work, *The Divine Comedy*—divine not only for its content but also for its beauty—gives the best introduction to the spirit of the times. Georges Duby, in *Saint Bernard: l'art cistercien* (Paris: Arts et Métiers Graphiques, 1976), examines the development of Gothic art, whose foundations are traced back to the then emergent Cistercian spirituality. Duby always offers worthwhile approaches to different aspects of medieval culture, such as *The Age of the Cathedrals: Art and Society 980–1420* (Chicago: University of Chicago Press, 1983), *The Three Orders: Feudal Society Imagined* (Chicago: University of Chicago Press, 1982), and *The Legend of Bouvines: War, Religion, and Culture in the Middle Ages* (Berkeley: University of California Press, 1990).

Chapter 9—The Emergence of Modernity

Some of the general ideas in this chapter concerning the evolution of modernity from the sixteenth century to the middle of the twentieth century are inspired by the works of the great specialists in the early Modern period: Peter Burke, *The Renaissance* (London: Palgrave Macmillan, 1997) and *European Renaissance* (Cambridge: Wiley-Blackwell, 1998); Carlo Ginzburg, *The Cheese and the Worms: The Cosmos of a Sixteenth Century Miller* (Baltimore: Johns Hopkins University Press. 1980); Anthony Grafton, *What Was History? The Art of History in Early Modern Europe* (Cambridge: Cambridge University Press, 2006); Simon Schama, *Rembrandt's Eyes* (London: Penguin, 2014); *The Embarrassment of Riches: An Interpretation of Dutch Culture in the Golden Age* (New York: Knopf, 1987); Natalie Z. Davis, *Society and Culture in Early Modern France* (Stanford: Stanford University Press, 1975) and *The Return of Martin Guerre* (Cambridge: Harvard University Press, 1983).

Art is also a key for understanding the foundations of modernity: Ernst Gombrich, *The Story of Art* (London: Phaidon, 1950).

Reading Shakespeare's dramas, Cervantes's novels, or Saint Teresa of Jesus's autobiography, *The Life of Teresa of Jesus*, also helps us understand the spirit of the period, just as Virgil's texts did for Classical Antiquity or Dante's did for the Middle Ages.

Chapter 10—The Modern State

To understand the tradition on which the modern state is founded, it is still necessary to turn to Ernst Kantorowicz's classic *The King's Two Bodies* (Princeton: Princeton University Press, 1957). See also the synthesis by Anthony Black, *Political Thought in Europe, 1250–1450* (Cambridge: Cambridge University Press, 1992); Walter Ullmann, *Principles of Government and Politics in the Middle Ages* (London: Routledge, 2011), George H. Sabine, *A History of Political Theory* (London: Dryden, 1973), and Quentin Skinner, *The Foundations of Modern Political Thought* (Cambridge: Cambridge University Press, 1978).

The state considered as a founding myth of the modern world and some of its meta-political manifestations are found in Ernst Cassirer, *The Myth of the State* (New Haven: Yale University Press, 1961) and William T. Cavanaugh, *Theopolitical Imagination* (New York: Bloomsbury, 2002). Studies by classic political thinkers such as Eric Voegelin, Leo Strauss, Alexandre Kojève, and Carl Schmitt, and the sociologist Norbert Elias are always useful and instructive. John G. A. Pocock, in *The Machiavellian Moment* (Princeton: Princeton University Press, 1975), and Quentin Skinner, in *Machiavelli* (Oxford: Oxford University Press, 1981), dissect Machiavelli's thinking, which is essential to understand the foundations of the modern state. Peter Burke, in *The Fabrication of Luis XIV* (New Haven: Yale University Press, 1994), describes how the modern state functioned in its absolutist phase, materialized in the person of the king.

Finally, exploration of the contemporary derivations of the modern state can be found in Samuel P. Huntington, *Political Order in Changing Societies* (New Haven: Yale University Press, 2006).

Chapter 11—The Origins of Capitalism

Introductions to capitalism from a historical perspective can be found in Michel Beaud, *A History of Capitalism, 1500–1980* (London: MacMillan, 1984) and Fernand Braudel, *Civilization and Capitalism, 15th–18th century* (New York: Harper, 1982–1984). A general vision is found in James Fulcher, *Capitalism: A Very Short Introduction* (Oxford: Oxford University Press, 2004).

Understanding the emergence of modern capitalism also requires knowledge of the vibrant mercantile society of the Middle Ages. The most successful syntheses include Roberto S. López, *The Commercial Revolution of the Middle Ages, 950–1350* (Cambridge: Cambridge University Press, 1976) and Henri Pirenne, *Medieval Cities: Their Origins and the Revival of Trade* (Princeton: Princeton University Press, 1969).

The figure of the late medieval merchant is analyzed in Jacques Le Goff, *Marchands et banquiers du Moyen Âge* (Paris: PUF, 1981) and Jaume Aurell and Alfons Puigarnau, *La cultura del mercader en la Barcelona del siglo XV* (Barcelona: Omega, 1996). The figure of the modern bourgeois is defined in Werner Sombart, *The Quintessence of Capitalism: A Study of the History and Psychology of the Modern Business Man* (New York: E. P. Dutton, 1915). Peter Burke offers an excellent comparison of two of the most dynamic cities in modern capitalism in *Venice and Amsterdam* (Cambridge: Polity, 1994). See also an interesting cultural-economic perspective in Paul Freedman, *Out of the East: Spices and the Medieval Imagination* (New Haven: Yale University Press, 2009).

Chapter 12—Modern Science

For this chapter, I referred to essays on the general evolution of science in the West, especially those of John Gribbin, *History of Western Science: 1543–2001* (London: The Folio Society, 2006), Patricia Fara, *Science: A Four Thousand Year History* (Oxford: Oxford University Press, 2010), and Alexandre Koyre, *From the Closed World to the Infinite Universe* (Baltimore: The Johns Hopkins, 1957). For the medieval foundations of modern science, Seb Falk, *The Light Ages: The Surprising Story of Medieval Science* (New York: W.W. Norton & Company, 2020).

Other key words on the history of science are Pierre Duhem, *Medieval Cosmology: Theories of Infinity, Place, Time, Void, and the Plurality of Worlds* (Chicago: University of Chicago Press, 1985); Marshall Clagett, *The Science of Mechanics in the Middle Ages* (Madison: University of Wisconsin Press, 1979); Edward Grant, *A History of Natural Philosophy: From the Ancient World to the Nineteenth Century* (Cambridge: Cambridge University Press, 2007); Alistair Crombie, *Robert Grosseteste and the Origins of Experimental Science, 1100–1700* (Oxford: Clarendon, 1971).

On the general theory of science, Michael Polanyi, *Personal Knowledge: Towards a Post-critical Philosophy* (Chicago: University of Chicago Press, 2000); Karl R. Popper, *The Logic of Scientific Discovery* (London: Routledge, 2009); Paul Feyerabend, *Against Method: Outline of an Anarchist Theory of Knowledge* (New York: New Left Books, 1975); Ludwik Fleck, *Genesis and Development of a Scientific Fact* (Chicago: The University of Chicago Press, 1979); Alexander Koyre, *From the Closed World to the Infinite Universe* (Baltimore: Johns Hopkins Press, 1957).

The theoretical foundations and functioning of modern science are well described in various works by Thomas S. Kuhn: *The Structure of Scientific Revolutions* (Chicago: University of Chicago Press, 1962), *The Essential Tension Selected Studies in Scientific Tradition and Change* (Chicago: University of Chicago Press, 1977), and *The Copernican Revolution: Planetary Astronomy in the Development of Western Thought* (Cambridge: Harvard University Press, 1957).

For a comparative study between the development of science in the West and other civilizations: Toby E. Huff, *The Rise of Early Modern Science: Islam, China and the West* (Cambridge: Cambridge University Press, 1993); Toby E. Huff, *Intellectual Curiosity and the Scientific Revolution. A Global Perspective* (Cambridge: Cambridge University Press, 2011); Joseph Needham, ed., *Science and Civilization in China* (Cambridge: Cambridge University Press, 1954–1999); Roger Hart, *Imagined Civilizations: China, the West, and Their First Encounter* (Baltimore: Johns Hopkins University Press, 2013); Arun Bala, *The Dialogue of Civilizations in the Birth of*

Modern Science (London: Palgrave Macmillan, 2008); and Seyyed Hossien Nasr, *Science and Civilization in Islam* (Cambridge: The Islamic Texts Society, 2007).

An excellent synthesis of the history of technology, which in this chapter I also connect with the evolution of science, can be found in Thomas K. Derry and Trevor I. Williams, *A Short History of Technology* (New York: Dover, 2003). More specifically for the Middle Ages, Lynn White, Jr., *Medieval Technology and Social Change* (Oxford: Clarendon, 1966).

I also consulted biographies of some great scientists, including James Gleick, *Isaac Newton* (New York: Vintage, 2004), Mariano Artigas and William R. Shea, *Galileo in Rome* (Oxford: Oxford University Press, 2003), and Denis Brian, *Einstein: A Life* (New York: John Wiley, 1996).

Other books that cover specific aspects of modern science, but that are comprehensible for those of us who are not scientists and instead come to the topic with a more humanistic background include Ed Regis, *Who Got Einstein's Office?* (New York: Basic Books, 1988).

Chapter 13—Religious Reformations

For an introduction to Protestantism's foundations and initial expansion, see Mark A. Noll, *Protestantism: A Very Short Introduction* (Oxford: Oxford University Press, 2011) and J. Gordon Melton, ed., *Encyclopedia of Protestantism* (New York: Facts on File, 2005).

Among the many biographies of Luther, Martin Brecht's three volumes are of special interest: *Luther. 1: His Road to Reformation, 1483–1521* (Philadelphia: Fortress Press, 1985): *Luther. 2: Shaping and Defining the Reformation, 1521–1532* (Philadelphia: Fortress Press, 1994); *Luther. 3: The Preservation of the Church, 1532–1546* (Philadelphia: Fortress Press, 1999). See also Le Roy Edwin Froom, *The Prophetic Faith of Our Fathers* (Washington: Review and Herald Publishing Association, 1948); Michael A. Mullett, *Martin Luther* (London: Routledge, 2004); Derek Wilson, *Out of the Storm: The Life and Legacy of Martin Luther* (London: Hutchinson, 2007).

See also Brad S. Gregory, *The Unintended Reformation: How a Religious Revolution Secularized Society* (Cambridge, Harvard University Press, 2012) and the classics of Lucien Febvre, *The Problem of Unbelief in the Sixteenth Century: The Religion of Rabelais* (Cambridge: Harvard University Press, 1982); Jacques Maritain, *Three Reformers: Luther, Descartes, Rousseau* (New York: C. Scribner's Sons, 1941); and Carlo Ginzburg, *The Cheese and the Worms: The Cosmos of a Sixteenth-Century Miller* (Baltimore: Johns Hopkins University Press. 1980).

Chapter 14—Enlightenments

To understand the immediate precedents and the origins of the Enlightenment, Paul Hazard's classic, *The Crisis of the European Mind, 1680–1715* (New York: New York Review Books, 2013), remains reliable.

A general introduction to the Enlightenment is found in John Robertson, *The Enlightenment: A Very Short Introduction* (Oxford: Oxford University Press, 2015).

For the most detailed account of the Enlightenment and its different phases and levels of radicalism, see the four monographs by Jonathan I. Israel, *Radical Enlightenment: Philosophy and the Making of Modernity, 1650–1750* (Oxford: Oxford University Press, 2001); *Enlightenment Contested: Philosophy, Modernity, and the Emancipation of Man, 1670–1752* (Oxford: Oxford University Press, 2006); *Democratic Enlightenment: Philosophy, Revolution, and Human Rights 1750–1790* (Oxford: Oxford University Press, 2011); and *A Revolution of the Mind: Radical Enlightenment and the Intellectual Origins of Modern Democracy* (Princeton: Princeton University Press, 2011).

Understanding the Enlightenment requires knowledge of the intellectual trajectory of its most representative pioneers and advocates. Excellent works in this regard include Leo Strauss, *The Political Philosophy of Hobbes* (Oxford: Clarendon Press, 1936), Peter Burke, *Vico* (Oxford: Oxford University Press, 1985), John W. Yolton, *John Locke: Problems and Perspectives* (Cambridge: Cambridge University Press, 1969), Alfred J. Ayer, *Voltaire* (New York: Random, 1986), and Alfred J. Ayer, *Hume* (Oxford: Oxford University Press, 2001).

The social dimension of this eminently intellectual phenomenon can be better understood with Peter Burke, *Social History of Knowledge: From Gutenberg to Diderot* (Cambridge: Polity, 2000).

Finally, an excellent summary of how the Enlightenment affects our age can be explored in Anthony Pagden, *The Enlightenment and Why It Still Matters* (New York: Random, 2003).

Chapter 15—Ideologies: Marxism, Fascism, Liberalism

To understand the ideologies that developed in the nineteenth century, we must look to their revolutionary origins toward the end of the eighteenth century. Among the most lucid interpretations of French revolutionaries' ideology: Francois Furet, *Interpreting the French Revolution* (Cambridge: Cambridge University Press, 1981), Lynn Hunt, *Politics, Culture and Class in the French Revolution* (Berkeley: California University Press, 2004), and William H. Sewell Jr., *Work and Revolution in France: The Language of Labor from the Old Regime to 1848* (Cambridge: Cambridge University Press, 1980).

A contextual introduction to the period in which these ideologies were created can be found in Eric J. Hobsbawm's trilogy, *The Age of the Revolution: Europe 1789–1848* (New York: Vintage, 1995), *The Age of Capital, 1848–1875* (New York: Vintage, 1996), and *The Age of Empire, 1975–1914*. See also Richard J. Evans, *The Pursuit of Power: Europe, 1815–1914* (London: Viking, 2016). The historical materialization of Marxist ideology is well summarized in Stephen A. Smith, ed., *The Oxford Handbook of the History of Communism* (Oxford: Oxford University Press, 2014). Despite the public commotion associated with its original publication, some of the nefarious consequences of Marxist praxis are well described in Stéphane Courtois, and others, *The Black Book of Communism* (Cambridge: Harvard University Press, 1999).

A good synthesis of fascism—its identity, concept, and historical development—can be found in Stanley G. Payne, *A History of Fascism, 1914–1945* (Madison: University of Wisconsin Press, 1995).

Some of the formulations of classical liberalism and its political and economic derivations are well summarized in Lawrence H. White, *The Clash of Economic Ideas* (Cambridge: Cambridge University Press, 2012). Capitalism's most current instantiation is dissected in Thomas Piketty's monumental study, *Capital in the Twenty-first Century* (Cambridge: Harvard University Press, 2017). It is always useful to come back to the basic theories of liberalism and capitalism as they were originally formulated, such as Adam Smith, *An Inquiry into the Nature and Causes of the Wealth of Nations* (Oxford : Clarendon Press, 1979, originally published in 1776) and John Maynard Keynes, *The General Theory of Employment, Interest and Money* (London: Macmillan, 1936).

Biographies of the main actors in this period, in this case the leaders of Fascism and Communism, are of great interest: Ian Kershaw, *Hitler: A Biography* (New York: W. W. Norton, 2010); Robert Service, *Stalin: A Biography* (London: Macmillan, 2004); and Robert Payne, *Mao Tse-Tung* (New York: Weybright and Talley, 1969).

Some of the ideas in this chapter are inspired by the dense book interview by Tony Judt, *Thinking the Twenty-first Century* (London: Penguin, 2013) and the remarkable autobiographies from my fellows historians, such as Eric J. Hobsbawm, *Interesting Times: A Twentieth-Century life* (London: Allen Lane, 2002), Annie Kriegel, *Ce que j'ai cru comprendre* (Paris: Le Gran Livre du Mois, 1991), Richard Pipes, *Vixi: Memoirs of a Non-Belonger* (New Haven, Yale University Press, 2003), Geoff Eley, *A Crooked Line: From Cultural History to the History of Society* (Ann Arbor: University of Michigan Press, 2005), and Robert A. Rosenstone, *Adventures of a Postmodern Historian: Living and Writing the Past* (London: Bloomsbury, 2016).

As I explain in this chapter, many of the excesses that contemporary ideologies generate are due to the fact that people often confuse them with religions, an idea documented in detail by Michael Burleigh, *Sacred Causes: The Clash of Religion and Politics, from the Great War to the War on Terror* (New York: Harper, 2008).

Chapter 16—The Crisis of Modernity

We sometimes fail to give sufficient attention to World War I, which was known at the time as 'the Great War' and which lies at the base of the modern (and postmodern) conscience's profound crisis. Good syntheses of the causes and development of the Great War come from Margaret MacMillan, *The War that Ended Peace: The Road to 1914* (New York: Random, 2014) and Michael Howard, *The First World War: A Very Short Introduction* (Oxford: Oxford University Press, 2007).

Many political and intellectual lines converge in this chapter, which makes summarizing them especially complex. To understand this, and to find a thread that unites it, I recommend a far-reaching text by Norman F. Cantor, *The American Century: Varieties of Culture in Modern Times* (New York: Harper, 1997). His clarity and ability to synthesize and define some of the most complex concepts from this period (especially the key concept of modernism, which is often so erroneously employed) are masterful. Peter Watson's synthesis, *The Modern Mind: An Intellectual History of the Twentieth Century* (New York: HarperCollins, 2002) is a dense, but well-ordered explanation of many of the interwar period's key intellectual concepts, as well as those from the postwar period (in this regard, it is also recommendable for the next chapter).

To understand the intellectual evolution of this period, I recommend exploring two key cities, namely Vienna at the end of the nineteenth century and Berlin during the interwar period, which are reflected in Carl E. Schorske, *Fin-de-Siècle Vienna: Politics and Culture* (New York: Vintage, 1993), Peter Gay, *Weimar Culture: The Outsider as Insider* (New York: W. W. Norton, 2001), and, for the political context of Weimar Germany, Eric D. Weitz, *Weimar Germany: Promise and Tragedy* (Princeton: Princeton University Press, 2007).

A few overall approaches are also useful for understanding the context of this period, including Ian Kershaw, *To Hell and Back: Europe 1914–1949* (London: Penguin, 2016), Anthony Adamthwaite, *The Making of the Second World War* (London: Allen and Unwin, 1977), and Niall Ferguson, *The War of the World: Twentieth Century Conflict and the Descent of the West* (London: Penguin, 2006).

On the influential Frankfurt school, whose shadow stretched throughout the twentieth century, see Martin Jay, *The Dialectical Imagination: A History of the Frankfurt School and the Institute of Social Research* (Berkeley: University of California Press, 1996).

Chapter 17—Liberations: the Struggle for Freedom and Equality

An ambitious and acclaimed general and contextual introduction to this period comes from Tony Judt: *Postwar: A History of Europe since 1945* (London: Penguin, 2006). Other useful texts include overviews from Paul Johnson, *Modern Times* (New York: HarperCollins, 2001) and Walter Laqueur, *Europe since Hitler: The Rebirth of Europe* (London: Penguin, 1982).

From a political perspective, introductions to the Cold War include John L. Gaddis, *The Cold War: A New History* (London: Penguin, 2006), an author who is also well known for his remarkable text on the practice of history: *The Landscape of History: How Historians Map the Past* (Oxford: Oxford University Press, 2004). On the United States, see Niall Ferguson, *Colossus: The Rise and Fall of the American Empire* (London: Penguin, 2005). On the Soviet Union, see Raymond Pearson, *The Rise and Fall of the Soviet Empire* (London: Palgrave, 2002).

For the precedents of the Declaration of Universal Rights of 1948, and its obvious connection with the Declaration of the French Revolutionaries, Georg Jellinek, *The Declaration of the Rights of Man and of Citizens: A Contribution to Modern Constitutional History* (New York: Henry Holt, 1901). On the history of human rights: Henry J. Steiner and Philip Alston, *International Human Rights in Context: Law, Politics, Morals* (Oxford University Press: Oxford, 2000); Johannes Morsink, *The Universal Declaration of Human Rights: Origins, Drafting, and Intent* (Philadelphia: University of Pennsylvania Press, 1999); Mary Ann Glendon, *A World Made New: Eleanor Roosevelt and the Universal Declaration of Human Rights* (New York: Random House, 2002).

On the revolution of 1968, see Mark Kurlansky, *1968: The Year that Rocked the World* (New York: Random House, 2004). On the crucial influence of French intellectuals: François Dosse, *La Saga des intellectuels français, II. L'Avenir en miettes (1968–1989)* (Paris: Gallimard, 2018). Some ideas herein concerning the cultural evolution of this period are from a somewhat naive, but tremendously expressive, text by Norman F. Cantor, *The Age of Protest: Dissent and Rebellion in the Twentieth Century* (San Rafael, CA: Leswing, 1969), written very shortly after the events he narrates, which, due to his proximity to the events described, gives the book a singular air of testimony.

Chapter 18—Challenging the West

I started this chapter by citing two essays that, beyond the controversy and debate that they incited at the time of their publication, are also good introductions to this period of enigmas, as well as contain valuable information on and interpretations of an already globalized world: Francis Fukuyama, *The End of History and the Last Man* (New York: Free Press, 1992) and Samuel P. Huntington, *The Clash of Civilizations and the Remaking of World Order* (Charlesbourg, Quebec: Braille Jymico, 2004).

Jean-François Lyotard's *The Postmodern Condition: A Report on Knowledge* (Minneapolis: University of Minnesota Press, 1989), originally published in 1979, is cited as a diagnostic model for the various ideas that contributed to the creation of the "postmodern" label that reigns at present.

On the new geopolitical scenario herein, see Walter Laqueur, *No End to War: Terrorism in the Twenty-First Century* (New York: Continuum, 2004). On the new economic context and its contradictions, see Thomas Piketty, *Capital in the Twenty-Frist Century* (Cambridge: Harvard University Press, 2017) and Niall Ferguson, *The Ascent of Money: A Financial History of the World* (London: Penguin, 2019).

A good introduction to globalization comes from two American intellectuals: Marshall McLuhan and Bruce R. Powers, *The Global Village. Transformations in World Life and Media in the 21st Century* (Oxford: Oxford University Press, 1992). Regarding the influence of new technologies, I relied on Asa Briggs and Peter Burke, *A Social History of the Media: From Gutenberg to the Internet* (Oxford: Polity Press, 2018), as well as on the more succinct, but not less interesting, text authored by Peter Burke, *A Social History of Knowledge: From the Encyclopedia to Wikipedia* (Cambridge: Polity Press, 2014).

For an introduction to authors as influential as Richard Rorty, Michel Foucault, Jacques Derrida, and Hayden White, see Ernst Breisach, *On the Future of History: The Postmodernist Challenge and Its Consequences* (Chicago: University of Chicago Press, 2007).

DETAILED TABLE OF CONTENTS

Introduction

The spirit of the book—The challenges of the West—The concept of genealogy— Civilization—Religion—Consciousness—The West still matters

Chapter 1

1000 BC—King David—The conquest of Jerusalem—The Temple in Jerusalem—The Chosen People—The colonization of the Promised Land—Israel and its neighbors (Egypt, Mesopotamia, Persia)—Monotheism—Compiling a history: The Bible—Exchange of ideas among ancient civilizations—The settling of a tradition—Alphabetic writing—Genesis: Fascination with the origins—Mythical and symbolic language—The privilege of divine election—The origins of anti-Judaism—Between providentialism and fatalism—The monarchy of Israel—Kings David and Solomon—From elective to hereditary monarchy—Kings and priests share a royal anointing—Kings and prophets and the search for wisdom—Messianic expectancy—The Messiah—Political and spiritual messianism—Jesus's crucifixion—Demolition of the Temple—Jews and Christians

Chapter 2

500 BC—Greece and Persia—The Emperors Cyrus and Darius—The Persian Wars—Marathon, Thermopylae, and Salamis—Reason against barbarism—Victors and the vanquished—The power of legend—Homer—Mythologized heroes—Pericles's Athens—Classic art—Phidias—The Greek Acropolis—The value of philosophy and reason—Myth and logos—Reality and fiction—Greek myths and modern films—The Father of History: Herodotus—The theater: The rationalization of rites—Tragedy and

comedy—Sophocles—Euripides—Aristophanes—The organization of the Polis—The Solonian Constitution—Athenian democracy—The legacy of classical Greece

Chapter 3

250 BC—Roman civilization—The origins of Rome—Romulus and Remus—Monarchy—Tarquin the Proud—Consuls—Patricians and plebeians—Italian Expansion—Alliances and conquests—The Punic Wars: Carthage and Hannibal—Hellenization—Hispania—Gaul—Julius Caesar—Augustus and the Empire—Transferring the empire—The rationalization of administration—Public works and engineering—A tax regime—Roman law—Roman citizenship—The Mediterranean, a commonwealth—Romanization—The legacy of Rome—Roman and Germanic legacy—Paganism and Christianity

Chapter 4

AD 30—The Christian era—Jesus's teachings—The Rich and poor—Masters and slaves—The death and the resurrection of Jesus—Saint Paul and the first great expansion—The rupture between Judaism and Christianity—Rome as the center of Christianity—The Gospels and the New Testament—The apostolic tradition—Divine revelation—A near and ever present God—Persecution and martyrdom—The liberalization of Christian worship—Constantine's conversion—Councils—Politics and religion—The second Enlightenment—Hellenization and Christianity—The social effects of Christianity: The case of slavery—Rome and Constantinople

Chapter 5

AD 622—Late Antiquity—The triple heritage of the Roman Empire: West, Orthodoxy, and Islam—The Byzantine world—Constantinople—Justinian—The recovery of Roman Law—The Byzantine Basileus—The emperor and patriarch—The Byzantine ceremonial—Religious schism—The Islamic world—The Arab substrate—Muhammad—The first Islamic expansion—Cultural heritage: The decimal system and the recovery of the classics—The Western world—Charlemagne—The unifying function of Latin—The Carolingian Empire—The emperor and the pope—The "restoration" of the Roman Empire in the West—Demystifying the Middle Ages—The Enlightenment's misunderstanding—Nine medieval values

Chapter 6

AD 870—Disintegration of the Carolingian empire—Invasions: Vikings, Normans, Magyars, and Muslims—Game of Thrones—Benedictines—Capetian France—Anglo-Saxon Britain—Holy Roman German Empire—Christianization of Central Europe: Poland, Bohemia, Hungary—The kingdom of Rus in Kiev—The Balkans—Christianization of Scandinavia—Vikings—Normans—Al-Andalus in Iberia—Christian kingdoms of Iberia—The Reconquista and the Convivencia—The Sicilian curse—Universitas Christiana

Chapter 7

AD 1100—Axial shift—Intellectual revolution—Bernard and Abelard—The Birth of the University—The Gregorian reform—Roman and Canonical Law—The Third Enlightenment: Scholastic theology—Abelard and the Logics—Thomas of Aquinas and the rational theology—Robert Grosseteste and the science—Legal reform—Institutionalization of Corporations—Roger Bacon and the laws of nature—The foundations of modern science—Chivalric codes—Courtly love—Urban development

Chapter 8

AD 1300—Dante and The Divine Comedy—Giotto and the artistic revolution—Geoffrey Chaucer and the new literature—Marsilius of Padua and the secularization—William of Ockham and the Human Rights—Christine de Pizan and the early feminism

Chapter 9

AD 1500—Modernity and modern—Where and when—Who: Key characters—Why: The causes of change—Humanism—Renaissance—Patronage: Lorenzo the Magnificent—Geographical discoveries: Christopher Columbus—Expansion and evangelization: conquerors and missionaries—Colonization—Iberian Expansion—Philosophical Rationalism — Political state, economic capitalism, scientific knowledge, and religious reformation

Chapter 10

The modern state—Definitions—Origins—Precedents—Feudal monarchy—Territorial monarchy—Authoritarian monarchy—The function of representative

bodies—Absolutist and enlightened monarchy—American Constitution—
The French Revolution—Descendent and ascendant theories of power—The
liberal state—Monarchy or republic—Division of powers: Legislative, executive,
judicial—State and nation—Totalitarianism—The role of a constitution—
The liberal-democratic system—Alternatives—Populism—The effects of
globalization—Supranational organization—The future of the state—From the
state to capitalism

Chapter 11

From merchants to capitalists—The rationalization of the economy—
The relationship between individual, work, and capital—Exponential
surplus—The mercantile bourgeoisie—The support of Franciscans and
Dominicans—The capitalist mentality—A society with mercantile values—
Financial activity—The creation of banks—Credit as a conventional
economic activity—Public debt in kingdoms and cities—Monetarization—
Deferred payment documents—The value of trust—Compliance with
rules—Corruption—The autonomous mercantile legal system—The birth
of insurances—Large mercantile companies—The first Dutch and English
global companies—The emergence of anonymous capital—Corporations—
Three problems: anonymization, delocalization, inequality—Marxist
criticism—Problems associated with the independence of capital:
Speculation—Capitalism today—The alternatives—The regularization
of markets—The promotion of growth from within—The economy of
capitalism and the economy of the gift

Chapter 12

Science and Technology—Knowledge and action—Western scientific
revolution— A comparison with other civilization: Islam and China—The
rationalization of science—From medieval scholasticism to modern science—
Faith and reason—Philosophy and theology—Inductive and experimental
English thought—Roger Bacon—From the philosophy of nature to natural
sciences—The development of mechanics—William of Ockham—Integral
humanism—Leonardo da Vinci—"Nature does not break her own laws"—
Calculus—Galileo—From astrology to astronomy—Isaac Newton—The
theory of gravity—John Locke and the spirit of tolerance—Scientific discoveries
and technological inventions—Industrialization and mechanization—
Transportation—Developing modes of communication—Einstein and

the theory of relativity—Bohr and quantum theory—The infinite and the miniscule—The enigmas of the universe—The legacy of scientific and technological development

Chapter 13

A new clash—The press and the Reformation: technology and ideas— Reformation: Luther, Zwingli, and Calvin—Counter-Reformation: Ignatius of Loyola and Teresa of Avila—Politics and Religion—The First European civil war: Thirty Years' War—Protestantism and capitalism—Disenchantment of the world—Freedom of conscience and subjectivism—Sola Scriptura—The transcendental self—The Protestant Ethics and the Capitalism—Protestantism, Catholicism, and Science—The expansion of Protestantism—Protestantism today—Protestantism and the West

Chapter 14

AD 1715—The Fourth Enlightenment—Substitution of religion—The symbolism of light—Rationalization and secularization—Precedents: The crisis of European consciousness—Spinoza, Bayle, Toland, Vico—Intellectual elitism—Enlightened despotism—The French Enlightenment—Voltaire and the public moral—The German Enlightenment—Kant and the autonomy of reason—The British Enlightenment—Hume and empiricism—Adam Smith and economic liberalism—Edward Gibbon and rational history—The American Enlightenment—Alexis de Tocqueville—Anti-Catholicism—Anticlericalism— Praise of tolerance—Religious freedom—Politics and religion—Freedom of expression—Jean-Jacques Rousseau and universal equality—Adam Smith and the Wealth of Nations—Universalism—The Encyclopedia—A new genre: The essay and the printing press—Enlightenment and revolution—The anti-liberal reaction—Enlightenment and Modernity: The Frankfurt School— Enlightenment and Postmodernity—The legacy of the Enlightenment

Chapter 15

AD 1789—The dawn of ideologies—Definition—Characteristics—Four ideologies: Liberalism, Marxism, fascism, nationalism—Nineteenth-century trends: Romanticism, historicism, positivism, evolutionism, and pragmatism— The origins: The French Revolution—The legacy of the French Revolution: Republicanism (Liberalism), socialism (Marxism), authoritarianism

(Fascism)—Dimensions of liberalism: Intellectual, political, economic, and social—Free thought—Parliamentary democracy—Liberal capitalism—Social democracy and the welfare state—Social fluidity—The hegemony of liberalism—Marx and Marxism—Theory and praxis—Social and class struggle—Marxism and Christianity—Political forms—Communism, nationalism, and empire—Global expansion—Disintegration—From communism to populism—Fascism—Political forms of fascism—Fascism and nationalism—Strategies: Propaganda, rites, political totalitarianism, messianism—Substitution of religion—The Crisis of Modernity

Chapter 16

AD 1914—Ideologies and nationalism—The crisis of Modernity—Modernism—Picasso's Guernica and the disfiguration of the art—Nietzsche and the "death of God"—Einstein and the theory of relativity—The regulation of science and technology—The world in war—Russian Revolution—The Crash of 1929 and the Great Depression—The regulation of the economy: Keynesian theories—The modernist crisis in the Catholic Church—Challenging modernity—Irrationalism—The avant-garde—Dadaism—Surrealism—Expressionism—Cubism—Functionalism and organic architecture—The Warburg Institute—Literary modernism—Nihilism in literature—Organicism in history—Existentialism in philosophy—Personalism in theology—Dystopias—Transhumanism—Humans and machine—A linguistic turn—Psychoanalysis—Marx, Nietzsche, and Freud—Modernism as anti-modern—Modernism as anti-historicist—Modernism as anti-enlightenment—Postmodernism and Postmodernity

Chapter 17

AD 1945—The aftermath—Political and military decline in Europe—The Cold War—Communism, capitalism, and nationalism—The globalization of armed conflicts—Southeast Asian wars—Latin American liberation movements—Terrorism and guerrillas—Independence in Africa and Asia—Liberation movements in the 1960s: race, class, nation, and gender—Racial liberation: Martin Luther King—The student revolt: Berkeley and Paris—Decolonization—Liberation and Marxism—Communist subversion and revolution—Russian dissidents—Gender liberation—Feminist claims—The counterculture—Beat generation—The Beatles—Relaxation of social conventions—Idealism and naivety—The sad 1970s—The economic crisis of

1973—The upsurge of armed conflicts: Vietnam, Cambodia, Afghanistan—The conservative revolution of the 1980s—The fall of the Berlin Wall—The legacy of the postwar period

Chapter 18

AD 1989—Fukuyama's "end of history"—Huntington's "clash of civilizations"—From ideologies to civilizations—A late Modern era—The fall of the Berlin wall and its aftermath—Post-communism—Leftist populisms—Right-leaning populisms—The 1990s—A new international geopolitical scene—The Middle East and the Persian Gulf—Political Crisis: Islamic Fundamentalism and Jihad—Economic Crisis: The Financial Crash of 2007—Alternatives to modern capitalism—Alternatives to the modern state—Globalization in politics—Supranational organizations—Alternatives to modern science—Scientific and symbolic language—What is essential is invisible to the eye—The postmodern condition: Lyotard—Postmodern authors: Rorty, Derrida, Foucault—Postmodernity or late Modernity—Current situation

Epilogue

Challenges—Transculturation—Identitarianism—Post-Christian age—Anti-universalism—Postcolonialism—Westernization and Modernization—Conclusion

INDEX

A

Aalto, Alvar 209
Abd al-Rahman III 89
Abelard, Peter 12, 19, 93–95, 100–104,
    116, 158
Abraham 25, 34
absolutism 134, 135
Achilles 37
Acropolis (Athens) 38, 39
Acts of the Apostles 62, 63
Adams, John 182
Adelard of Bath 100
Adenauer, Konrad 13, 196, 251
Adorno, Theodor 186
Aeneas 45
Afghanistan 35, 228, 233, 238
African Americans 224
Agrippa, King of Israel 51
Ahijah, prophet of Israel 32
Ajax 37
Al-Andalus 89
Albert of Saxony 160
Albert the Great (Albertus Magnus) 100,
    103, 158, 159
Alexander the Great 46, 128
Alexandria 68
Alfonso II the Troubadour, King of
    Aragon 133
Alfonso VI of Castile 89, 90
Alfonso X the Wise, King of Castile 227
Alfred the Great of England 85
Algeria 218
Ali, cousin to Muhammad 77
Allah 77

Amazing Grace (2006) 67
Ambrose of Milan 65, 66, 81
American Awakenings, the 176
American *Bill of Rights* (1791) 256
American Civil War 220
American Independence 194
American Revolution 136, 182, 185, 194
Américo Castro 90
Amsterdam, Netherlands 144
Anabaptism 174
Anglo-Saxon, people 85–87, 130, 148, 253
anonymization of the economy 150
Anselm of Canterbury 99, 100, 116
anti-clericalism 183
Antioch of Syria 61, 68
Antiquity 20, 29, 50, 68, 72, 97, 103, 151
anti-Semitism 27, 31, 186
Antwerp, Belgium 144, 145
Anubis, Egiptian God 27
Apostles 62
Aquinas, Thomas 100, 101, 103, 104,
    112, 158
Arab Muslim 88
Arabia 35, 68, 76, 84
Arabian Peninsula 76
Arabic Islam 79
Arabs 128, 239
Aragon, Spain 89, 90
Aragonese Pyrenees 81
Archbishop of Rheims 85
Archduke Franz Ferdinand 87
Arendt, Hannah
    *Eichmann in Jerusalem: A Report on
    the Banality of Evil* 202

Aristophanes 43
Aristotle 39, 99, 103, 111, 117,
    158, 160
Armesto, Felipe Fernández 14
Armitage, David 17
Arthur, King of England 37
Asia Minor 63, 73
Asturias, Spain 89
Athanasius of Alexandria 66
Athenian civilization 38
Athens 36
Augsburg, Germany 144, 145
Augustine de Hippo, Saint 19, 66
Augustus, emperor Rome 12, 38, 48
Austria 80
Austro-Hungarian Empire 87
authoritarianism 134, 140, 187, 193
avant-garde 9, 208, 209, 214, 215
Averroes 79, 156
Avicenna 79, 156
axial age 18, 20

B
Babeuf, François 193
Bacon, Francis 178
Bacon, Roger 103, 107, 158, 159
Baez, Joan 233
Baghdad 91
Balkans, the 35, 87
Barcelona, Spain 89, 144, 145, 149
Baretti, Giuseppe 162
Barth, Karl 210
Basil of Caesarea 66
Bathsheba 32
Baudelaire, Charles 173
Bayle, Pierre 178, 179
Beard, Mary 13
beat generation 231
Beatles, The 16, 231, 232, 233
Beauvoir, Simone de 229
Becket, Thomas 98
Beckett, Samuel 210
Belgium 80, 196
Bell, David A. 7
Benedict of Nursia 84
Benedictine 82, 84, 85, 94, 95, 102, 107,
    110, 144, 171

Benson, Robert H.
    Lord of the World 211
Bergson, Jean 117
Berlin Wall 16, 201, 234, 237
Bernard of Chartres 4, 94, 95, 99
Bernard of Clairvaux 94, 95, 101, 110
Bernini, Gian Lorenzo 127
Bethlehem 33, 58
Bible 13, 27, 28, 31, 33, 162,
    178, 241
Biblical faith 65
Black Nationalism 223
Blade Runner (1982) 164, 212
Blatand, Harold 88
Bohemia 85
Bohr, Niels 101, 158, 165, 205
Boleslaw, King of Poland 13
Boston, Bernie 233
Botticelli, Sandro 114, 124, 127
Bourdieu, Pierre 135
Bradford, Lillie Mae 221
Bradwardine, Thomas 103, 160
Braque, Georges 208
Braudel, Fernand 14, 17
Bridget of Sweden 119
Britain 52, 67, 207, 232
British Empire 53, 134, 138
Brown, Peter 72
Bruges, Belgium 144, 145
Brunelleschi, Filippo 127
Bruno, Giordano 167
Buber, Martin 211
Buddhism 66
Bulgars 87
Buñuel, Luis 208
Buonarroti, Michelangelo 114, 124, 127
Buridan, Jean 160
Byzantine Christianity 94
Byzantine civilization 73, 75
Byzantine Empire 74–76, 79
Byzantine Orthodox Christianity 87
Byzantium 72, 73, 75, 78, 93

C
Calvin, John 168, 171, 174, 175
Calvinism 174
Cambodia 8, 218

Cambridge, England 17, 97
Campbell, Joseph
  The Hero with a Thousand Voices 40
Camus, Albert 210
Canute II, king of Denmark 85
capitalism 1, 4, 9, 10, 15, 17, 130, 134,
  136, 141, 143, 148–154, 158,
  173–176, 186, 195–198, 201, 235,
  237, 238, 240–242, 256, 258
capitalist economy 154, 196, 206
capitalist imperialism 226
Caravaggio 127, 214
Carolingian Empire 71, 85
Cassirer, Ernst 186, 210
Castile, Spain 89
Castro, Fidel 218
Catalonia 81
Catherine II of Russia 135, 179
Catherine of Siena 119
Catholic 73, 134, 162, 170, 171, 174, 211
Catholic Church 168, 182, 194, 207, 234
Catholic Reformation 168
Catholicism 173, 174, 180
Catlos, Brian
  Kingdoms of Faith (2019) 90
Cervantes, Miguel de 109, 124
Chaplin, Charles 150
Charlemagne 12, 30, 49, 68, 71, 79–81, 170
Charles I of England 134, 136
Charles III of Spain 135, 179
Charles V of Spain 49, 147, 170
Charles X 83
Charles, Duke of Lower Lorraine 85
Chaucer, Geoffrey 113, 115
Chechnya 78
Chesterton, G.K. 249
China 7, 20, 72, 93, 94, 106, 128, 129,
  153, 155, 156, 167, 195, 197, 200,
  236, 239, 249, 253, 255–257
Chinese civilization 17, 157, 236
Chivalry 108, 109
  medieval 109
Christian civilization 183
Christian faith 158
Christian God 125, 140, 177
Christian religion 256
Christian scholasticism 160
Christian Trinity 64
Christian values 18
Christian West 7, 93, 107
Christianity 66
Christianity 15, 18, 27, 34, 54, 55, 57–67,
  73, 84, 85, 88, 111, 167, 171, 176,
  200, 240, 249, 250, 257
Christianization 62, 86, 250
Christians 34, 55, 61, 64, 65
Chrysostom, John 66
Churchill, Winston 12, 251
Cicero 51, 53, 103
Cid, The Poem of 40, 109
civic responsibility 148
civilization 13, 14, 45
  ancient 155
  clash of 218, 236, 238, 239
  concept of 14–16, 236
  diversity of 20
  stationary 255
civilizational analysis 17
civilizational complex 15
civilizational identity 14
Clark, Kenneth 13
Classical Antiquity 84, 125
Clovis, king of the Franks 13
Coeur, Jacques 124
Cohn-Bendit, Daniel 226
Cold War 9, 72, 140, 201, 218, 232,
  233, 234, 237, 239
Collingwood, Robin G. 12
Cologne, Germany 144
Columbus, Christopher 12, 124, 128
commercial revolution 82, 93,
  144, 198
communism 193, 201, 234, 250
Communist Party 257
Communists 151
community 107, 171
  discourse 13
  religious 107
Comte, Auguste 192, 209
Concordat of Worms 65
Condorcet 186
Confucianism 18, 66
Congress of Vienna 136, 186
Conrad, Joseph 173

conscience 18, 103, 104, 171–173, 175, 223, 251, 256
consciousness 13, 15, 16, 18, 19, 99
Constantine 49, 54, 55, 64, 65, 73, 81, 112, 178, 218
Constantinople 68, 73, 74, 124
Copernicus, Nicolaus 12, 101, 124, 158, 162, 165, 174, 175, 205
Córdoba 89–91
Corpus iuris civilis Justiniani 74
Cortés, Hernán 129, 251
Council of Nicaea 65
Council of Trent 168
counterculture 231
Counter-Reformation 168
Cromwell, Oliver 134
Cubism 209, 215, 244
cultural liberation 219
cultural reality 229
Cultural Revolution 200
cultural studies 242
Cyrus the Great 35

D
d'Alembert, Jean 184
d'Eiximenis, Francesc 145
da Vinci, Leonardo 12, 114, 124, 125, 158, 160, 161, 163
Dadaism 208
Dali, Salvador 2, 208
Damascus 89, 91
Daniélou, Jean 210
Dante Alighieri 2, 12, 112, 113, 240
The Divine Comedy 2, 111, 115
Danzig 144
Darius, king of Persia 35, 36, 49
Darwin, Charles 192
Datini, Francesco 143
David, king of Israel 25, 31–33, 58
Dawson, Christopher 14, 18
de Chateaubriand, François-René 19
de-Christianization 62
de Gaulle, Charles 226
de Saussure, Ferdinand
Course in General Linguistics 1916 212
Dean, James 231
Declaration of Independence 182

decolonization 9, 152, 185, 201, 221, 227, 229, 238
Decree of Gratian 98
democracy 4, 20, 43
Denmark 85, 88, 237
Derrida, Jacques 242, 244
Descartes, Rene 100, 130, 158, 159, 161, 171, 174, 175, 178, 209
Dickens, Charles
Oliver Twist 214
Diderot, Denis 184
Dilthey, Wilhelm 192
Diocletian, emperor Roma 64
Dostoyevsky, Fyodor 160
Brothers Karamazov 214
Douglas, Mary 18
DuBois, W.E.B. 221
Dudintsev, Vladimir
Not by Bread Alone 1956 229
Duhem, Pierre 101
Durkheim, Émile 14, 179
Elementary Forms of Religious Life 18
Dutch merchant 149
Dylan, Bob 233

E
Eastern Christianity 81, 247
Eastern civilization 5
Eckhart, Meister 113
economic liberalism 184, 195
Edict of Milan 64
Edmund Ironside 85
Edward the Confessor 86
effective consciousness 5
Egypt 7, 12, 33, 35, 47, 49, 58, 63, 76, 84, 238
Einstein, Albert 12, 101, 158, 161, 163, 165, 203, 205
Elcano, Juan Sebastián 129
England 85, 86, 88, 123, 127, 129, 134, 145, 168, 185, 196, 206, 212, 217, 218, 228, 238
English Civil War 136
English merchant 149
Enlightenment 6, 8, 14, 40, 66, 171, 177, 178, 180, 182–187, 203
Erigena, Scotus 116

Etruscans 46
EU. *See* European Union
Euripides 43
Eurocentrism 7
Europe 8, 73, 81, 83, 84, 94, 97, 102, 106,
    118, 124, 138, 144, 147, 155, 156,
    170, 171, 182, 187, 191, 192, 197,
    201, 203, 206, 207, 210, 217, 219,
    231, 245, 252
European Union (EU) 13, 141, 240
Evans-Pritchard, Edward 183
evolutionism 192
exclusivism 253
Eyck, Jan van 124

F
fascism 118, 186, 193, 198, 201, 202
Fathers of the Church 65
Feijoo, Benito Jerónimo
    Teatro crítico universal 185
feminism 119, 120, 229
Ferdinand III the Saint of Castile 133
Ferguson, Niall
    Civilization: The West and the Rest 15
feudal system 133, 144, 151, 240
feudalism 4, 54, 84, 87, 108, 156, 198, 265
Feuerbach, Ludwig
    The Essence of Christianity 1841 18
Fichte, Johann Gottlieb 173
Fidanza, Giovanni di (Bonaventure) 100,
    103, 158
Fiore, Joachim de 167
First World War. *See* Great War, World
    War I
Flanders 38, 81, 127, 144
Florence, Italy 144, 145
Ford, John
    The Man Who Shot Liberty Vallance 89
Foucault, Michel 11, 173, 186,
    242–244, 248
    The Government of the Living 1974 171
Four Asian Tigers 154
France 80, 85, 86, 123, 127, 128,
    145, 168, 185, 196, 206, 217, 218,
    228, 238
Francis of Assisi, Saint 144
Francis of Marchia 160

Franciscan Juníper Serra 251
Franco-Carolingian empire 83
Franklin, Benjamin 136, 182, 251
fraternity 18, 60, 107, 232
Frederick II Hohenstaufen 133
Frederick the Great 135, 179
French Revolution 4, 93, 115, 123, 136,
    177, 183, 185–187, 191–194
Freud, Sigmund 173, 208, 213
    Civilization and its Discontents 213
Fugger, Jakob 124
Fukuyama, Francis 236
    The End of History and the Last Man 16,
    140, 235, 253

G
Gadamer, Hans-Georg 5
Gaius Julius Caesar 47, 48
Galileo Galilei 100, 101, 110, 124, 158, 160,
    162, 163, 165, 171, 174, 175, 205
Game of Thrones 83
Gandhi, Mahatma 223
Garvey, Marcus 223
Gasperi, Alcide de 13, 196, 251
Gates, Bill 160
Gaudí, Antoni 213
Geertz, Cliffort 18
gender theory 230
genealogy 6, 7, 10–13, 176, 243
Genesis, Book of 13, 27–30
Genoa, Italy 144, 145
German nationalism 138
Germania 54
Germany 80, 85, 123, 127, 129,
    138, 148, 167, 170, 192, 196,
    206, 228
Ghent, Belgium 144
Gibbon, Edward
    *The History of the Decline and Fall of
    the Roman Empire* 182
Gilbert de la Porrée 101
Gilson, Étienne 211
Giotto 12, 113, 114, 119
globalization 17, 141, 149, 198, 236, 240,
    245, 247, 254, 258
God 26–28, 30, 31
Goethe, Johann Wolfgang 173, 180

Golden Age, culture 78
Golgotha, Israel 61
Gombrich, Ernst H.
    A Little History of the World 38, 108
    The Story of Art 210
good and evil 3, 28, 30, 37, 43
Goody, Jack 29
Gorbachev, Mikhail 234
Gospels 57, 60–64, 178
Goya, Francisco de 214
Graf, Friedrich Wilhelm 175
Grafton, Anthony 7
Great Britain 118, 136, 148, 240, 242
Great Depression 207
Great War. *See* First World War,
    World War I
Greco-Roman legacy 6
Greece 7, 20, 31, 35–38, 41, 47, 57, 62,
    63, 72, 91, 141, 177, 237
Greek civilization 44, 47
Gregory of Nazianzus 66
Gregory the Great 66
Gregory VII, Pope 98, 107
Gropius, Walter 209
Grosseteste, Robert 159
    De Machina Universitatis 107
Guardini, Romano 211
    The Essence of Christianity 1929 18
Guevara, Che 218, 228
Guiscard, Robert 90
Guldi, Jo 17
Gutenberg 124

H
Habermas, Jürgen 244
Hamilton, Alexander 182
Hannah Arendt 2012 202
Hannibal 46
Harari, Yuval Noah
    Homo Sapiens 6
Haskins, Charles H. 93
Hazard, Paul
    The Crisis of European Mind 178
Hector 37
Hegel, Georg Wilhelm Friedrich 173
hegemonism 5, 10, 54, 252
Heidegger, Martin 173, 211

Heisenberg, Werner 165
Heloise 102
Henry VIII of England 133, 135, 168
Hepburn, Audrey 14
Heraclius 75
Herod the Great 51
Herod, king of Israel 33
Herodotus 7, 41, 42, 261
Hindu civilization 17
Hinduism 7, 18, 66, 250
historical reality 20, 42, 113, 139, 249
Hobbes, Thomas 131, 132, 136
Hobsbawm, Eric 3
Holland 196, 237
Holocaust 3, 9
Holy Roman Empire 49, 80
Holy Roman German Emperor 86
Holy Roman German Empire 83, 167
Holy War 238
Horkheimer, Max 186
Huff, Toby E. 16
Hugh Capet 30, 83, 85
Hugo, Victor 100, 212
    Les Misérables 214
Huguenots 168
Huizinga, Johan 210
    The Autumn of the Middle Ages 214
Humanism 125
Hume, David 130
    The History of England 185
    The Natural History of Religion 182
Hungarian revolt 1956 228
Hungary 85
Huntington, Samuel P. 248
    *The Clash of Civilizations and the Remaking
        of World Order* 16, 236
Huss, Jan 167
Husserl, Edmund 211
Huxley, Aldous
    Brave New World 211
Huxley, Julian 211

I
Iberian Peninsula 78, 88, 89, 129
ideologies, definition 191
imperialism 253
India 20, 35, 49, 72, 78, 106, 156, 218, 223

Indies 128
Indonesia 78, 147, 257
Industrial Revolution 123, 171
industrialization 6, 9, 147, 150, 151, 163,
    164, 176, 193, 197, 198, 200, 250,
    253, 254, 258
Innocent III, Pope 104
Inquisition Courts 162
international communism 206, 207
International Monetary Fund 240
interwar period 7, 9, 16, 138, 201,
    203–205, 208, 210, 212, 221, 233, 256
Ionesco, Eugene 210
Iran 35, 238, 239, 250
Iraq 35, 238
Irish rebellion 224
Islam 7, 18, 78, 156, 239, 257
Islamic civilization 17, 71
Islamic science 93
Islamic tradition 158, 160
Islamic world 81, 103, 156, 233, 236
Islamize modernity 250
Israel 20, 25–34, 62
Israelites 27, 29–31
Istanbul 72, 73
Italian peninsula 46
Italy 45, 80, 113, 123, 128, 138, 144, 185,
    192, 237

J
James I the Conqueror of Aragon 133
Japan 153, 154
Jaspers, Karl 18, 20, 93
Jay, John 182
Jefferson, Thomas 136, 182
Jerome of Stridonium 66
Jerusalem 25–34, 45, 61, 68
Jesus Christ 12, 57–67, 75, 107
Jewish people 25, 27, 31, 33, 34, 58
Jews 12, 14, 33–35, 45, 51, 58–62, 94,
    149, 220, 238
Joan of Arc 119
Joas, Hans 175, 250
Jobs, Steve 160
John of Salisbury 95, 100
John Paul II, Pope 234
Jordan 238

Jordan River 25
Joseph II of Austria 135, 179
Joseph of Arimathea 60, 61
Joyce, James 173
    Ulysses 210, 213
Judaism 34, 63
Judeo-Christian West 7
Judgment at Nuremberg 1961 202
Jung, Carl Gustav 173
Justinian 12, 68, 71, 73, 75, 98

K
Kafka, Frank 9, 173, 210
Kagan, Robert 140
Kandinsky, Vasili 205
Kant, Immanuel 180
Keele, Kenneth D. 161
Kepel, Gilles 250
Kepler, Johannes 158, 175, 205
Kerouac, Jack 232
Keynes, John M. 4, 196
Keys, Sarah Louise 221
Khmer Rouge 8
Khomeini, Ayatollah 257
Khrushchev, Nikita 227, 228
King, Martin Luther 124, 167, 221–224,
    269, 280
Kierkegaard, Søren 173, 210
King of Aragon and Navarre 89
King of England 85
King of Leon and Castile 89
Klimt, Gustav 208
Kneale, Martha 109
Kneale, William 109
Kohl, Helmut 234
Korea 218
Koselleck, Reinhard 186
Krakow, Poland 144
Ku Klux Klan 220
Kubrick, Stanley 212
Kuhn, Thomas 4, 109
Kuran, Timur 106

L
Lacan, Jacques 244
Lang, Fritz 208
Langer, William 227

Las Casas, Bartolomé de 117, 129, 251
Las Navas de Tolosa 89
Lateran (1123) Council 98
Le Corbusier 209
Le Goff, Jacques 93
Lebanon 26, 238
Leibniz, Gottfried 130, 158, 174, 178, 180
Lennon, John 231, 233
Leon, kingdom of Spain 89
Lessing, Gotthold Ephraim 180
Lévinas, Emmanuel 211
Lévi-Strauss, Claude 183
Lewis, C.S. 249
liberal capitalism 195, 197, 207
liberal democracy 135, 136, 235
liberal economics 136
liberalism 17, 20, 193, 194, 197, 198, 235
Libya 35
linguistic turn 101, 212, 242
Lisbon, Portugal 144
literary criticism 125
Llull, Ramon 113, 158
Locke, John 12, 136, 163, 178, 179, 194,
    198, 248, 257
    An Essay Concerning Human Understanding
    1690 163
Lombard, Peter 100, 101
London, England 144, 145, 150, 151,
    203, 209, 238
López, Roberto S. 93
Lord Palmerston 51
Lorenzo de' Medici 124, 127
Louis V of France 85
Louis VI the Fat of France 133
Louis XIV of France 133, 135
Louis XVI of France 136
Lubac, Henri de 211
Lucas, Georges 40
Luther, Martin 12, 110, 124, 167–175
Lyon II (1274) Council 98
Lyotard, Jean-François 244
    The Postmodern Condition 9, 241

M
Macedonia 63
Mach, Ernst 101
Madison, James 182

Mahler, Gustav 21
Malcolm X 223
Mallorca, Spain 149
Malthus, Thomas 192
Malthusianism 192
Mann, Thomas 173
Mao Tse-Tung 8, 200
Marathon, battle 37
Marcel, Gabriel 210
Marcuse, Herbert 226
Mare Nostrum 52
Marrou, Henri-Irénée 72
Marseille, France 144, 145
Marsilius of Padua 113, 115
Marx, Karl 12, 151, 180,
    199, 213
    The Capital (1867) 199
Marxism 17, 118, 151, 198, 200,
    227–230, 257
materialism 250
Matrix, The 164
Maxwell, James Clerk 164
McLuhan, Marshall 242, 244
McNeill, William H. 14
    History of Western Civilization.
    A Handbook 7
meaculpism 1, 4, 245
Mediterranean Sea 25, 52
Mendelssohn, Moses 180
Menocal, María Rosa
    The Ornament of the World (2002) 90
mental illness 243
mercantile bourgeoisie 144
Merton, Robert K. 237
Mesopotamia 63, 76
Methodism 174, 176
Michael Cerularius 76
Michelet, Jules 186
    The History of the French Revolution 214
Middle Ages 1, 8, 50, 81–83, 97, 102,
    105, 108, 109, 113, 115, 123, 125,
    143, 149, 151, 174, 240
Mieszko I of Poland 87
Milan, Italy 144
Miró, Joan 209
Modern Age 116, 142, 170
modernism 9, 203, 207, 207, 213–215, 250

modernity 93, 123, 130, 134, 174, 186,
    207, 209
  crisis of 7, 10, 203, 205, 208, 210, 213
  dawn of 123, 141, 155, 207, 240
  emergence of 255
  great narratives of 242
  zenith of 19, 187, 244
modernization 14, 94, 106, 174, 176, 248,
    250, 253–258
Mongols 94
monotheism 28, 63
Monroe, Marilyn 231
Montaigne 184
Montesquieu 52, 136, 137, 186, 195
More, Thomas 21
Morgan, Irene 221
Morocco 78
Mounier, Emmanuel 211
Muhammad 46, 58, 68, 71, 77, 236
Munch, Edvard 9, 208
Muslim religion 77, 78
Myron
  Discobolus 38

N
Naples, Italy 127, 145, 179
Napoleonic Empire 193
nationalism 138, 192, 201, 203, 218, 250
NATO. *See* North Atlantic Treaty
    Organization
natural reality 162
Navarre, Spain 89
Nazism 139, 206, 210, 211
Nelson, Benjamin 14, 16, 19, 20, 93, 110,
    173, 254, 255
Nemo, Philippe 93, 100
neoclassical liberalism 4
Nero, emperor Roma 64
Netherlands 129, 147, 168, 170
New Testament 33, 57
New World (Age of Discoverings) 117,
    127, 167
Newton, Isaac 12, 158, 160–163, 165,
    174, 178, 205, 209
Nicodemus 61
Nietzsche, Friedrich 9, 11, 101, 173, 205,
    213, 242

Nigeria 78
1968 Revolution 12, 168, 183
Normandy 88
Normans 87, 88
North Atlantic Treaty Organization
    (NATO) 141, 240
North Korea 151
Northern Spain 80
Norway 85, 88

O
Old Continent (Europe) 8
Old Testament 27, 30, 33, 57, 63, 65
Oresme, Nicolas 160
Orwell, Georges 211
Otto I of Germany 83, 86
Oxford, England 95, 159–161

P
paganism 54, 61, 111, 178
Palazzo Vecchio in Florence 113
Palermo, Sicily 99, 145
Pankhurst, Emmeline 229
Panofsky, Erwin 210
Paris, France 49, 85, 102, 144, 145, 160,
    203, 225, 226, 238
Pascal, Blaise 130, 158, 171, 174, 175, 184
Patriarch of Constantinople 250
Paul of Tarsus. *See* Paul, Saint
Paul, Saint 51, 52, 57, 61–63, 67, 172
Pax Romana 16, 48, 235, 236
Peirce, Charles 192
Pelayo, King of Astur-Leonese, Spain
    13, 30
Peregrinus, Petrus 103
Pericles 12, 38, 43, 127
Persia 7, 25–31, 35–39, 76–79, 250
Persian Empire 26
Persian Wars 35, 41, 46, 49
Peter of Poitiers 101
Peterson, Jordan 249
Philip Augustus the Conqueror
    of France 133
Philip II of Spain 49, 124, 133,
    135, 147
Philo of Alexandria 62
physical reality 159

Picasso, Pablo 9, 12, 208
  Guernica 9, 204
Pietism 174, 176
Piketty, Thomas
  Capital and Ideology 152
  Capital in the Twenty-First Century 152
Pinker, Steven 249
Pirenne, Henri
  Muhammad and Charlemagne 1937 54
Pisa, Italy 144
Pius X, Pope 207
Pizan, Christine de 118, 119
Pizarro, Francisco 129, 251
Planck, Max 101, 165
Plato 39, 111, 225
Poincaré, Henri 101
Poland 85, 129, 237
Polish Solidarity 228
political religion 77, 180
political theology 171
Polo, Marco 93, 143
Polybius 41
Pontius Pilate 59
populism 4, 141, 154, 180, 201–203, 234,
  237, 238, 240, 249, 254
Portugal 78, 123, 128, 141, 167, 217
positivism 114, 118, 174, 192, 193, 205
post-Hispanic Cuba 151
post-modernism 215, 258
postmodernity 1, 9, 11, 205, 213, 215,
  242, 244, 258
pragmatism 192
Prague, Czech Republic 144
Presley, Elvis 231
Pritchard, James B. 28
Protestant Ethic 153, 171, 174, 175
Protestant Reformation 124, 168,
  171, 207
Protestantism 168, 170–176
Proust, Marcel 9, 173
  In Search of Lost Time 210, 213
psychoanalysis 173, 208, 212, 230, 244
public intellectuals 179
Public Limited Company 150, 151
Punic Wars 46
Puritanism 176

Q
Queen Cleopatra 47

R
racism 220, 253
radical feminists 230
Raphael 114, 124
rationalists 102, 180
rationalization 2, 9, 50, 53, 94, 98–100, 102,
  103, 106, 108, 130, 131, 135, 158,
  164, 171, 174, 176–178, 252, 255, 258
Ratzinger, Joseph 211
  Introduction to Christianity 1968 18
Reagan, Ronald 225, 234
reality 16, 20, 21, 54, 67, 68, 102, 114,
  130, 131, 141, 159, 180, 186, 191,
  192, 197, 208, 210, 211–212, 215,
  223, 224, 225, 243–245
Redon, Odilon 208
religion 13, 17, 138, 250
  wars of 139, 170, 236
religiosity 45, 53, 90, 250
Renaissance 93, 110, 113, 125, 160,
  177, 203
Renaissance Art 127
Renaissance Florence 38, 54
Ricci, Mateo 157
Rimbaud, Arthur 173
Robert de Curzon 103, 104
Robert Grosseteste of Lincoln 103
Robert the Strong 85
Robertson, William
  The History of Scotland 185
Robespierre, Maxilmilien 12
Robin Hood 37
Rogan, Joe 249
Roger II of Sicily 90
Roldan 37
Roman Catholicism 176
Roman civilization 45, 48, 51, 73
Roman Empire 47, 49, 52, 54, 71, 74, 82,
  86, 247
Roman imperialism 33
Roman law 52, 98, 102, 105, 106
Roman Republic 136
Roman society 106

Roman tradition 54, 68, 73, 75, 79
Romanesque Pantocrator 115
Romanization 2, 45, 52, 53, 129, 253
Romanized Africa 78
Romanticism 139, 192
Rome 45–56, 68
Romulus and Remus 30, 45
Roosevelt, Franklin D. 207
Rorty, Richard 186, 212, 242, 244
Roscelin of Compiègne 100
Rosenstone, Robert A.
  The Man Who Swam into History 13
Rousseau, Jean-Jacques 19, 136, 173, 183,
  184, 186
  Émile 185
Royal Academies 185
Royal Prussian Academy of Sciences 185
Russia 7, 67, 72, 87, 129, 195, 197, 200,
  206, 207, 238, 248, 250, 255
Russian nationalism 206
Russian Revolution 202, 206
Rustin, Bayard 221

S
Said, Edward 79
  Orientalism 5, 10
Saint Ignatius of Loyola 169
Saint Teresa of Avila 169
Saint-Exupéry, Antoine de 241
Salamanca, Spain 95
Salamis, battle 37
Sancho Ramirez, king of Navarre 89
Sartre, Jean-Paul 211, 226
Saudi Arabia 238
Savio, Mario 225
Savonarola, Girolamo 167
Scandinavia 88
Schama, Simon 13
Schleiermacher, Friedrich
  The Christian Faith 1922 176
Schlesinger, Arthur 227
Schmitt, Carl 131, 171
  *The Planetary Tension Between Orient and
  Occident* 5
Schuman, Robert 13, 251
Schumann, Maurice 196

science 155
  contemporary 211
  experimental 100, 103, 116, 159, 160,
    165, 255
  modern 156–158, 161, 163,
    171, 205
  and technology 155, 158, 165, 241
Scientific Revolution 156
Scott, Ridley 212
Scott, Walter
  Ivanhoe 214
Scotus, Duns 100, 103, 116, 158
Second World War 9, 117, 118, 141, 170,
  186, 196, 201, 215, 217
secularization 62
secularized religions 180
Seignobos, Charles 214
self-esteem (of the West) 3, 5, 10, 14
self-satisfaction (of the West) 14
Seneca 53, 103
Sepúlveda, Juan Ginés de 118
Serbia 87
Seville, Spain 144
Shakespeare, William 12, 47, 109, 124
Shapiro, Ben 249
Shaw, Bernard 249
Sicily 46, 78, 86, 88, 90, 91
Skötkonung, Olaf 88
slavery 4, 44, 60, 66, 67, 198, 220
Slavic Orthodox tradition 87
Smith, Adam 12, 136, 182, 184, 194
  The Wealth of Nations 1776 183, 185
Social Democracy 4
Social Revolution 200
Socrates 11, 12, 39, 225
Solomon, king of Israel 32, 33
Solonian Constitution 43
Solzhenitsyn, Alexander
  One Day in the Life of Ivan Denisovich
    1962 229
Song of Roland, Poem 40
Song of the Nibelungs, Poem 109
Sophocles 40, 43
Soviet Empire 228, 229, 234
Soviet imperialism 206
Soviet Union 53, 217, 228, 234

Spain 123, 127, 128, 136, 145, 167, 185, 217, 237
Spanish Civil War 204
Spanish Empire 53, 170
Spengler, Oswald
    The Decline of the West 9, 210
Spinoza, Baruch 130, 178, 194
spiritual fraternity 107
spiritual reality 208
spirituality 25, 30, 165, 173, 207, 227, 242
Spivak, Gayatri
    A Critique of Postcolonial Reason 10
Stammesherzogtum 86
state, definition and development 131–142
state, liberal 135–137
Stephen Langton of Canterbury 104
Stephen of Hungary 87
Stockholm, Sweden 144
Strayer, Joseph R. 255
Sudan 78
Suger of Saint-Denis 100
supremacism 5, 10, 20, 187, 251–253
Sweden 85, 88, 91
Switzerland 168, 196
Syria 76, 77, 238

T
Tacitus 53
Tarquin the Proud 46
technology 155, 162, 163, 165, 168, 171, 206, 211, 212, 230
    history of 164
Teresa of Ávila 19, 124
Terminator 164
Tertullian 66
Thatcher, Margaret 234
The French Declaration of the Rights of Man and Citizens (1789) 256
The Hague's Human Rights Tribunal 141
Themistocles, General 36
Thermopylae, battle 12, 36, 37
Thessalonica 65
Third Reich 49
Thirty Years War 49, 170
Thomas, William I. 237

Thompson, Edward
    The Making of Working Class 19
Thucydides 41
Tocqueville, Alexis de 12, 52, 135–137, 182, 186, 194, 195, 257
Toland, John 179
Toledo, Spain 99
totalitarianism 139, 193, 201, 207
Toynbee, Arnold 12, 14, 210
transhumanism 211
Treaty of Versailles 1919 206
Troeltsch, Ernst 175
    Protestantism and Progress 1906 175
Trojan 45
Troy, battle 37
Trygvesson, Olaf 88
Turkey 35, 84, 248
Turks 239
Turner, Frederick Jackson
    The Significance of the Frontier in American History 1893 89
Turner, Victor 18
Twin Towers 16, 90
2001: A Space Odyssey (1968) 164, 212

U
Ukraine 85, 87, 88, 91
UN. *See* United Nations
Unamuno, Miguel de 211
Union of Soviet Socialist Republics (USSR) 206, 227, 228, 233, 234
United Nations (UN) 141, 217, 240
United Nations Universal Declaration of Human Rights (1948) 256
United States 12, 13, 52, 67, 79, 137, 148, 196, 197, 207, 217, 219, 232, 233, 238, 239, 242, 249
Universal Declaration of Human Rights 217, 253
universalism 34, 184, 249, 251–253
USSR. *See* Union of Soviet Socialist Republics

V
Valencia, Spain 144, 149
Valla, Lorenzo 124

van der Rohe, Ludwig Mies 209
Vatican Council I 168
Vatican Council II 194, 208
Vega, Lope de 135
Velázquez, Diego 209, 214
Venice, Italy 118, 127, 144, 145
Vico, Giambattista 179
Victoria, Francisco de 117
Vienna, Austria 203, 272
Vietnam 151, 218
Vietnam War 233
Vikings 88, 127
Virgil 2, 53, 111, 112
Virgin Mary 178
Vitello, Pole 103
Vitoria, Francisco de 67
Vivar, Rodrigo Díaz de 37, 89
Vladimir of the Kievan Rus 87
Voltaire 179, 183, 184, 187, 194
von Balthasar, Hans Urs 211
von Harnack, Adolf
   The Essence of Christianity 1900 18
von Hayek, Friedrich 207
von Humboldt, Alexander 158
von Ranke, Leopold 42, 182, 192, 214

W
Wagner, Rudolf G. 257
Walesa, Lech 228
Wallerstein, Immanuel 14
Walter of St Victor 101, 110
War of Secession 220
Warburg, Aby 209
Washington, Booker T. 221
Washington, George 12, 182, 251
Watt, James 164
Weber, Max 14, 106, 131, 171, 174, 175,
   179, 255
   *The Protestant Ethic and the Spirit of
   Capitalism* 173
Weimar Republic 206
Wenceslas I of Bohemia 87
West Indies 128
West, The 12, 49, 84, 156, 203,
   239, 247
   criticism of 13

history of 2
rejection of 258
Western Christianity 12, 81, 94, 247
Western civilization 1, 6, 7, 13, 14, 16,
   17, 19, 25, 29, 66, 71, 75, 93, 98, 99,
   106, 157, 161, 170, 172, 176, 217,
   236, 247, 249, 253, 258
Western consciousness 19, 258
Western culture 164
Western Europe 5
Western legacy 1, 8, 11
Western modernity 9
Western science 93
Western society 158, 164
Western tradition 3, 8, 11, 47
Western values 7
Westernization 253
Westphalia, peace of 170
Weyden, Roger van der 124
White, Hayden 212
William of Heytesbury 160
William of Ockham 103, 113, 115, 116,
   158, 159
William the Conqueror of England 13,
   30, 86, 133
Wojtyla, Karol 211
Wolff, Cristian 180
Woolf, Virginia 9, 229
   Mrs. Dalloway 210
World Bank 240
World War I 87, 138, 186, 192, 202, 206,
   207, 218, 236
World War II 9, 117, 118, 141, 170, 186,
   196, 201, 215, 217
World Wars 170
Wright, Frank Lloyd 209

X
Xerxes 36

Y
Yiannopoulos, Milo 249

Z
Zweig, Stefan
   The World of Yesterday 9

Printed in the USA
CPSIA information can be obtained
at www.ICGtesting.com
JSHW021446180324
59436JS00004B/27